COUTURE

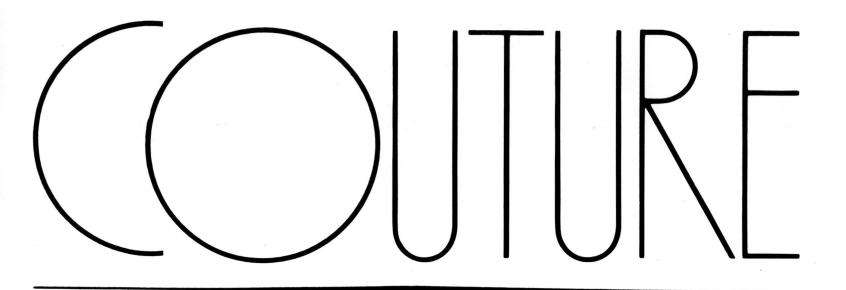

COUTURE

The Great Fashion Designers

With 176 colour and 222 duotone illustrations

Caroline Rennolds Milbank

Thames and Hudson

For my husband

THE FOUNDERS
20

Worth *24*
Doucet *38*
Paquin *42*
Lanvin *48*
Callot Soeurs *60*
Lucile *64*
Boué Soeurs *70*
Poiret *74*

THE ARTISTS
88

Fortuny *92*
Gallenga *100*
Liberty & Co. *102*
Mary McFadden *106*
Zandra Rhodes *112*

THE PURISTS
116

Chanel *120*
Jean Patou *138*
Molyneux *144*
Grès *150*
Augustabernard *156*
Louiseboulanger *158*
Vionnet *160*
Mainbocher *166*
Valentina *174*
Halston *178*
Sonia Rykiel *184*

THE ENTERTAINERS
192

Schiaparelli *196*
Adrian *204*
Maggy Rouff *212*
Karl Lagerfeld *216*
Marcel Rochas *222*

THE EXTRAVAGANTS
228

Dior *232*
Nina Ricci *246*
Balmain *252*
Jacques Heim *258*
Jacques Fath *264*
Jacques Griffe *270*
Jean Dessès *274*
Norman Hartnell *276*
Valentino *280*
Givenchy *286*
Galanos *294*
Oscar de la Renta *298*
Bill Blass *302*
Yves Saint Laurent *308*

THE ARCHITECTS
316

Balenciaga *320*
Charles James *328*
Roberto Capucci *336*
Pierre Cardin *338*
Courrèges *342*

THE REALISTS
348

Claire McCardell *352*
Vera Maxwell *360*
Bonnie Cashin *364*
Norma Kamali *366*
Norman Norell *372*
Pauline Trigère *378*
Hardy Amies *382*
Geoffrey Beene *388*
Perry Ellis *392*
Ralph Lauren *398*
Kenzo *404*
Giorgio Armani *408*
Issey Miyake *412*

BIBLIOGRAPHY
416

INDEX OF DESIGNERS
419

Introduction

Things have a signature, if you use your eyes.
— Nancy Mitford
Love in a Cold Climate

That an article of clothing, made from a mere yard or two of fabric, could be recognizable as the work of a specific individual is a relatively new idea in the history of fashion. It has only been for the past hundred and thirty years—since Worth built an international business out of dictating styles to his customers—that couturiers and designers have followed their own inspiration, using the medium of women's clothing to express personal views of fashion, style, beauty, and life. In the twentieth century, the most important changes in fashion have been started purposely, by couturiers who design the most luxurious of clothes made to order and fitted individually to each client; or by designers who create ready-to-wear clothing reproduced by the tens or the thousands. Even when a style has seemingly come from the street (or out of thin air), or has erupted in emulation of some highly celebrated person, it often has achieved widespread popularity only after receiving a designer's imprimatur.

Therefore, it is to couturiers and designers—not historical events, not political personages or accidents—that we owe developments such as Worth's abolishment of the crinoline and adoption of the bustle silhouette, Poiret's banishment of the corset in favor of the lean and narrow look, or Chanel's campaign for a truly easy "uniform" in which women could move freely. Similar couturiers' concerns led to Vionnet's discovery of the bias-cut, and Fortuny's patented invention of a finely pleated dress. Madame Grès originated the genre of the classically draped jersey dress, while Patou and Louiseboulanger paved the way for the longer silhouette of the Thirties, which then gave way to the more abrupt, wide-shouldered look attributed variously to Adrian, Schiaparelli, and Rochas. The New Look sprang from many designers' minds, but Dior received credit for making it the widespread post-World War II look. Balenciaga's steadfast allegiance to the chemise dress prepared the way for the sheath shape dominant in the Sixties, and then it took Courrèges to hack off that sheath above the knees, creating the first miniskirt. Yves Saint Laurent in Paris and Norell in New York designed the first universally adopted uniform since Chanel's suit: the pantsuit. A whole new generation of ready-to-wear sportswear designers owe their inventiveness to Claire McCardell, the first designer to concentrate on Everywoman, whose sportswear renounced previous associations with men's clothing.

An examination of these and other designers, phenomena of little more than the last century, shows how this new form of artist thinks and creates. This book is not intended to be a history of the couture, or of recent

Chanel beach pajamas.

fashion, but rather it is a brief look at the work of each of these artists of fashion. Worth is the obvious starting point for, although there were great and able couturiers before him, he established the couture house on which all subsequent ones would be based. For the most part, the designers included in this book were chosen for the strength of their individual signatures as well as, in terms of the earliest, for their obvious popularity as determined by how well their clothes are represented in private and museum collections.

In France before Worth, couturières were far from creative instigators.

Mostly women, they (like their counterparts, household seamstresses) held onto their jobs not through originality, but by following orders. A couturière, *or dressmaker as the word then implied, whether in her storefront shop or by travelling from family to family, might show her prospective client a dress made up for another woman, or perhaps a miniature sample made for a doll. Usually, though, each garment was created for, and with, the client. The client usually already knew what she wanted, and would already have the fabric and the trimmings. She possibly even had an illustration from a ladies' magazine.*

What she had in mind would not have been, by our standards, particularly inventive. Fashions prior to the last half of the nineteenth century changed slowly, a new silhouette sometimes taking decades to evolve. (There were really only two silhouettes up to this time: the wide-skirted "bell" of the Renaissance and eighteenth century, and the Classical, Medieval, and Empire "tube.") Those who could afford to have their clothes made wore practically the same thing as those who could not, with variances occurring only in quality of workmanship, fabric, or lace and embroidery. Luxury was determined less by what one could afford than by one's station in life: for every place in society, and for every occasion, there were rules about what constituted suitable attire. As a result, dressmaking was mostly decorative and primarily consisted of making the choices of fabric, trimmings, and kinds of handiwork.

Into such a staggeringly undeveloped market walked Charles Frederick Worth, the first dressmaker whom we would not hesitate to call a couturier. He was the first to put his signature on the clothes he made for his clients—both literally on a label, and metaphorically, by creating clothes

W*orth evening dress.*

that were readily attributable to him. Equally important was his role as first designer to establish the supremacy of his own taste, and then to use it to set new styles. His back-draped, flattened crinoline look, which became the bustle, was the first new silhouette ever singlehandedly introduced by any individual. Even though it was merely the combination of the two existing silhouettes, it had never been seen before. He did require help in launching his styles, usually from his wife or a prominent figure in the court; nonetheless, he became the first couturier to do so, and those who have followed in his footsteps have been able to set new styles all on their own as a result.

In effect, Worth personified the new kind of artist, one who used his ideas of feminine beauty to influence the actual beauty of women. Like architects and designers who worked to produce useful commodities, the new couturiers were restricted by the needs, and blind spots, of their clientele. The couturier-artist had to work with the limitations of the etiquette of the time as well as with each client's particular appearance and disposition. He had to know the habits of the socially prominent and convey this knowledge through the clothes he made for them. The more he became a part of society, the better he understood the nuances of clothes for visiting or for receiving, country clothes and court clothes, dinner dresses and ball gowns, clothes for morning and for mourning.

Just as being a manufacturer had become "respectable," and just as a king was now able to dine with a stage actress, couturiers were now socially acceptable, a status from which they could even more forcefully dictate the terms of their artistic vision. By the turn of the century, a client who patronized the "right" couture house expected not only an ingeniously conceived, and perfectly executed, dress, but also the assurance that she would be impeccably dressed.

During World War I, when women entered the workforce and social life diminished, both daytime and evening clothes necessarily became less elaborate; curiously, this strengthened the couturiers' roles even further. Many of the new designers, Chanel and Vionnet for example, were women, and their intuition, as shown in their clothes, led the client of the couture to another expectation from her favorite house: along with displaying quality and suitability, the clothes must encourage her growing acceptance of physical and mental freedom. A designer's vision of the client's needs, based on the life she led, became an integral part of his or her artistry.

Designers who were too tyrannical, or who failed to keep up with what had become rapid changes in fashion and in the world, found that women were making up their own minds more and more, and hence were unwilling to subscribe to a single couturier's vision. Making his job even more demanding, a couturier's clientele now typically encompassed women from all over the world, from queens to film idols, and of all ages, beginning with debutantes. The couturier now needed to come up with a collection that included something for everyone as well as for every hour of the day. He had to produce what would become the "Fords" of his collection for, if he were astute, he knew that every woman needed to replace her favorite little black or navy dress periodically. But at the same time, he had to create those works of art that fanned the flames of his reputation and sated a growing addiction to novelty.

At the semiannual and smaller, mid-season collections, those in attendance now included growing ranks of manufacturers and store buyers

H*eim evening dress.*

from department stores and the smaller, out-of-town couture houses, in addition to private clients. Manufacturers paid admission with hopes of finding those "Fords" that would be most popular when mass-produced and advertised as "Copies of Original Paris Creations." Buyers attended in order to purchase actual models, which they would export at great expense, sell at a loss, and thus increase the cachet of their own establishments. They hoped to make up this loss by cadging a few free ideas to incorporate into their own designs. Also present were reporters from newspapers and magazines such as Vogue *and* Harper's Bazaar *(spelled "Bazar" until 1929) whose pages included fewer and fewer tips on frugal household management and more on the latest modes in dress.*

The fashion magazines fed on Paris and, as the Twenties and Thirties progressed, became increasingly dictatorial. Occasionally their pages would include a design by an American or an English couturier, but usually only if that design had been shown in Paris. American "designers" prior to World War II remained primarily anonymous appendages to manufacturers' labels. Parisian couturiers meanwhile found that they needed to add public relations skills to their roster of talents.

World War II nearly brought the frenzied activities of the Paris couture to a grinding halt. The houses closed or considerably cut down on their operations, and the magazines filled their pages with articles on career women (sometimes shown in the Paris clothes they had worn before the war) and with ways to cope with clothing rationing and shortages. Not only did the clothes themselves change, becoming less frivolous and less likely to be credited with a designer's name, but Paris couture began to lose ground to what was actually available: affordable, practical, ready-

made clothing. During the war there was talk of New York supplanting Paris as a fashion center. Although when it ushered in the New Look, the Paris couture resurrected itself admirably, even spectacularly, fashion had become internationalized and from then on, the couture would face strong competition from the ready-to-wear industry.

Parisian couturiers—who had experimented with boutique lines in the Thirties, mostly whimsical accessories and amusing items of clothing— now began to follow the lead of American designers. They even went so far as to import American sewing machines and operators. Many of the French prêt-à-porter lines (well-made ready-to-wear items based on sportswear and separates dressing and also sometimes on their more fanciful couture) were aimed at a college-age audience, a younger, and definitely more casual, clientele.

In the Sixties, when everyone wanted to look like a sixteen-year-old, couturiers found their made-to-order collections irrelevant. Youth-inspired fashions translated into the best fabrics and workmanship seemed absurd, and couturiers, seeing the custom end of their businesses lose money, and losing many of their workers to other professions, began to think about dispensing with the couture altogether. Some retired. By 1974, Time magazine would pronounce that the couture had not died, but it was "breathing very hard."

The designer, however, was not dead. Rather he had begun, in France and America, England and Italy, and eventually Japan, to be an international celebrity. The decline of interest in genuine quality curiously resulted in a heightened appreciation for the designer-designed article, whether a shoe, a pair of jeans, a bikini, a piece of chocolate, a radio, or

Saint Laurent evening dress.

an automobile—all were sprinkled liberally with the designer's monogram, logo, and sometimes with an actual signature. The signature was now literally the signature and not the look, and all the buyer seemed to care about was the logo.

Recently, though, the fashion magazines have begun to write of "investment" dressing, and the days of the throw-away fad have been proclaimed over. The idea of quality, both in its outward appearance, and as a standard of construction and workmanship, has found a new champion in the woman who has truly begun to make her own way in the world. This attraction to quality, to luxury, even to conservatism, has resulted in the recovery of the couture, not in its original omnipotent role, but as the arena for a designer's most creative and finest work.

In the seven chapters that follow, designers and couturiers have been grouped in categories according to how their clothes look. Each artist-couturier is presented individually in order to best examine his or her signature. The first chapter, The Founders, is not based on a shared aesthetic vision as much as on the fact that these were, beginning with Worth, the first to bring about what we now perceive as the system of the couture. Other chapters unite designers according to visions and styles that have changed fashion, sometimes simultaneously, sometimes over a period of time. The Artists treats a group important both because their urge to create was as strong as any painter's or sculptor's, and for the fact that their clothes were worn by women who chose to present themselves artistically—as opposed to fashionably—avoiding artifice but not art.

The Purists, on the other hand, have worked very much within the

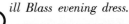
ill Blass evening dress.

system of fashion, but always theirs was an allegiance to the natural female figure, beautiful in its own right. The Entertainers and The Extravagants include the showmen, those who revelled in all the escapist frivolities of fashion, in beauty for beauty's sake; the first group specialized in fantasy and wit, the second in luxury. These two chapters, like The Purists and The Architects, consider both designers of couture and ready-to-wear.

The couturier-as-artist reaches new heights in The Architects. By mastering cut to such a point as to begin to play with it in relation to the human form, and by abstracting that form, Balenciaga and his colleagues used cut and construction to create altogether new forms. The Realists, theirs an almost opposite point of view, worked primarily with an allegiance to the practical needs of their clientele, using or discarding traditional elements of sportswear and active clothes to create clothing suitable for wearing at all times, clothing that is first and foremost comfortable but is still fully imbued with the ingenuity and creativity of the couture at its most hothouse.

Naturally, there are designers who belong in more than one chapter, particularly those whose careers have spanned many decades. The death of a couturier might result in a change of signature for that house, occasionally for the better with the hiring and nurturing of young and talented designers and sometimes for the worse, resulting in the demise of the house. Still, by grouping the designers according to the kinds of clothes they made, it is possible to see their individual strengths and styles of art even more clearly.

RIGHT:
Charles James adjusting the hem of a black faille suit, 1948. The sleeves of the jacket curve out from the shoulders and into the waist; the hat was inspired by a Yugoslavian cap.

BELOW:
Saint Laurent dinner suit.

THE FO

The history of the couture begins on a specific street—the rue de la Paix—in Second Empire Paris, the center of a world lustily following Napoleon III's example of putting on a big show. The nineteenth century saw a great burgeoning of industry and those who benefitted from this progress were faced with finding ways of spending their freshly gotten gains. Status no longer had to be inherited; it could be acquired. But it needed to be displayed to be acknowledged. The newly wealthy, with no ancient reputation to maintain and no ancient breeding to guide them, sought assistance in building an image appropriate to their financial position. They availed themselves of the advice of an art dealer in assembling the right painting collection; they turned to architects to build them houses in the right spots; and they relied on fashionable couturiers to provide them with the right clothes. In becoming willing reflections of the taste of others, they provided the means by which these experts' images became fully developed.

Charles Frederick Worth was not just the first person to apply an artist's standards to the design and construction of a dress and the first to sign his work; he was also the first couturier to develop a saleable image. He forged a career as a dictator of modes and thus built an empire that enabled him to live in style and comfort, as did his clients. By refusing to behave like a tradesperson, he was treated like a great man. The standing of the couturier was further advanced through the efforts of Jacques Doucet and Paul Poiret. Doucet's reputation as collector and cultural philanthropist increased his clientele's assurance of his taste. Poiret was a star, and, whereas Worth had been known to turn away prospective cus-

tomers from his maison de couture, *Poiret had uninvited guests escorted from his legendary parties.*

Mesdames Paquin and Lanvin and the Callot Soeurs were responsible for the tremendous achievement of developing small storefront businesses into thriving international couture houses. As the first woman in her field to be awarded the Légion d'Honneur, Paquin further solidified the position of the couturière. *The Boué Soeurs and Lucile (Lady Duff Gordon) comprehended the potential in the American market and, surmounting the obstacle of crippling export taxes, did their best business in New York where designers were not thought to exist. Like Poiret, Lucile understood the power of the press. Both couturiers not only wrote highly popular illustrated fashion articles, but also somehow saw to the publication of their highjinks. These* couturières *possessed extraordinary style and courage, and none can fall prey to the criticism often levelled at today's women designers: that they design only in their own image.*

By World War I, these couturiers had all contributed considerably to expanding the types of businesses inherent in the couture. Poiret and Lanvin were among the first to grasp the value of applying their imprint to scents. Poiret left nothing undesigned, and today it is somehow expected of a couturier that he or she costume whole environments. Lanvin was the first to design men's clothing and today's designers likewise make clothes for every member of a family. Although it would be farfetched to credit any of the founders with specific styles still applicable to today's clothing, they are responsible for having created our notion of the designer: someone who, as in Poiret's definition of an artist, puts himself into everything he does.

Worth

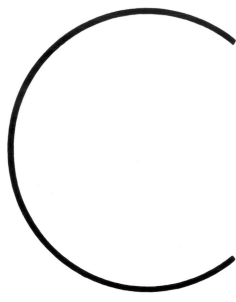

HARLES FREDERICK WORTH WAS NOT THE FIRST CELEBRATED FASHION designer—that honor belongs to Rose Bertin, Minister of Fashion to Marie Antoinette—but, unlike his predecessors, whose careers danced around the flame of a specific monarchy, he was the first couturier whose career outlasted the passing of governments and spanned international boundaries. Although he may be credited with many design innovations that established how women dressed in the last half of the nineteenth century, Worth is most remembered for changing the entire way in which clothing was produced. As a result of his example, the designer was established as an arbiter of taste and a catalyst of change.

Worth was an unlikely candidate for the position of first modern couturier. He was an Englishman in Paris at a time when English fashion was constricted by a national fascination for tailoring methods and when Paris, the center of fashion deluxe, was home to an assemblage of female dressmakers who indulged their clientele in random frivolity. It was Worth who first realized that aesthetic perfection must be built on a foundation of technical excellence and who, not incidentally, first thought to sign his work. The word *couturier*, adapted from the feminine *couturière*, had to be invented for him.

When his lawyer father lost his job and all his money gambling, Worth was apprenticed at the age of thirteen to Swan & Edgar's, a London mercer's establishment that specialized in ladies' dress fabrics. When his seven-year stint came to an end, he found employment at Lewis & Allenby, then the most fashionable fabric business in town.

In 1845, at the age of twenty, Worth left this secure but dead-end post for Paris where, until he learned the language, he occupied himself with menial jobs. After a year, he was hired by Gagelin's, an important emporium offering the finest fabrics as well as mantles and shawls. Promoted to the position of salesman, Worth met Marie Vernet, a young woman of innate elegance and charm, whose job was to model the wraps before interested clients. They fell in love and soon married. Worth's relationship with Marie seemed to inspire his creativity, and it was not long before he had designed a few dresses for her to wear when showing off the wares of the shop. The simplicity of these dresses piqued the interest of customers, and Worth was asked for orders. His suggestion that he open a small department devoted to dresses made from Gagelin's fabrics was at first vetoed by the shop's management, but, in 1850, they relented. By the following year the management saw fit to include several Worth dresses in their display in the Great Exhibition at London's Crystal Palace.

Throughout his career, Worth's wife functioned as his muse, inspiring him to create clothing of beauty and originality. With Marie to

n this 1885 evening dress, patterned silk frames a panel of eighteenth-century point d'Angleterre.

wear his creations and thus give credence to his ideas, he developed a confidence in his abilities, an assurance that would stand him well in his attempts to promote new styles. His clients could not help believing that he was right. In time, Marie Worth's wearing of a new style in public was enough to ensure its acceptance.

One of Worth's first innovations was a novel treatment of the train of a court dress—suspended from the shoulders rather than from the waistline. The dress, of gold and bead-embroidered moiré, won a medal at the 1855 Exposition Universelle. But despite his growing reputation, Gagelin's would not offer him a partnership. Frustrated in his ambitions, in 1856, he and Marie left to form a partnership with a wealthy Swede named Otto Bobergh. Worth et Bobergh opened in 1858 at 7, rue de la Paix.

The story of their first success is well known. Worth sent Marie with a sketchbook of his designs to the Princess de Metternich, wife of the Austrian ambassador to France and a close friend of the Empress Eugénie. The princess, a self-described *belle-laide*, possessed great influence in matters of fashion and deigned to look at the Englishman's drawings. Pleased with what she saw, she ordered two dresses. One of these, worn at court, attracted the notice of the empress, who summoned the English dressmaker herself. When she too ordered dresses, it was akin to a mandate that the rest of society follow suit. Worth came to design all of Empress Eugénie's official court clothes; and his label—the first in fashion history—bore the royal crest. For the next decade Worth made almost all the clothes for members of her court, as well as for such other crowned heads as Grand Duchess Marie of Russia, sister of Czar Alexander II; Margaret, Queen of Italy; and Empress Elizabeth of Austria.

In 1870, as the Prussians advanced on Paris, the House of Worth was forced to close its doors. When the house reopened in 1871, Worth felt that a great age of elegance had passed and wondered how he could continue his success without the patronage of the court.

Shortly thereafter, Bobergh sold his shares of the business and returned to Sweden. Worth's name now stood alone on the label, in golden block letters. His fears about the future of his business, however, were unfounded. Even without the Empress Eugénie and the Princess de Metternich, his business prospered, and his reputation extended to all the corners of the globe. Over the years he had created a demand for something made by *him*, and Worth on the rue de la Paix became an imperative stop on anyone's Grand Tour of Europe.

The reputation of Worth had as much to do with the quality of his garments and the status they conferred as it did with his innovations

*W*orth debutante dress, 1888.

in silhouette, although he, more than any other person, can be said to have presided over the growth in popularity of the crinoline. From the 1840s onward, skirts continued to grow in size until they required, to fill them out, a multitude of petticoats, including one made with *crin* (horsehair). The weight of these combined layers severely prohibited movement. Attempts to release women from this fashionable bondage resulted in such absurd inventions as the inflatable petticoat and, in 1856, what came to be called the crinoline, or cage. This undergarment was a collapsible contraption composed of a series of concentric metal circles, connected by fabric tapes; it allowed the skirt to bell out without unwieldy multiple underskirts.

The crinoline was much ridiculed—and not without reason. It could be lifted easily by a breeze and was easily caught on a carriage door or piece of furniture; its size made it difficult for women to move easily in a crowded room (tales were told of girls burning to death after their skirts had brushed against a fireplace grate). Women continued to wear these dangerous things because they were flattering —nothing made a waist look tinier—and because they were better than the alternative: the return to layered petticoats.

To someone of Worth's sensibility, the cage, as it grew and grew, must have seemed unnatural and stiff, but, although he was not solely responsible for its increasing absurdity, credit was given him in numerous newspaper cartoons and satires. Exasperated, the couturier enlisted the aid of the Princess de Metternich in launching a less full silhouette. With his great responsibility to the French silk-making industry, he could not dispense with the full skirt altogether. To protect the jobs of the weavers (as well as his own), Worth's new silhouette was actually a modification of the crinoline. He flattened the skirt in front and swept the fullness around to the back. Because the newly revealed abdomen seemed risqué, he developed all sorts of camouflaging tunics and overskirts. The skirts themselves became more elaborately draped. By 1868 to 1869, women had adjusted to the new silhouette, and it, too, inevitably began to be exaggerated. The crinoline disappeared, and the back fullness evolved into the bustle. By the early 1870s the front of a dress was flat to the body (but curved at the sides in an hourglass shape), and the back jutted out over the support of a half-cage. In 1888, Worth dispensed with the shape, and he worked, in the 1890s, with the prevailing look of gigot sleeves, a curved corsage, and a stiff and flat skirt flared in the back to form a short train.

Worth's early training in the fabric business proved useful throughout his career, allowing him to combine the most beautiful fabrics

FOLLOWING PAGES:
*W*orth capelet, ca. 1885, *of velvet voided in a characteristically bold pattern. PAGE 29: This wedding gown, trimmed with swansdown, crystals, and pearls, had a covered-up bodice for the church ceremony, and the décolleté shown here for the grandest of dances.*

with each other and providing him with expert knowledge of the capabilities of the mills. When Worth left Gagelin to form a couture house, he was careful always to include displays of fabrics, trimmings, embroideries, and lace. And once his business had grown, the Lyons manufacturers reserved the best of their output for his exclusive use and made up special weaves and widths to his specifications.

Worth's ingenuity in combining different fabrics was disciplined and honed by his work for the women of the Second Empire. Not only was a woman required at that time to wear white for evening court occasions, but it was a serious political mistake to appear twice in the same *toilette*. Worth had the typical couturier's task of making different (but always white) dresses for the same client season after season, and he also had the opportunity of designing many of the dresses for a single event. Thus he grew skilled at designing variations on a theme and from there went on to design whole collections—today the basis of every designer's work. Working with white, Worth was forced to experiment with texture and light and proved deft at interlacing white tulle with the palest of silk flowers or rendering white bold with touches of imperial reds and golds.

The frosted and confectionary colors of the candlelit balls at the Tuileries gave way, in the Republican Seventies, to stronger, more somber tones. Worth admired all the shades of purple, garnet, and deep green, but was always adamant about choosing a color for a client that suited her own complexion. The backswept bustle skirt that had begun appearing in the Sixties allowed for an almost painterly fall of fabric, and Worth exploited all the possibilities of pattern in the vertical, horizontal, and angled use of material. Both his highly developed ability with cut and his sense of ornament led to geometric patterns of great intricacy, caused by the play of fabric with itself as well as by the addition of bands of lace, rows of chenille fringe, and meandering bands of passementerie or jet embroidery.

In the late 1870s, Worth began to work with the large-scaled patterned fabrics that look so vivid and modern to us today. These were a departure from existing designs in that they did not hark back to eighteenth-century materials and in that they were woven to follow the figure once it was cut into a dress. The designs were asymmetric, simply silhouetted, and larger than life: colossal parrot tulips, leaves the size of those on a cornstalk, plumes of ostrich, and staffs of wheat. The repeats, too, were immense. These bold and freewheeling patterns were well suited to the less complicated silhouette that came to the fore in the 1890s, and Worth balanced the size of the pattern with the size of the sleeve (the gigot sleeve was just then reaching its

Worth evening dress showing a mid-Thirties nostalgia for the bustle.

prime). He abandoned the ingenious color combinations of the previous decade in favor of gentler tones and trimmings, so as not to detract from the graphic force of the material.

Worth had become interested in cut when aiming for a perfect fit and, now that the silhouette was simpler, experimented with cut for decorative and not always functional effects. Among his most interesting creations was the princess dress, masterfully cut in one piece at a time when most dresses were still being made with a separate bodice and skirt. Another was a skirt with bias panels described in *Vogue* in 1893 as resembling "a series of cornucopia."

Worth had a reputation as a fearful dictator, but his sense of perfection is what made his business so successful. In one of his salons, the windows were blackened and the wall sconces lit by gas so that a lady could see herself as she would appear at night on the dance floor. Another salon could be turned into a waiting room where ladies amused themselves with *pâté de foie gras* and madeira while waiting for the final touches to be applied to their *toilettes* by the great master.

Worth accommodated his clientele in other ways as well. Dresses were modelled by mannequins Worth chose because of their resemblance to specific clients—and whom he ordered to gain or lose weight as their respective "doubles" did. A lady might send her unset jewels or heirloom lace to be sewn onto a dress at the last minute. One customer, who made a religious vow to wear only brown wool for the rest of her life, had no reason to regret her promise when Worth outfitted her with morning, afternoon, and evening *toilettes* fashioned from this humble stuff. He designed mourning wardrobes, fancy-dress costumes, maternity clothes (modelled by a specially padded mannequin), and, for important future clients, christening dresses. The beauty of the stage designs of the House of Worth were also well known (and became even better known when Worth's son Jean-Philippe dressed the great Eleonora Duse).

Charles Frederick Worth died in March 1895. He was on the premises at 7, rue de la Paix until just two days before he died. His sons then officially assumed the positions they had filled since 1874: Gaston ran the business and Jean-Philippe designed the clothes.

Gaston was an astute businessman who was careful to see that the house remained solvent and that profits were invested wisely. He initiated the opening of a House of Worth in London. Sensing that with a new century the house needed to change with the times, he approached the young Paul Poiret to make simple daytime clothes. Poiret's sojourn there did not last long, however, and the house's reputation continued to have little to do with practicality and more to do with its designs for

Gazette du Bon Ton illustration of a 1921 Worth evening dress.

FOLLOWING PAGES: Lillie Langtry dressed by Worth for the role of Mrs. Trevelyan in The Degenerates.

grand and traditional affairs. No one could come close to Worth in preparing a client for her social responsibilities. Fortunately for the house, the requirements of meeting these persisted and even increased until just before World War I.

Jean-Philippe's designs reflected the then burgeoning taste for Art Nouveau. His patterned fabrics were woven, printed, or embroidered with the life-size flowers popularized by his father, as well as with the scrolling lines and curlicues so prominent in the decorative arts in the early years of the new century. Like his father, Jean-Philippe sought inspiration from the paintings of the great masters, claiming that a visit to the Louvre or Versailles "will yield the seeing eyes a thousand ideas."

Gaston retired in 1922 and Jean-Philippe shortly thereafter. The new directors of the house were Gaston's sons: Jacques, who became the financial director, and Jean-Charles, the new couturier. Jean-Charles was known for his fertile imagination; the *Gazette du Bon Ton*, the most prestigious fashion periodical of the era, described his style as embracing both sumptuousness and sobriety. Under his guidance, the house responded easily to the new simple and practical styles of the Twenties.

In 1936, the House of Worth showed its first collection at 120, rue du Faubourg Saint-Honoré, under the direction of the fourth generation of Worths—Jacques and Roger, the latter the new couturier. But it was finally the beginning of the end. Forced to close during World War II and unable to establish a coherent and pertinent design image, the Paris Worth sold out to London in 1946. The London division, with less competition, was able to continue filling a demand for sedate made-to-order clothing until 1954, when it too was sold—to a perfume manufacturer. Today the Worth label can be found only on perfume.

The legacy was a great one: Charles Frederick Worth developed a system of pattern parts that provided for near-perfect fit with fewer fittings; he was the first to present annual collections from which his clients could chose their personal wardrobes and from which foreign buyers and manufacturers could order toiles and patterns; he made visiting the couture house a social event in its own right—a place to see and be seen. In the strictly aesthetic realm, he is remembered for developing the idea of the mutable silhouette and, with it, the concept of the "new" in fashion. Furthermore, he brought the superb tailoring of England across the sea to meld with the chic of Paris, thereby setting the standard for elegance in women's dress for a period of nearly 100 years.

*M*any houses accommo-
dated out-of-town clients
by sending them draw-
ings accompanied by
fabric swatches, as with
this Forties day dress.

9407
Précieuse

Doucet

ACQUES DOUCET WAS IN LOVE WITH ELEGANCE AND WORKED TOWARD its achievement both in his couture designs and in his private life. His couture house was, by the turn of the century, the source for clothes of perfect taste and unostentatious luxury, his name the only one whispered in the same breath as Worth's. The first of the couturiers to promote himself to the rank of gentleman, he built a reputation as a connoisseur by assembling a superb collection of eighteenth-century works of art and paintings. He went on to become a patron of the Impressionists and to collect African sculpture and the most avant-garde art: it was Jacques Doucet who, in 1909, bought Picasso's groundbreaking *Demoiselles d'Avignon* and installed it in a specially built wing of his house at the head of a crystal staircase.

The Doucet legend began early in the nineteenth century with Jacques's grandmother, a bonnet seller turned lace merchant. Under her direction, Doucet became an emporium that offered lace and lace-trimmed articles—christening gowns, handkerchiefs, and lingerie of point d'Alençon and Valenciennes. Her son, Edouard, expanded the inventory to include linens for gentlemen. As a *chemisier* selling and laundering *linge pour les hommes*, Doucet's attracted the notice of the French court and the Parisian carriage trade. In 1871, the lace merchant's grandson took things one step further. Like Worth before him, he opened a department selling the most luxurious ladies' evening gowns, reception dresses, and *toilettes de visite*. The grandson was Jacques Doucet, the perfectionist and soon-to-be-gentleman.

The late 1800s was a period of graceful profusion and controlled excess whose ideal woman labored to appear fragile, delicate, and ornamental. Doucet provided this clientele with concoctions made, not surprisingly, of lace and trimmed with other costly confections: silk ribbons and flowers, feathers, braid, beadwork, and embroidery. He used rare gros point de Venise for entire dresses, or re-embroidered panels of more fragile Alençon with pale flowering vines to match the barely tinted silk underneath. Lacelike patterns were achieved by cutting floral patterns into tulle or mousseline and sewing the outlines with shimmering paillettes. For luxurious contrast, Doucet fashioned bodices out of taffeta-thin ivory chamois, lined opera capes with swansdown, and made liberal use of chinchilla and marten or soft, lustrous zibeline. His *ensembles* were as romantic and opulent as the dresses in the eighteenth-century Watteau and Fragonard canvases he loved so well.

Doucet's clothes were worn by the most famous actresses of the day, most notably Réjane, celebrated for her performance as Sardou's Madame Sans-Gêne (Napoleon's laundress, who married one of his marshals). Vivacious and known for her taste as much as for her talent,

Réjane was a special friend of Doucet's and wore his clothes to great effect both onstage and off. During Doucet's heyday, the stage became the most visible showcase for a couturier's talents. Fashion periodicals could not yet be counted on to attribute the designs they showed, and the races had not yet become the place to observe the latest modes. Doucet's dresses appeared in production after production, and his work for the theatre colored his perception of how clothing should look. For Doucet, a dress had always to be grand, regal, and gala.

It may seem surprising that someone with such a sympathy for avant-garde art should suppress its parallel in fashion. But for Doucet, dignity and luxury were always more important than novelty. Such an attitude, unfortunately, was not well suited to the increasing simplicity and ease of wartime and postwar styles. His designs lacked the contemporary simplicity of Vionnet or the shock value of Poiret, both of whom had worked for him. The days were over when a client needed her couturier in order to acquire legitimacy. The *grande cocotte* Liane de Pougy recalled in her *Blue Notebooks*: "Doucet fitted us out like good mothers of families—or like colonel's ladies."

By 1923, Baron Adolph De Meyer, the fashion arbiter and photographer, had to defend Doucet against accusations that he was stuffy, noting that it was to Doucet's credit that he did not cater to a spirit of commercialism. But De Meyer couldn't reverse what was obvious: by the time of his death in 1929, the couturier's reputation had come to center less on his fashion and more on his connoisseurship. His obsession with elegance and his desire to be accepted into a grander social milieu than was his by birth had resulted in his being known precisely for his accomplishments as a leisured man of taste. Consequently, he never shook his conviction that women should want to look like ladies. He dressed one generation of women but never really attracted the custom of their daughters.

In 1929, Doucet's house was merged with that of Doueillet, a couturier of more modest reputation who had once worked as a silk merchant and as the manager of the House of Callot. The merger was not successful. The new house closed in 1932. The Doucet's begun by Jacques's father, Edouard, however, still does business selling gentlemen's accoutrements in the rue de la Paix.

A typically grand Doucet
dinner dress as seen in
Les Modes *in 1909.*

Paquin

THE HOUSE OF PAQUIN, LOCATED NEXT DOOR TO THE GREAT WORTH on the rue de la Paix, was famous from its founding in 1890 right through the Twenties for its originality and opulence. At its height, it dressed queens and duchesses, actresses and *cocottes*. Although determined and able to compete with the neighboring Doucet and Worth, the Paquins astutely chose not to concentrate on the haute aspect of the couture. A 1906 Paris guidebook captures the house's warmth:

> [Its] success was first and foremost a success of personality. Monsieur Paquin is a handsome man. His manner is a thing to conjure with —and he has worked it to its conjuring limit. Madame Paquin is pretty, she is gifted, she is charming. Everyone is fond of Madame Paquin. From the first this clever and ornamental young couple followed a new system. No haughty seclusion, no barred doors, at the Maison Paquin. Madame was probably met at the door by Monsieur Paquin himself, and to be met by Paquin was a treat.

Unlike the houses of Worth and Poiret, where the husband was the creator and the wife acted as muse and mannequin, at Paquin it was the wife who was the *animatrice*, while the husband ran the business and provided the administrative skills. Madame Paquin had trained at the highly regarded Maison Rouff, then opened her own small dressmaking establishment in one of Paris' less fashionable quarters. In 1890, her new husband, fresh from a success on the Bourse, found backers and joined her in establishing a *maison de couture* at 3, rue de la Paix. By 1900, it was Madame Paquin who was chosen to organize the fashion segment of the Exposition Universelle; her house's display included a mannequin of herself dressed to the nines. She was the first of the couturiers to send mannequins to the trend-setting and trend-spotting races at Longchamps and Chantilly. In 1910, she sent a dozen of them off to tour the major cities of America. Paquin was the first of the couture houses to open branches outside Paris, beginning, in 1896, with one in London and following it with others in Buenos Aires, Madrid, and a special shop for furs in New York. In 1913, Madame Paquin became the first woman in her field to be awarded the Légion d'Honneur.

From the beginning, Paquin's designs displayed her liveliness, as well as her graphic ability with vivid colors emphasized by the use of black. She rescued black from its dignified and frequently mournful nineteenth-century role, tempering its severity by lining an 1896 town coat in bright, glossy red silk, or using it as a foil for brilliant jewel-tone embroideries or fabulous lace. Her turn-of-the-century designs, while echoing the period's "silhouette serpentine," as well as its pref-

RIGHT:
Paquin race gown, ca. 1914.

BELOW:
Madame Paquin.

A 1905 summer evening
dress trimmed with
silver lace and rose
garlands (top); a 1911
evening dress.

A Paquin fur-trimmed
evening coat, ca. 1932.

Paul Iribe fan, from the
1911 Paquin album.

erence for soft swirls of lace and tulle and floral garlands, made use of exuberant raspberry or Dutch blue rather than the "swooning" pastels decried by Poiret. Like him, she embraced exoticism in the Teens, outshining even the Sultan of Fashion with her Chinoiserie opera cloaks and evening dresses worn with headdresses of Chantilly lace shaped like butterfly wings and sporting bird-of-paradise antennae. Paquin also collaborated with the artists of her day. In 1911, she produced an album of designs for accessories, fans, and clothing by the fashion artists Georges Barbier and Paul Iribe and in the years following made up dresses after designs by Léon Bakst and Drian.

Paquin also made tailored clothes, however. There, her sensibility showed itself in soft pale wool felt decorated with finely traced scrolling braids and inserts of Irish crochet lace. These luxurious tailleurs came to be trimmed with furs, and fur became part of the image of the house. In particular, Paquin had a reputation for coats, and year after year the best sellers were trimmed with collars, cuffs, and hems of sable, fox, chinchilla, and monkey. And for thirty years after Madame Paquin's abdication, the house made practically nothing else.

Client relations—Monsieur Paquin's doing—played a larger part at this house than perhaps at any other. A client would write with her upcoming season's requirements, and Paquin would make everything she might need. Madame Paquin relied upon—and promoted—her knowledge of how women actually moved in their clothing, rebelling against increasingly narrow skirts in the Teens and including, as she once remarked, "those Parisians who must battle with the Métro" in her thoughts when designing.

When Monsieur Paquin died shortly after World War I, Madame Paquin, suffering from the loss of his encouragement and guidance, gave up her role as house designer to a Mademoiselle Madeleine, who created the collections throughout the Twenties. In the early Thirties, Madame Paquin retired. Although the house remained open until 1956 (under the direction of a Madame del Pombo) at 120, rue du Faubourg Saint-Honoré, its output, mood, and reputation changed completely in the absence of its charming and gifted founder.

The Paquin pavilion at the 1911 Turin exposition.

A "bacchante gown," ca. 1914.

Lanvin

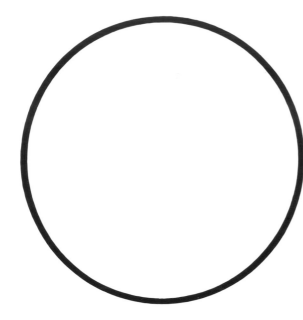

F ALL THE HOUSES IN PARIS, LANVIN IS THE OLDEST AND THE ONE that has displayed the most continuity. Its beginnings were inauspicious: in 1890, a twenty-three-year-old woman, Jeanne Lanvin, the eldest of ten children of a pair of Breton concierges, went into business as a milliner in a two-room apartment at 22, rue du Faubourg Saint-Honoré. It was this woman who for more than fifty years presided over her own constantly growing corner of the haute couture, never losing her popularity and never abandoning her aesthetic. For Jeanne Lanvin, women were meant to wear clothes of unabashed femininity, in colors that were frankly pretty, and whose shapes had always more to do with the *jeune fille* than with the *garçonne*. She has a special place in the hearts of those women who remember the anxious wait and the delicious pleasure of their first "good" dress from her house, a house that remains in the Lanvin family (and, not incidentally, in the building where she began by making hats).

Jeanne Lanvin (she reverted to her maiden name after her divorce) branched out of the millinery business slowly, first making dresses for a younger sister and then for her daughter Marie-Blanche. At a time when children were dressed in fussy and restrictive reproductions of adult clothing, Lanvin's suitably youthful creations seemed refreshing and new. By 1909, she was making dresses for mothers who had noticed Marie-Blanche's beautiful clothes and asked if she could dress their daughters as well. Her reputation, and her versatility as a designer, grew as her daughter did, and in time Lanvin, in much expanded quarters, was making dresses and all kinds of clothing for elegant people of all ages.

As can be seen in photographs of Lanvin-garbed mothers and daughters, the Lanvin aesthetic was independent of age. She has been justly credited with blurring the distinction between women's and children's clothing, the youthfulness of both being an important aspect of twentieth-century fashion. The beginning of this century saw a division of women into "types," these only occasionally based on age. No longer was it necessary for a woman to dress according to her stage in life as a debutante, bride, wife, and finally, matron or widow. Whether she was girlish, athletic, exotic, or "smart," she could carry her look with her throughout life, and likely enough, Lanvin would design something that suited her. Lanvin possessed an uncanny awareness of the varied sartorial needs of the modern woman and could dress her appropriately for any occasion. She had as well a great awareness of the varying moods of a woman, and would, for example, design a black taffeta dress with either short sleeves and demure beribboned flowers or a slashed neckline outlined with diamanté

*J*eanne Lanvin, in the Thirties.

PSYCHÉ.

Typical Lanvin ribbons
on a Twenties robe de
style.

FOLLOWING PAGES:
Gilda Gray photographed
in a Lanvin picture
dress before a Drian
screen.

arabesques. Both dresses were appealing, both undeniably "Lanvin," and both could be and were worn by the same woman as the social occasion required.

Lanvin worked by delivering oral instructions to a team of artists who would then sketch her ideas and return the drawings to her for editing. Color was always primary among her concerns. She maintained her own dyeworks and, while her hues were seldom the *dernier cri*, they were always clear, subtle, and feminine: pale pink, begonia, fuchsia, cerise, almond green, periwinkle blue, cornflower blue, and, especially, Lanvin blue, the deep robin's-egg shade inspired by medieval stained glass. Silver was combined with every color, but is especially recognizable as a Lanvin touch when used with black. Her graphic skill resulted in striking black-and-white patterns.

Lanvin's sense of color and pattern had its roots in an active appreciation of the visual arts. Her painting collection included works by Vuillard, Renoir, Fantin-Latour, and Odilon Redon, painters she favored for their grace and charm. In her search for inspiration in museums, monasteries, and costume libraries, she would not overlook a glimpse of a garden through a window, a botanical etching, or the pages of a history book. Throughout her collections, embroideries appear that are reminiscent of Aztec, Renaissance, eighteenth-century, Impressionist, or Cubist art. Where another *couturière* might have been tempted to translate these elements literally, Lanvin's taste and vision were so strong that they became instantly "hers."

Lanvin's designs seemed to exist in a time of their own and, while modern, were never slavish to prevailing modes. In the early Teens, even while working with the slim silhouette and occasional egret-sprouting turban, she managed to avoid the obvious histrionic references so prevalent in the clothing of other designers. Lanvin set her own mood with narrow, empire-waisted dresses sewn with burnished gold Persian vines; *robes capucines* with hoods, and simple dresses that acted as backgrounds for her already stylized and Cubistic flowers. In her hands, a medieval look was evoked by long, trailing sleeves, gently re-interpreted in lace for an afternoon in a rose garden.

She even remained true to her aesthetic during what could have been a difficult era—the reign of the flapper. In 1929, Lanvin repeated her assertion that "modern clothes need some sort of romantic quality" and that couturiers "should be careful not to get too prosaic and practical." During periods when fashion consisted of only one fashion, and skirt length or silhouette never varied but by general consensus, Lanvin always offered an alternative. As early as 1914, she showed full-skirted dresses, first called "1830 frocks," then pan-

LEFT:

A Twenties cloche from Lanvin.

BELOW:

A mother's dress and daughter's dress.

RÊVERIE

ROBES. DE JEANNE LANVIN

LEFT:

Representative Lanvin afternoon dresses trimmed with couched thread embroideries, ca. 1917.

ABOVE RIGHT:

Lanvin evening dresses showing characteristic use of line stitching.

nier gowns, and finally *robes de style*. Each season, the press predicted the demise of these romantic and ornamental picture dresses, but Lanvin proved their lasting appeal. The House of Lanvin showed *robes de style* throughout the Twenties and Thirties, and while other houses also made them, it is Lanvin's that set the standard. Most frequently made in silk taffeta, they were also available in velvet, sheer silk chiffon, organdy, or metallic lace, with shirred or cartridge-pleated skirts and shawl collars or net-filled wide necklines. In 1922, the artist Paul Iribe immortalized the style by sketching Jeanne and Marie-Blanche, each in a *robe de style*; the image has ever since been a signature of the house, appearing on its labels and perfume bottles.

Jeanne Lanvin's early training as a seamstress (she had served her apprenticeship at a house called Talbot, long before becoming a milliner) gave her an intimate knowledge of fabrics. These she used in a readily identifiable style—applying taffeta to tulle so that the appliqué appeared to float in thin air; attaching free-flowing ribbons at the neck or hip, or petals to other petals; and winding ruffles so that they undulated like ribbon candy. She seldom used patterned fabrics, preferring to work with appliqués and embroideries. Beginning in the Teens, she experimented with the modern look of machine parallel stitching and, by the Thirties, was using lamé and satin worked in parallel stitch and in honeycomb quilting to form shoulder "wings," belts, and bibs on otherwise simple columnar evening gowns. Many of the patterns were graduated in size, just as colors were worked in ombré gradations. Her favorite motifs, next to flowers, were bow-tied ribbons and firework-like sunbursts.

Children's clothing and hats were always part of the Lanvin

collections. In 1926 she opened a men's division, becoming the first *couturière* to dress whole families. (There was also a separate sports division and one for furs.) Lanvin's way with accessories was characteristic. She designed the loveliest of Art Deco evening envelopes, Pierrot collars of her favorite tulle, hairbows made of rhinestones, belts suspending medieval pouches. The house grew in other ways as well: My Sin was introduced in 1925, Arpège in 1927. Branches were established in Nice, Cannes, and Biarritz. Her illustrious clientele included the princesses of England, the Queens of Italy and Roumania; the actresses Mary Pickford, Marlene Dietrich, and Yvonne Printemps; the poet Anna de Noailles, and Louise de Vilmorin, novelist and *femme de lettres*.

The House of Lanvin, like all the French houses, suffered during World War II. Although she designed bright felt or black tweed gas-mask holders, Lanvin's strengths were not suited to the oppressive requirements of war. She was now old. Her greatest contribution—the conviction that youthfulness in dress need not be the exclusive province of young girls—was no longer news. But the house, even after her death in 1946, endured under the direction of the family and two younger couturiers. Antonio del Castillo, a Spaniard who had trained as an architect, joined the firm in 1950. His Spanish heritage was reflected in his penchant for black lace, jewel-encrusted embroideries, and the use of vivid colors. Marie-Blanche, who on her marriage became the Comtesse de Polignac, now ran the house and worked closely with Castillo in upholding certain Lanvin traditions, especially that of magnificent embroideries. In line with the tastes of the 1950s, Castillo's evening clothes often incorporated details adapted many years before by Lanvin herself: bouffant skirts, fichu collars, off-the-shoulder necklines, and the use of parallel stitching to stiffen and ornament evening coats and skirts.

Since Castillo's departure in 1963 to found his own house, the couture collections have been designed by Jules-François Crahay, a Belgian. His first design was the wedding dress worn at the marriage of Maryll and Bernard Lanvin, the grand-nephew of Jeanne and now the owner of the house. The present Madame Lanvin, a former model and a great beauty, has worked closely with Crahay through the years and, in 1982, began creating the prêt-à-porter collections herself. In the brief time she has been designing she has already established certain hallmarks for the house: a cheerful color sense, a fondness for jacquard and damask-patterned fabrics, the use of the tulip shape for skirts and of asymmetry for necklines. Her designs for day and for grand evenings continue in the Lanvin tradition of a happy elegance.

LEFT:
Romantic evening looks by Jules-François Crahay for Lanvin.

FOLLOWING PAGES:
Antonio del Castillo adjusting a 1951 evening dress. PAGE 59: Silver wedding dress designed for the Princesse d'Alcantra in 1936.

BELOW:
For the finale of a recent show, the house made up this Thirties Lanvin evening dress.

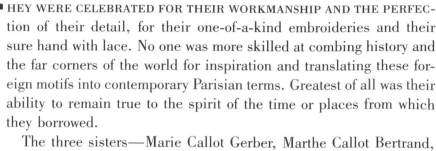

Callot Soeurs

THEY WERE CELEBRATED FOR THEIR WORKMANSHIP AND THE PERFECtion of their detail, for their one-of-a-kind embroideries and their sure hand with lace. No one was more skilled at combing history and the far corners of the world for inspiration and translating these foreign motifs into contemporary Parisian terms. Greatest of all was their ability to remain true to the spirit of the time or places from which they borrowed.

The three sisters—Marie Callot Gerber, Marthe Callot Bertrand, and Regina Callot Chantrelle—set up their business in 1895 on the rue Taitbout, where they worked with antique laces and ribbons to fashion shirtwaists and lingerie. They had inherited their love of fine lace and their artistic ways from their father, a painter and teacher of design, and their mother, a lacemaker from a family that had always made lace. Gradually the three formed a couture house that purveyed all manner of mysterious and breathtaking concoctions. In 1914, the Callots moved into grander quarters at 9-11, avenue Matignon, where they remained until 1928, when Madame Gerber's son took over the reins and moved the Maison Callot to 41, avenue Montaigne. The business was absorbed into Calvet in 1937.

Madame Gerber, the oldest sister, was in charge of designing. She had worked as a *modéliste* for Raudnitz et Cie. before starting a small lace shop that she abandoned in favor of Maison Callot. Madame Gerber was, no less than her designs, a study in exoticism: tall, with her hair hennaed red, she wore shapeless dresses so as not to detract from her masses of freshwater pearls and Oriental jewelry. Known for her superb sense of color, she borrowed tints from antique porcelains, Chinese cloisonné, a Louis Treize fabric, or a handful of wildflowers and combined them daringly in embroideries evocative of Persia, China, or Renaissance Italy. All the sisters were fond of gilt brocades, sheer silver and gold tissues, and gilt lace.

The Callot oeuvre can be divided into distinct categories: day clothes and lingerie, dresses made from antique fabrics, period gowns, clothes made of lace, and Oriental, or exotic clothing. The period gowns were among the sisters' first endeavors. Turn-of-the-century versions were made in the style of Louis XV, with pointed bodices, panniered skirts, and delicately floral-patterned silks garnished with Alençon lace ruffles. These evolved into what would be known as *robes de style*, or "picture dresses." These sweet dresses, with their full skirts and close bodices, were usually realized in yellow, mauve, rose, or pale green petalled tulle and appeared throughout the Teens and Twenties.

More sophisticated were the Callots' Oriental offerings—the first, which appeared in the early Teens, were called *robes phéniciennes*

—evening dresses that bore no discernible relationship to Phoenician works of art but nonetheless appealed to a clientele enamored of the rare and unusual. *Orientalisme* was conveyed in dresses of embroidered satin or velvet, overlaid with panels that crossed at the neck and continued down the sides, in lines suggesting a tunic. These panels incorporated, and ended in, paisley medallions, turret shapes, or Chinese scroll-topped *ruy-i* bands. The Near-Eastern and Eastern motifs were expressed in appropriate colors: kingfisher blue and black, highlighted with copper and gold; Nile green satin strewn with coral beads; or peach velvet stitched in beads of blue, mauve, and rose. For the beaded chemises so popular in the Twenties, Callot embroidered silks with birds hovering over plum blossoms or fierce dragons spewing fire, reinterpreted in subtle, smoky tones. Their efforts in more contemporary decorative modes benefitted from this love of the Orient: a Cubist pattern, for instance, might be worked out in all the colors of a Chinese hardstone tree—jade greens, rose quartz, and crystal.

Clothes from Callot were known for their exotic details—kimono sleeves, tasselled girdles, various kinds of tunics. Day clothes of plain or checked wool might be enlivened with passementerie or a multitude of crocheted buttons and loops. A simple mid-Twenties black wool chemise was trimmed with bits of crisp white organdy and, to differentiate it from a Patou or Chanel frock, was belted in green kid stamped in gold, Russian style. Even in sports clothes, Callot made use of unusual materials like rubberized gabardine or pearl-gray calfskin. The lingerie made by the house was extraordinarily feminine: nightgowns and chemises of the most gossamer silks, worked with bands of golden lace or bouquets of pendant silk flowers.

By the late Twenties, the house had passed into the hands of Pierre Gerber, and his efforts to maintain his mother's standards resulted in criticism that the house wasn't keeping up with the times. In truth, throughout this period Callot was a well-kept secret among women who appreciated quality and sought to avoid the harsh lines of the late Twenties or the severe simplicity of the Thirties decade. The house was especially adept at working with quality laces and demand continued for its use in such at-home wear as pajamas and tea gowns. Madeleine Vionnet, who trained at Callot Soeurs, paid the house the supreme compliment: "Without the example of the Callot Soeurs, I would have continued to make Fords. It is because of them that I have been able to make Rolls Royces."

PRECEDING PAGES:
A*Callot headdress, ca. 1912. PAGE 61: A turn-of-the-century Callot dinner dress, from* Les Modes.

LEFT:
T*wo Thirties evening dresses.*

Lucile

ETWEEN THE STERN REIGN OF QUEEN VICTORIA AND "THE WAR TO end all wars" there was a brief period of unabashed and promiscuous "living well." The Edwardian era in England paralleled the Belle Epoque in France and, in Lady Duff Gordon's words, "the luxury trades were kept alive by the princely expenditures of American millionaires and Russian grand dukes." All the world watched avidly as royalty, the haute monde, the very, very rich, and their mistresses spent money like water, worshipping at the altar of beauty. The newspapers and magazines delighted in each new excess, chronicling the chamois sheets, monogrammed cigarettes, and hothouse lilies-of-the-valley (sewn in her garters twice a day) of lady so and so.

It was against this backdrop that Lucile, Ltd. became the first English-based couture house to achieve international recognition. (Worth, while founded by an Englishman, was utterly French in its tone and output.) From the turn of the century until the late Teens, Lady Duff Gordon strove to sate the sartorial appetites of her worldwide clientele. Lucile, Ltd. turned out dance frocks, day clothes, street ensembles, and elaborate lingerie, but especially it was known for its glorious tea gowns, those dresses worn over loosened stays at home for intimate dinners or at country houses for the century's new diversion, five o'clocks, when houseguests assembled for tea (and, increasingly, cocktails). Lucile's tea gowns dripped with lace, ribbons, silk flowers, and "it," a word given new meaning in this century by the *couturière*'s sister, the novelist Elinor Glyn.

Lucy Christiana Sutherland was born in 1863, married at the age of eighteen, had a child, and was divorced in 1889. In order to support her daughter, she began dressmaking on a small scale, and slowly the creations of Mrs. James Wallace grew in demand. Mrs. Wallace was fortunate to have her sister as a showcase. Elinor Sutherland wore her sister's models at house parties; and Lucy designed her wedding gown as well. Adopting a name that better suited her creations, Mrs. Wallace opened the Maison Lucile in 1894 at Old Burlington Street and moved twice before establishing Lucile, Ltd. at 23 Hanover Square. In 1900, she married Sir Cosmo Duff Gordon, and following a 1910 Christmas visit to New York, she opened a branch of Lucile, Ltd. on West 36th Street. A year later saw the inauguration of the Paris branch on the rue Penthièvres.

Lady Duff Gordon's most visible work was in the performing arts. She provided the stage wardrobe for Lily Elsie in *The Merry Widow* in London. As a result the narrowed silhouette topped by a gigantic hat became the established mode. She dressed Irene Castle for her dance performances; the combination of Lucile's airy dance frocks and Irene's

The Dolly Sisters, famous twin clotheshorses, wearing Lucile's robes de style in 1914.

lithe body and charismatic beauty exerted tremendous fashion influence on both sides of the Atlantic. Florenz Ziegfeld was in the audience when Lucile presented her first theme fashion show based on the Arabian Nights. Ziegfeld bought the entire collection, whisked away four of her most beautiful models, and included the show in his "Miss 1917." Lucile's next fashion show, done to support her sister's war charity and called "Fleurette's Dream at Perrone," toured the vaudeville circuit. Indeed, Lucile's clothes received so much publicity that she was satirized as "Lady Muff Boredom."

A glance through the scrapbook Lucile kept of nineteenth-century fashion illustrations reveals the sources for many of her favorite details: bertha collars, layered puff skirts, sheer batiste undersleeves, pointed bodices that laced up the front, and wire-framed hats, as well as motifs built around bows, tassels, ruffles, and ribbons. She herself acknowledged a debt to Fragonard, the eighteenth-century Rococo painter, extolling "the wonderful grace of the full skirts, the feminine coquetry of flowers and lace and puffs, and the charm of delicate color combinations" in his delightful canvases.

Many of her own dresses have a comparable ingénue quality, reinforced by such eighteenth-century "milkmaid" details as aprons, panniers, and garlands of posies. This innocence contrasted in a rather interesting way with the boudoir mood set by the soft fabrics, these seen to best advantage floating over a dance floor or spread out beguilingly on a fainting couch. To heighten the sense of romantic fantasy, Lady Duff Gordon christened each dress with a seductive name: "Hesitate No Longer," "His Lullaby," "Why So Lonely," "Lolita." The fabrics and colors for these dresses were misty and languorous: palest pink ribbons plaited through silver lace; wind-gray tulle combined with silver lamé and silver fox; iridescent taffeta the color of a moonlit rose petal; and orchid-gold lamé used in conjunction with mauve and rose chiffon.

The designs of Lucile were created directly on the mannequins. Lady Duff Gordon presided over a workroom filled to overflowing with fabrics of every imaginable hue and texture, and she chose from these as she draped and fitted on the figure. For these sessions, her mannequins wore a pale flesh-colored satin underdress trimmed with lace that became the actual foundation of the dress being created. After achieving the desired effect, she made a quick sketch; the dresses were made up using these. Even in the Teens, Lady Duff Gordon was relatively uninterested in tailormades, but when the need arose, they were designed, under her supervision, by her tailor.

The twice-yearly collection always included romantic picture dresses

RIGHT AND FOLLOWING PAGE: Dinarzade in a 1917 evening dress of bright blue and black brocade.

BELOW: Dinarzade wearing a 1916 wedding dress of white satin liberally ornamented with "pearls."

as well as exotic Oriental *toilettes*, notable for their daring color combinations and bejewelled headdresses. Year after year, a dress called the Elinor Glyn was included (these were prominent in her own wardrobe and were always made of softly draped mousseline or chiffon). Silk roses, her signature, were sewn to picture dresses and lingerie and were made in her workrooms. The notion that Lady Duff Gordon invented the split skirt is apocryphal. She does, however, deserve credit for making the fashion show an event and for glamorizing the role of the mannequin. With a photographer's eye, she chose young women whose striking looks and unusual height denied them other posts, and in her typically histrionic manner christened them with such names as Dinarzade, Ruby, and Arjamando. These beauties brought gasps from the audience—she highlighted the effect by presenting them clothed in her exquisite concoctions without the customary black high-necked underdresses.

Each of Lucile's *maisons de couture* featured a Rose Room, its wall and daybed hung with pale pink taffeta overlaid with lace. Here one could find all kinds of tea gowns, nightdresses, and chemises made of diaphanous pale-hued silks awash with ribbons and flowers. Although tinted lingerie came into use just as she was beginning her business, and she cannot lay claim to its invention, Lady Duff Gordon was astute in realizing that women, even nice women, had become as interested in their appearance *en déshabillé* as they were in the impression they might make at a dinner party.

The international reputation of Lucile, Ltd. was not due to Lady Duff Gordon's business acumen. In a way, it was precisely the lack of pragmatic consideration that led to the house's phenomenal growth and inevitably to her ruin. Her enthusiasm led her to accomplish things no practical person would have dared to try. And since her fiascos made headlines as much as her fantastic utterances and clothes, she profited from her own lack of discipline. Her businesses were bought and sold, went bankrupt and were bought back again. A legal dispute with a manufacturer is still a subject in first-year law contracts courses. She continued to make clothes well into the Twenties, but her interest and appreciation of contemporary clothing declined. By 1930 she could write: "No more commercial aims, thank God! I have done enough real work in my life. It bores me now to make ordinary clothes. I design nothing but special dresses for special people." Soon she designed nothing at all. Although her 1932 autobiography was popular, she died in obscurity and poverty in 1935, having come to rely on the generosity of such friends as Edward Molyneux, whom she had trained as a couturier many years before.

Boué Soeurs

THE BOUÉ SOEURS HAD ONE OF THE MOST RECOGNIZABLE STYLES IN the history of fashion. Every piece of clothing they made had a gently feminine quality enhanced by a use of lace, delicate colors, and folded silk ribbon rosettes. These roses were, in the opinion of the sisters, "the signature of Boué." Although their romantic mien can be likened to that of Lucile or Lanvin, the Boué Soeurs never achieved the reputation of a major house. Their popularity was greatest in America, and today there is a small cult of devotées who remember the Boué lingerie or *robes de style* in their grandmothers' attics or have coveted them at museum costume exhibitions.

The house was founded in 1899 by two sisters, Madame Sylvie Montegut and the Baronne Jeanne d'Etreillis, both née Boué. Together they established couture houses, first in Paris, then in New York. The house perfume, Quand les Fleurs Rêvent, was concocted at their ancient Château de Maison Rouge outside Paris. By the mid-Twenties, their reputation rested mainly on lingerie; by 1933, they had ceased to advertise and, probably, to exist.

Madame Sylvie seems to have been the artistic spirit; Jeanne, the translator, adaptor, and missionary, travelling around the world to gather inspiration and promote their wares. Both sisters had long been known by their circles for their original manner of dressing and their remarkable hairstyles when they realized a longstanding dream of founding a *maison de couture*.

Many of Sylvie's most profound influences seem to have derived from a childhood fascination with fairy-tale personifications of the sun, the wind, and the moon. In an interview she once spoke of her preoccupation with these elements as well as with transparency and light. In her creations she sought to portray the harmonies of nature, to capture the essence of the constantly changing sky, the reflection of the setting sun, the poignancy of falling leaves. She felt that a dress, as well as a poem, could express the melancholy beauty of twilight, *l'heure bleue*, and she attempted to do so in a dress christened Ciel d'Orient.

The Boué Soeurs made great use of light-refracting silver and gold cloths, which, since such fabrics were unobtainable from the usual sources, were purchased from theatrical supply houses. They were also fond of silver and gold lace, made in their own workrooms, and of embroideries made with gilt threads applied in a scrolling tracery. Their staff of lacemakers also provided them with *filet Boué*, a floral-patterned lace worked on a grid mesh. This became another house signature. The transparency so important to Madame Sylvie can be seen in the ankle-revealing lace scallops of her petalled skirts, in the

LEFT:

nstallation photograph
with a "lingerie" robe
de style *shown at right.*

ABOVE RIGHT:

wo Boué robes de
style, *ca. 1922.*

U-shaped bibs lined in blush-pink silk at the bodice, and in the way she layered embroideries under lace or sheer silks. Embroidery for the Boué Soeurs was done in Venice on another sheer fabric, organdy, which was used both in inserts and for entire "lingerie dresses," afternoon gowns popular from the turn of the century through the Twenties and fashioned out of fabrics formerly reserved for lingerie. The moods created by light at different hours of the day, as fascinating to Madame Sylvie as they had been to the Impressionist painters, were translated into changeable taffeta, a fabric that reflects different colors in different lights. Boué colors were usually pale and muted, reminiscent of tinted almonds or spring flowers; these were frequently used in combination with each other and with gold, silver, and white.

A French artist of the day dubbed the Boués, who made an extraordinary six to eight trans-Atlantic crossings a year to manage their New York house, "the seagulls of lace." It is a fitting epithet for two sisters whose work was a pure flight of fancy.

Poiret

N HIS AUTOBIOGRAPHY, *KING OF FASHION*, PAUL POIRET ASKED, "AM I a fool when I dream of putting art in my dresses, a fool when I say dressmaking is an art?" Although Worth had avowed that a dress could be a work of art—just as he himself was an artist—it was Poiret who first realized the couture's place in the realm of the arts, especially in its relation to the avant-garde. He felt that the great artists of his day were his colleagues—"fellow workers," as he called them. He believed that an artist was someone who put himself into everything he did, and he breathed his passion for fantasy and his rare individuality into each endeavor—writing, painting, theatrical and interior design, and schemes for fabrics, objects, scents, and dresses.

The first of the fashion celebrities, Poiret had a personality as newsworthy as his clothes. Everything he touched turned to headlines. His name, more than that of any other couturier, is linked with the life that died forever with the outbreak of World War I. The age of Poiret —begun in 1908 when he published the first of two albums of fashion designs and concluding with his departure for the front in 1914 in a uniform of his own design—was over almost as soon as it began.

During that brief period, Poiret, as he said, "freed the breasts [and] shackled the legs." Gone forever was the rigid hourglass silhouette and the Belle Epoque's blurred profusion of fabrics and colors. The Poiret woman was as slender as a will-o'-the-wisp in her long, straight dress, and as fresh as a child's drawing in primary colors and simple decoration.

Poiret, in his memoirs, did not claim to have effected a permanent fashion revolution: "It is neither by restoring life to the color scheme, nor by launching new styles that I think I rendered the greatest service to my epoch." Rather, he admitted, "It was in my inspiration of artists, in my dressing of theatrical pieces, in my assimilating and response to new ideas, that I served the public of my day." Although Poiret's clothes were revolutionary, and truly "modern" in relation to those they replaced, their validity would not last. The Second World War changed women's lives and clothes forever, and Poiret was not present to assimilate the new currents.

Paul Poiret was born in 1879 to a pair of cloth merchants whose business was in a section of Paris near the market quarter of Les Halles. It was during his enforced apprenticeship to an umbrella maker that his artistic personality began to emerge. Frustrated by his menial tasks, he lost himself in creating little dresses on an artist's figure given to him by his sisters. He then drew the resulting designs and took twelve of these renderings to Madame Chéruit, then at the house

of Raudnitz et Cie. She encouraged him by buying the lot and soon he was selling his sketches to the houses of Doucet, Paquin, Worth, Redfern, and Rouff. In 1898, Jacques Doucet made the ambitious and talented young man an offer of a job as a junior assistant.

Doucet was a great influence on Poiret, serving both as an encouraging teacher and as a model of an assured, elegant man-about-town interested in the arts. He put Poiret in charge of the tailoring department where his first design—a red cloth cloak with lapel and lining of gray silk that buttoned at one side with six enamel buttons—sold 400 versions. Doucet soon entrusted his protégé with the design of costumes to be worn onstage by Sarah Bernhardt and Réjane. Flushed with success, Poiret began to overstep his bounds, and by the time he left to serve in the military in 1900, Doucet had had to reprimand him for designing his own actress-mistress's clothes and for having sneaked into one of Sarah Bernhardt's rehearsals.

After his stint in the French army, Poiret returned to Paris, where he was engaged by the House of Worth, a considerably less satisfactory arrangement than he had enjoyed at Doucet, for Jean-Philippe was not the mentor Doucet had been. Poiret's dream of opening his own house was realized in 1904, when he learned of a vacancy in the rue Auber and borrowed funds from his mother. It opened to the public on September 1, at 5, rue Auber.

A year later, Poiret married Denise, a slender, dark young woman whom he had known as a child. Of her he wrote, "She was extremely simple, and all those who have admired her since I made her my wife would certainly not have chosen her in the state in which I found her. But I had a designer's eye, and I saw her hidden graces." Like Worth's wife, Marie, Denise was a source of inspiration to her couturier husband. Without her he may never have experimented with the empire style so suitable to her figure, or with the Oriental themes that complemented the slightly Slavic cast of her features. As they travelled around Europe, attending exhibitions and making the house known, Madame Poiret gained confidence. Poiret's clothes and the way his wife wore them became the desirable mode.

The very mention of Poiret evokes a feeling of sumptuousness, the thought of a line of mannequins parading in lavish brocade cocoons over Oriental pantaloons bound at their cuffs with silver and gold embroidery, their heads swathed in silk turbans festooned with jewels or sprouting bird-of-paradise feathers. In reality, however, Poiret's first designs were radically simple. As early as 1906, Denise had worn one of his plain, straight-line gowns, designed to show off her reedy figure, and, possibly, since she had her first baby that year,

*P*oiret *robe de style,*
"Mirage," illustrated in
the May 1920 Gazette
du Bon Ton.

intended to be worn both while pregnant, when a corset would have been most cruelly binding, or afterward. To Poiret, the corset was a horror. He complained that it "divided its wearer into two distinct masses: on one side there was the bust and bosom, on the other, the whole behindward aspect, so that the lady looked like she was hauling a trailer." He advocated the adoption of the brassière, which, thanks to his influence, won the day. In his early one-piece straight-falling dresses, line was everything, and it was critical that the corset and the then-fashionable ruffled petticoats be abandoned. In the next two years, every couturier began to see the wisdom of simplicity as a foil for youth. The emerging new silhouette was first called "Directoire," and, by 1908, when *Les Robes de Paul Poiret* (illustrated by Paul Iribe) was published, other details were incorporated that harked back to the period of the First Empire. Poiret's dresses featured wide necklines, pleated muslin underblouses, and simple patterns such as stripes or pin dots. Decorations were kept to a minimum: a line of buttons, a band of braid or fur, a tasselled belt.

For women accustomed to being transformed into flowerlike beauties by their couturiers and corsetières, the new silhouette seemed unfairly camouflaging of their graces. So that there would be no question as to the svelte figure underneath, Poiret narrowed the skirt even further, enclosing his women in a fitted tube, which, unlike Fortuny's clinging pleated gowns, had no elasticity and therefore gave no freedom of movement. Devices to promote movement, such as slit skirts and trouser-legged dresses, were as shocking as the hobble skirt they replaced, adding to Poiret's reputation as a startler. As important, though, as the new silhouettes, was Poiret's palette. Not only did he banish the spectrum of the Belle Epoque, he inaugurated one of extraordinary, and influential, brilliance, full of reds and vermilions, royal blues, yellows, and greens, colors made more dramatic by his simple lines and patterns.

During the period of his rising popularity, Poiret's thinking began moving in two simultaneous and not necessarily uncomplementary directions. While striving to clothe women simply, as they had been in ancient Greek and Neoclassical times, he also began to indulge a great interest in the Orient stimulated by his visit to Russia in 1911. Specifically, he was taken by "the whole phantasmagoria of half-Eastern life that is Moscow" as well as by the researches into ancient Sumerian, Persian, and Turkish costume required for his theatrical endeavors. From other eras and places he borrowed the simple shapes of kimono jackets, dalmatic copes, long tunics over trousers, and sari-like scarves to be worn any number of ways. He also made free with Persian

This 1926 evening dress was forward-looking less for its audacious skirt than for its halter neckline which presaged the Thirties.

Art - Goût - Beauté

brocades, naïve Slavic embroideries, the flying beads of a bodhisattva, and the blinding colors of India. Although he claimed not to have been influenced by Serge Diaghilev's Ballets Russes, then the rage in Paris, his new interests reflected what was most au courant. Paris had embraced the new exoticism, and Poiret's star rose.

In 1911, Poiret threw his great 1002nd Night fête, in which his garden was transformed into one of earthly delights. Persian costume was the order of the evening, and Poiret's wife, as the Sultan's favorite, wore an *ensemble* of sheer silk pantaloons under a wired tunic of cloth of gold edged with gilt fringe. A similar tunic made waves when it appeared in the Poiret-designed play *Le Minaret*, and soon every woman in Paris wanted one. Poiret's new shapes, worn over his signature narrow skirts, were conical lampshades, corollas, and bells.

Poiret had, as part of his artistic nature, a great curiosity and ability to learn. After a trip to Joseph Hoffmann's Wiener Werkstätte in Vienna, he founded an art school (named Martine after one of his daughters), where French girls were encouraged in a radically free atmosphere to play with paints and colors and to draw after nature or from their imaginations. Poiret subsequently took their bold prints, converted them into fabrics, and used the fabrics to make cushions, curtains, rag rugs, wall coverings, and, of course, articles of clothing. These, along with the painted pottery and lacquered furniture made by the young women, were sold in a special shop on the rue du Faubourg Saint-Honoré. 1911 also saw the advent of Poiret's perfume business (this named after another daughter, Rosine). The students at Martine painted the perfume bottles and packages according to the particular scent: Le Minaret in a turret-shaped box, Le Fruit Défendu in a bottle made like an apple, and Borgia, with a motif of a coiled snake. Rosine also produced lotions and other cosmetic preparations, among them what is reputed to be the first colored nail polish.

During this fertile year, Poiret engaged the painter Raoul Dufy to design fabrics. Dufy's bold patterns, along with the naïve ones produced at Martine, began to shape a new look for Poiret, which was exotic without being especially Oriental. He designed cloaks, shawls, and dresses in Dufy's woodblock prints; he also used brocades woven with brightly colored and gilt birds, foliage, seashells, and human figures for these designs. The Martine patterns—stylized dahlias, rosebuds, and artichokes—were carried out as beaded and embroidered motifs on dresses and accessories.

When World War I was declared, Poiret went to fight in the army, leaving his house in Paris to exist with such models as he had designed prior to leaving, and keeping his name in the news by writing

Two views of a 1926 evening dress.

tems from Martine: a
flower-decorated parasol,
a shoe, a pair of
gloves. The perfume,
Le Balcon, came in
its own miniature
gilt balcony.

articles from the front. In 1915 he returned to town for a short visit to put together a fall collection, but one of his daughters died suddenly, and he abandoned the idea. Between 1915 and 1918, Poiret's house was dormant, and those who were being written about in the fashion magazines were those couturiers who were too old to fight, or who were female.

Poiret's only wartime creation—a perfume called Sang de France, which was tinted red and came in a bottle shaped like a heart—was banned by the authorities. When he reopened his *maison de couture*, Patou and Vionnet were reopening and showing their decidedly un-Oriental designs. Molyneux was showing his restrained clothes, and Chanel was playing with Poiret's idea of a wire tunic for her little black dresses overlaid with black lace. In contrast, Poiret's clothes, though still dashing and imaginative, seemed loud and obvious. With increasing simplicity had come the expectation of perfect dressmaking. Poiret's clothes, unfortunately, remained theatrical—grand from a distance but poorly made when seen close up. By 1925, Liane de Pougy, herself one of a dying breed of "Grand Horizontals," after a visit to his new *maison de couture*, wrote about the "enormous premises, rich and tasteless. His struggle to be unusual has wound up making it all impossible. It's like a sweetshop."

Poiret's exuberance could not help him clothe the women of a new decade. Women wanted to wear their clothes, not be worn by them, and they had come to expect efficiency from their couturiers. Exoticism was moved indoors and reserved for dinner pajamas and tea gowns. Poiret sold the rights of his business to backers in 1925, but proved unreliable as an employee rather than an impresario. Short-lived affiliations, like one with Liberty's of London, did not work out. More and more, the designer occupied himself with diatribes against what he saw, not wrongly, as an increasingly masculine style of dress for women, and was reduced to making a list—rather a long one—of former friends he felt had betrayed him. His last days were bitter and hopeless. In 1944 Poiret, the man who had exacted fidelity from a fickle clientele, who had manipulated the press with deftness and enthusiasm, who had made the couturier a bona-fide celebrity, died in near-total obscurity.

P oiret cape, "C'est moi," drawn by A. E. Marty for Gazette du Bon Ton, *1922.*

FOLLOWING PAGES:
P oiret's wife and muse, Denise.

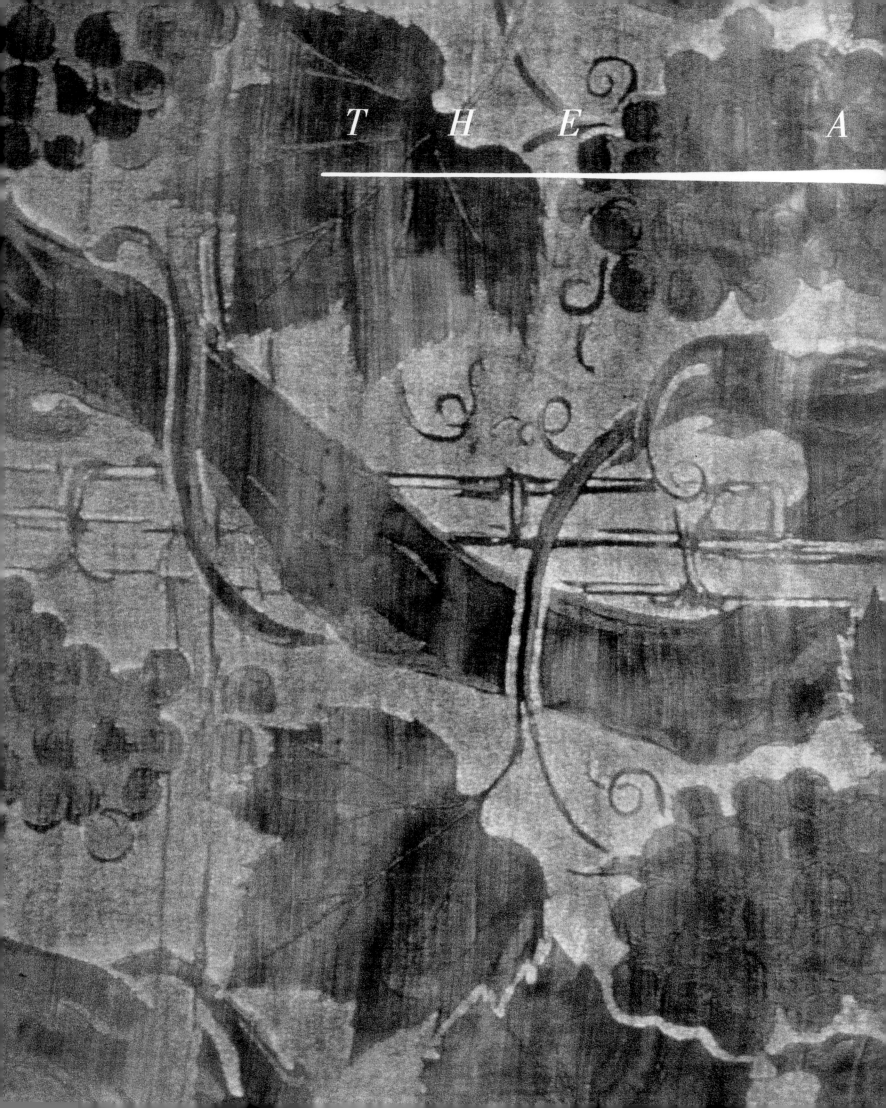

Most designers work within a framework dictated by their epoch. Given the current modes in color, textiles, and silhouette, their primary concern is to lend their individual stamps to what women will need and want. For others, the desire to make clothes or fabrics has nothing to do with fashion, but is simply an outlet for their special creativity. Because the present tends to be of little account to these clothing artists, their clothes are never "in" fashion—and never out of it.

Fortuny and Gallenga were fabric artists. They studied the whole of art history and derived their decorative elements, garment shapes, and the very feel of a fabric from a wealth of sources. The clothing and fabrics of Liberty & Co. very strongly reflected Arthur Lasenby Liberty's desire for a freedom in dress that would have both spiritual and physical ramifications.

Fashion's single most distinguishing characteristic today is diversity, and although many of the clothes worn "at home" now resemble those of "The Artists" in their flowing comfort and ethnic references, those made most strikingly in this Artistic tradition are certainly intended for grand, public moments. The very wearing of an evening dress today breathes a nostalgia for the past, and by using hand detailing, historical motifs, and sumptuous and personal fabrics, Zandra Rhodes and Mary McFadden justify an appreciation for the past, for the textile arts, and for the art of fashion. Because their fabric choices tend to dictate what their clothes will look like, they are less inclined to rely on any prevailing silhouette. And thanks to their use of such a wealth of references, these two designers, like all The Artists, hover outside the realm of fashion.

PRECEDING PAGES: Stencilled Fortuny velvet.

RIGHT: Isadora Duncan with her children, her son wearing a miniature Fortuny Delphos gown.

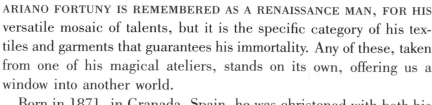

Fortuny

ARIANO FORTUNY IS REMEMBERED AS A RENAISSANCE MAN, FOR HIS versatile mosaic of talents, but it is the specific category of his textiles and garments that guarantees his immortality. Any of these, taken from one of his magical ateliers, stands on its own, offering us a window into another world.

Born in 1871, in Granada, Spain, he was christened with both his parents' names: Mariano Fortuny y Madrazo. His father, Mariano Fortuny y Marsal, was an internationally known painter, sometimes referred to as the Spanish Meissonier. His mother's family, the Madrazos, included several painters, and her father, Federico Madrazo, was a celebrated portraitist whose royal subjects included the Empress Eugénie.

Mariano Fortuny, in fact, inherited more than his family's art-making skills. Like his father, he experimented in mediums besides painting, drawing, and printmaking. He was well versed in physics and chemistry; and in the first three decades of the twentieth century, Fortuny would work on designs as varied as lighting devices and work tables and a reflective, collapsible theatre dome.

Mariano was only three when his father died. His mother, devoted to the memory of her husband, brought her son up to be an artist, providing him from an early age with teachers from among her family's circle. In homage to Fortuny y Marsal, she did her best, wherever the family lived, to re-create the environment her husband had painstakingly created, seeing that the collection lived by adding to it, especially in the area of textiles.

After a sojourn in Paris, the family moved, in 1899, to Venice, where they lived in a palazzo on the Grand Canal. Here, for a decade, Mariano Fortuny lived in the past, painting, drawing, etching.

Eighteen ninety-two was a pivotal year for Fortuny. The young man then made a pilgrimage to Bayreuth to the theatre founded by Wagner for the performances of his work. Fortuny was and would always remain mesmerized by Wagner's works; and his stay in Bayreuth cemented his conviction that, in its union of technology and the arts, opera was the perfect art form.

By 1899, when he left his mother's palazzo and moved into the Palazzo Orfei, Fortuny had begun to experiment with making Wagnerian maquettes and to study the uses of electricity in the creation of stage lighting and sets.

In 1906, he designed a theatre for the private house of the Parisian music patroness, the Comtesse Bearn, and for its inaugural performance Fortuny made his first textile/garment. This long, sheer silk rectangle, called a Knossos scarf, was printed with antique motifs and worn wrapped around the dancers in a number of ways.

RIGHT:

A rare stencilled and pleated tea gown photographed at the Palazzo Fortuny, Venice.

BELOW:

Fortuny bill of sale for a black Delphos gown.

These scarves (as well as the theatre's curtain) opened up a new world of experimentation to Fortuny. Already possessed of a profound admiration and knowledge of textiles nurtured by his mother's and his own collections, he began to apply himself to the production of textiles.

To the making of these textiles, Fortuny brought the methods learned in his other artistic endeavors: the manufacture and the mixing of tints for painting, the layering of color necessary to build a watercolor or gouache, the steps involved in making an aquatint print, and the technology of photographic printing. Because of the dyeing method, rarely were any two pieces exactly alike. Aniline and man-made dyes had been in use for several decades, but Fortuny chose to work mostly with dyes from natural sources: South American cochineal insects for red, Brittany straw for yellow, Indian indigo for blue. Although his inherited collection of textiles included many examples of rare brocades and embroideries, weaving and stitchery were not included in his battery of skills, and he never used them. Instead, he adopted their motifs and translated them into stencilling, as he adopted the motifs, but not the techniques of lace-making.

As for his method of pleating, it continues to be a subject of much discussion. Despite the fact that the patent filed for it by Fortuny shows diagrams, experts disagree on many details. What is known is that the pleats were formed by hand—probably when the fabric was damp—held in place with stitches, and set with heat. While subsequent technology has been able to accomplish Fortunyesque pleating on man-made fabrics, few attempts have come close to the magic of a real Fortuny.

It is interesting to note that although Fortuny had an inveterately curious mind, he remained immune throughout his life to the intricate problems of construction. Everything he made was flat, like the clothing of the past, achieving form only when put on the body. His dresses and robes slipped over the head or onto the shoulders, fastening with a drawstring or tie. Clearly his main interests were color and the preparation of the actual fabric, which he used as a ground, like a canvas, painting a picture of light. His actual decorative patterns were also flat, a contrast of light and dark; their complexity and depth is due to the layers of tints applied to the ground.

The year after the Knossos scarf—1907—was the year of the first Delphos. The Delphos was a columnar dress of thin silk satin more finely pleated than anything seen before. Christened by Fortuny's wife, the garment was named for the pleated linen chitons worn by maidens in Delphic Greek sculpture. For the next forty years, Fortuny made many variations on this dress. The early Delphos gowns had short,

Natacha Rambova (Mrs. Rudolph Valentino) wearing a Delphos tea gown.

bat-wing sleeves, laced along their tops. A later version—called a
Peplos—was given a peplum, a tunic attached at the shoulders and
falling, in points, to the hip. Sleeveless Delphos and Peplos dresses
appeared in the 1920s, at which time a fifth panel was added to their
construction. Occasionally Fortuny used the pleated silk for trousers,
for pleated dresses that were also stencilled, and for undulating pleated
dresses in which the pleats ran both horizontally and vertically. And
at times he used a very thin, fine cotton for the Delphos dresses.

Because of the elastic quality of the pleating, Fortuny weighted his
dresses by sewing cords strung with beads down the sides; these beads,
the most common of which were amber colored with squiggly stripes
of brick red and brown, were hand-blown on the Venetian island of
Murano. To keep their pleats, the dresses were twisted like skeins of
yarn, nestled in Fortuny watermarked tissue, and packed in a small
cream-colored box, tied with a black ribbon.

Over these pleated dresses, which some clients chose to belt with
narrow bands of matching (but stencilled and unpleated) silk or with
lengths of knotted cord, could be worn a Fortuny design in gauze or
silk velvet. Using a slightly ribbed gauze dyed some musty, muted
color, Fortuny turned out long vests; jackets with slit side seams based
on Chinese prototypes; short, sometimes tiered capes lined in opaque
white silk; and long, bat-wing-sleeved tunics. He stencilled his gauzes
and other fabrics with patterns culled from the paintings of Carpaccio
and Jan Memling as well as from textiles and artifacts of Chinese,
Persian, Coptic, North African, Arabian, Moroccan, Japanese, and
Italian Renaissance origin.

For the velvet garments (as well as for wall panels, cushions, pocket
bags, and simple beret hats) Fortuny used a thin, supple silk velvet
that was sent to him unbleached. He then treated the velvet with a
succession of dyes, stippling the tints by hand and brushing the pile
back and forth with one color after another until he achieved a patina
that improved upon that of antique textiles. Fortuny then applied the
gold, silver, and occasionally another color to a ground prepared with
the whites of specially aged eggs from China in the places where the
pattern was meant to be. Because the stencilled color is deep in the
pile of the velvet, the velvets have a slightly crusty texture. To apply
the patterns themselves, Fortuny used woodblocks, Japanese *katagami*
stencils, or a method of his own devising that utilized silk screens in
a photographically inspired printing process.

The velvet was then made up into medieval tabard gowns with sides
of pleated silk, Persian jackets, Moorish capes, knee-length robes
with belts and piping in another velvet, high-waisted Directoire gowns,

LEFT:

Mrs. Sloan wearing a
velvet Fortuny jacket
over her Delphos.

BELOW:

A collage of pleated tea
gowns.

and simple tunics, as well as a variety of theatrical and ecclesiastical garments. Variations were occasionally requested by customers, who could choose a fabric and then ask that it be made into something particular. Fortuny velvets were also bought and made into articles of clothing by several couturiers, including Poiret.

Travellers to Venice stopped in at the Fortuny store in the Palazzo Orfei, and when they returned home bearing his creations, demand for them grew. Fortuny had authorized the houses of Babani and Poiret to sell his fabrics and clothing when, in 1912, he opened his own emporium on the rue Marignan. There one could buy not only the stencilled velvet and gauze garments and the pleated dresses but also cushions, wall hangings, stencilled-silk lampshades, and desk lamps, all from the Palazzo Orfei in Venice. In New York, his wares were exhibited in the Carroll Galleries and, beginning in 1923, at the Brick Shop on Lexington Avenue. In 1929, Elsie MacNeill (who later became the Contessa Gozzi) opened a Fortuny store at 509 Madison Avenue. Here, the fabrics were and still are available, as well as the pleated dresses, which, because of import taxes, were sent to New York in pieces and stitched together on the premises. Also sold were jackets and other garments designed from Fortuny fabrics by MacNeill, the designs approved by Fortuny but bearing little resemblance to his own.

Shortly after Fortuny's death, in 1949, Contessa Gozzi, by then the director of the Fortuny fabric-manufacturing facilities on the island of the Guidecca, across the Grand Canal, decided to cease production of the pleated silks and stencilled silk velvets. Today, she still presides over the production of the stencilled cotton fabrics, with their watery jewel colors and peculiarly three-dimensional feeling. In any given season, she oversees the production of cloth in some fifty (of the 50,000 catalogued) Fortuny patterns. She alone mixes the dyes and prepares the ground.

Many of Fortuny's inventions (notably in theatrical design) have become obsolete with increasing mechanization. His invention of a boat motor designed to emulate the swimming of an eel is simply a curiosity. His paintings, and he considered himself above all a painter, are regarded as insights into a special mind. But his clothes, more perhaps than any ever made, are still able to astound and inspire. As long as they exist, they shall continue to do so.

Two Fortuny velvet garments. At left, a robe directoire *with a pattern of seventeenth-century lace; at right, a hooded cape stencilled in a Renaissance pattern.*

Gallenga

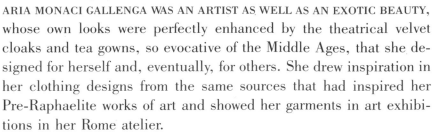

MARIA MONACI GALLENGA WAS AN ARTIST AS WELL AS AN EXOTIC BEAUTY, whose own looks were perfectly enhanced by the theatrical velvet cloaks and tea gowns, so evocative of the Middle Ages, that she designed for herself and, eventually, for others. She drew inspiration in her clothing designs from the same sources that had inspired her Pre-Raphaelite works of art and showed her garments in art exhibitions in her Rome atelier.

The turn of the century had seen a resurgence of interest in the period of the early Renaissance. Americans, looking for a past older than their own, built houses and apartment buildings that consciously aped Gothic and Tudor architecture. Into them went anything remotely Italianate. Gallenga's fabrics and garments reflect perfectly the passion for this rarefied past. Those who frequented her shop in Florence on the via de' Tornabuoni preferred her clothes to those of Fortuny because of the naïve, Gothic quality of the large, flat patterns.

Worn at a theatre opening in New York in 1916, a Gallenga "moyen âge" gown attracted much notice for its miraculous gold pattern, which appeared to float on the weightless black silk and did not seem "painted yet woven." Such a garment—a medieval tabard tea gown formed of two practically flat rectangular panels, the rear one long enough to form a train—became a Gallenga signature. These gowns had square, boat, or V-necklines, long tapered or panelled sleeves, and, often, panels of floating chiffon set into their side seams. They were sewn at the shoulders, and sometimes at the wrist or hem, with tubular Venetian glass mille fiore beads, larger and heavier than those used by Fortuny. For these gowns, Gallenga used silk velvet or crepe de Chine, sometimes dyed in ombré shadings and stencilled with up to nine tones of gold and silver paint. Her husband, a professor at the University of Rome, helped devise the method by which the metallic paint seemed to float on the fabric, not tarnishing and not flaking off.

The stencilling, which did not affect the depth of the velvet's pile, was applied in a variety of patterns. Most popular was a Gothic ironwork-inspired design that incorporated pointed ovals inside of which were birds and floral motifs. Another—a border of wave-splashed *li-shui* stripes—was quoted verbatim from a Chinese embroidery. Sometimes, Gallenga, who occasionally sewed a printed label into her garments, would include an almost illegible stencilled signature somewhere in the pattern of the fabric.

Gallenga also made garments that were contemporary in feeling, and for all their allusions to the past, her clothes were very much part of the Twenties idiom.

Detail of stencilled velvet from a Gallenga tabard tea gown.

Liberty & Co.

N THE NINETEENTH CENTURY, ARTISTS AND THEIR CIRCLES BEGAN TO perceive contemporary dress as an unbeautiful folly. It was not just that the creative mind tended to sniff at a slavish following of the latest modes, but also—from a painter's point of view at least—when a dress became passé, so did the painting in which it appeared. Starting in 1850s England, an Aesthetic Movement, composed of artists possessed of an evangelical zeal to elevate art to a realm untouched by fashion, started to become known.

The relation of art to everyday life was an important consideration to a group of London Royal Academy students, who decried all that the Victorian Age had done in the name of "advancement," and sought to return to what they saw as the last innocent age, that of their favorite painter, Botticelli. Naming their group the Pre-Raphaelite Brotherhood, they avoided contemporary clothing and settings in their paintings, and they chose instead backgrounds from nature and flowing Greek drapery, medieval garb, or Oriental costume.

"Aestheticism" became a popular and influential concept in the late 1870s, when Oscar Wilde emerged from Oxford. Through the importance he placed on dress and the need for its reform, in his lectures and essays, as well as by his own manner of dressing, he aligned himself with the Rational Dress Society. Wilde also stood in favor of E. W. Godwin, the architect and costume historian, who lectured on the practicalities of following the guidelines of hygienic (healthy) dress espoused by the German Dr. Jaeger.

At the heart of a bewildering variety of opinions about such issues as the benefits of divided skirts, woollen underwear, or clogs as opposed to high heels, was the belief that, in dress, the corset was the root of all evil. As the literal foundation for the crinoline and the bustle, it summed up all that was unhealthy (and therefore lacking in grace) about fashion.

Those who espoused freedom in dress also shared a desire for freedom of movement, the opinion that all clothing should be suspended from the shoulders, as well as the more merely aesthetic notion that colors should be pale, clear, and subtle. The ideal garment was waistless or casually girdled, hung in seemingly natural folds, and of a fabric in the light colors of nature, as can be seen in the works of Whistler, Alma-Tadema, and Burne-Jones.

The person who saw to it that the Aesthetic Movement was realized in actual clothing that could be purchased and worn by a general public was not a designer or an artist, but the founder of a great emporium that originally concentrated on Oriental wares, then fabrics, and then on clothing made from those fabrics. Arthur Lasenby Lib-

This gown was called "Maria" and appeared in the 1911 Liberty Catalogue of Picturesque Dresses.

erty was most influential in implementing the thinking of the artists and critics of his day—artists he had either met through their patronage of one of his stores, or whom he knew by reputation only. Along with E. W. Godwin, Liberty established a fabric and clothing department that strove to improve upon current, ungainly fashions and, as a result, produced designs that predated Paris by several decades. It was not until the Teens that Poiret championed the idea of suspending a garment from the shoulder, dispensing with the corset once and for all. Liberty's clothing, displaying only those tints found in nature as well as "out-of-fashion" shapes borrowed from history or other cultures, also predated the work of Fortuny.

When it first opened in 1875, Liberty's East India House reflected what had in the past two decades become almost a mania for things Japanese. The store, at 218A Regent Street, offered an assortment of fabrics, mats, screens, lacquerware, porcelains, and printed papers. Its showrooms were lined with Pre-Raphaelite paintings and leather-bound editions of works by Burne-Jones and by Christina and Dante Gabriel Rossetti. By 1883 Liberty had opened a second store, Chesham House, which stocked Chinese robes and Persian shawls along with goods from a variety of Oriental sources. The Paris branch opened in 1890 at 38, avenue de l'Opéra, and moved in the early Twenties to the boulevard des Capucines, where it remained until its closing in 1932.

Liberty's, as the original store came to be known, began producing its own wares in 1879, importing unbleached cashmeres, gauzes, woollens, and silks, and dyeing them in "art colors" like Nile green and soft Indian reds. The quality of the dyeing was so fine that it was considered an Occidental coup—the West had finally mastered an art formerly thought to be solely the province of the East. Soon Liberty's was printing its fabrics with intricate woodblocks similar to those used in Indian fabric manufacture. Liberty silks, most celebrated for their soft-flowing qualities, were used by Parisian couturiers as well as by artists draping their models for a pose, and the term "Liberty" came into use as a generic term for soft silk.

In 1884, Liberty's initiated a clothing department whose inventory was made from the store's fabrics. Headed by Godwin, the department featured two clothing categories: "Novelties for the New Season" and "Costumes Never Out of Fashion." The "Novelties" were modified versions of current styles, ornamented with smocking and embroideries meant to look hand-crafted. "Costumes Never Out of Fashion" relied heavily on Greek and Roman dress, as well as medieval and Empire influences, all eras notable for their undefined or raised waistlines and simple principles of construction. In the late 1880s, for example, Liberty's offered toga dresses of cotton or silk, with braided cord girdles and Greek key embroidery. (Similar styles were not to be shown in Paris until around 1910.) Long, dropped-waist velvet dresses with wrist-length sleeves laced with gilt cord and girdles embroidered with flowering vine motifs showed a medieval inspiration. Popular with Liberty's clientele for wear as tea gowns, these dresses were worn by the store's sales force until 1932.

One of Liberty's most popular items was the burnous, loosely based on a Middle Eastern cloak, and worn by Aesthetic and fashionable dressers alike as an evening wrap. The burnous was made of velvet or supple satin, sewn down the front with an embroidered floral band. It was fastened with two large self-covered buttons embroidered with florets, and connected by a loop of twisted braid. The end of the rectangle formed a graceful hood, which culminated in a braided silk tassel. The satin burnous was available in soft colors like blush pink, mauve, white-jade green, and ice blue; the velvet, in shades of black and claret. The burnous was the perfect embodiment of Aesthetic notions of beauty. Loosely fitted and therefore not constricting, it moved with the wearer, and its vaguely ethnic source rendered it otherworldly. Another of Liberty's characteristic garments was made for wear indoors: a cocoon-like "combing sacque" (designed for wear at one's toilette) made of fine ombré silk ornamented with an embroidered floral band and large embroidered buttons with braided loops.

Ladies' day and afternoon dresses and children's clothes were embellished with smocking, a decorative feature borrowed from ethnic and peasant clothing, for which the house is still famous. Liberty's also transformed such Oriental motifs as peacock feathers and irises into Art Nouveau patterns which were used in a variety of woven and printed fabrics.

By the early Thirties, Orientalism and nostalgia had ceased to be pertinent in a world obsessed by sports clothes, and Liberty's battle for freedom of movement in dress had long been won. Though the company continued to make its famous Liberty prints and smocked dresses, Liberty's had to wait until the Sixties for a resurgence of interest in its Art Nouveau prints (then produced in psychedelic colors) and its collections of Thai, Pakistani, Tibetan, Indian, and Japanese curiosities.

Detail of a Liberty & Co. velvet-cut-to-chiffon cape from the Teens.

Mary McFadden

PLEATED FORTUNYESQUE DRESSES WITH MACRAME DETAILS; CHANNEL-quilted coats, jackets, and tunics of hand-painted silk; hammered gilt-brass jewelry; belts of knotted cord dangling golden leaves and ancient symbols: these are the things for which the designer Mary McFadden is known.

Slender, with black, black hair, and white, white skin, McFadden was born in New York City in 1936. Part of her girlhood was spent on a cotton plantation in Memphis, Tennessee; later, the family moved to Westbury, Long Island. She attended the Foxcroft School in Middleburg, Virginia, the Ecole Lubec and the Sorbonne in Paris, and the Traphagen School of Design in New York, before taking up sociology at Columbia University and the New School for Social Research. Her first, short-lived job was with Christian Dior, New York; marriage to an executive for DeBeers, the diamond firm, took her to South Africa, where she found work at that country's edition of *Vogue*. A second marriage brought a move to Rhodesia, where her intense interest in African art led her to found a workshop for local artists. In 1970, she returned to New York, where American *Vogue* hired her as a special projects editor.

At *Vogue*, McFadden's individual style attracted the attention of the other editors, who described her entertaining and decorating ideas and even her change of hairstyle in the pages of the magazine. Most newsworthy in a period of increasingly casual pants dressing were the clothes, based on forms of clothing seen in her travels, that McFadden had made for herself. Geraldine Stutz, president of the innovative Henri Bendel, bought samples of her quilted silk "fencing" jackets or batik coats, one-shoulder "Masai" tunics, and slim Chinese tunics to wear over trousers. From there, business escalated rapidly, and, in 1976, McFadden formed Mary McFadden Inc., with headquarters in New York. Ever since, she has been putting together two collections a year, each based on a specific historical period or cultural phenomenon. Her themes have included Egypt, Pompeii, water, the twelfth-century Saracen sultan Saladin, Las Vegas, Napoleon, pre-Columbian artifacts, and the works of Austrian painter Gustav Klimt. A collection's theme may determine its coloration, decoration, and presentation, but it is always translated into McFadden's particular vocabulary.

The most noteworthy constant in McFadden's designs is the special pleated (and man-made) fabric that she referred to as "Fortunyesque" when she first introduced it in 1975 but now calls marii. Because of the fabric's nature, the pleated evening dresses, both long and short, are fairly tubular in silhouette. They may have a peplum one year, be one-shouldered or one-sleeved the next; they may be composed of two

RIGHT:

A Horst portrait of Mary McFadden in her apartment.

BELOW:

M arii hood and evening dress.

or more different colors and enhanced with lace, velvet, suede, gauze, or with—that McFadden signature—a macramé insert, a knotted belt, a ruffly edge. In every collection is a sampling of dresses in striking combinations of black and white.

McFadden also makes watercolor-like fabrics that are used in her cardigan-style coats and jackets. The patterns may be simple blocks of color or ornate, according to the theme. White is always a strong element in the pattern. Such a jacket (or coat) is line-quilted and worn with a McFadden pleated dress or floating silk pants. McFadden is also known for her roughly woven chenille shawls, which she displays, knotted, in her showroom in a hemp basket. She also makes use of batiks, brocades, gold- and pewter-embroidered lace, silk gazar, or mohair, depending on the theme of the collection. Always she combines modern technology with both her historical researches and the wonderful craftsmanship of her workrooms.

Like most contemporary designers, McFadden has ventured into other projects: pleated marii scarves, dress patterns, eyeglass frames, writing paper. Her upholstery fabrics and wallpapers are reminiscent of her watercolored prints; her style of interior decoration, as she practices it for herself and others, makes use of the very objects that inspire her collection.

McFadden is part of a certain twentieth-century phenomenon—the woman of style turned dress designer. But, unlike the Venezuelan Carolina Herrera and the Vicomtesse Jacqueline de Ribes, best-dressed women who have turned taste into a profession, for McFadden, making clothes and fabrics is but one of many expressions of a finely tuned artistic sensibility.

RIGHT:
An Antonio illustration of a McFadden pants ensemble from the early Eighties.

FOLLOWING PAGES:
Marii braid-trimmed evening dress, ca. 1982.

BELOW:
Even the simplest McFadden ensemble has an exotic feel.

Zandra Rhodes

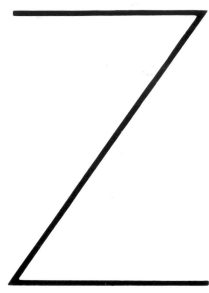

Z ANDRA RHODES EVENING DRESSES ARE AS INDIVIDUAL AS THE PALM of a hand. The dresses are born of the prints she designs for her fabrics; the prints are born of a drawing here or there, an incident that intrigued or charmed, a period in history or an illustration in a children's book. When making a print, Rhodes does not restrict herself to working in a rectangular, pattern-repeating format; rather, her fabrics are freewheeling and spirited—with no beginning, no end, and no straight edges. The fabric inspires the shape of the dress, the print decreeing the contour of the skirt, the neckline, and the sleeve. Much thought goes into each process, and each print and dress grows out of the last, making the whole of her work much like the output of a painter, with its recurrent themes, favorite subject matter, and characteristic coloring and light.

Zandra Lindsey Rhodes was born in Kent, England, in 1940. Her first experience with fashion was through her mother, who had worked as a fitter at the Paris Worth before being appointed senior lecturer in fashion at the Medway College of Art, which was not far from the family's home. When she was nineteen, Zandra enrolled in Medway to study fabric design and, two years later, entered the Royal College of Art, in London, where she continued with her specialization. She was graduated in 1964 with first-class honors and a special design award.

During the Sixties, Rhodes taught at the Royal College and designed for a printworks she had set up with Alexander McIntyre. It was not long before she grew dissatisfied with how fashion designers were treating her fabrics, and, in 1967, she became a partner in a boutique called the Fulham Road Clothes Shop, where she began to make clothes out of her own fabrics. The first designs to be featured under her own name included chiffon scarves described in *Vogue* in 1969 as "fascinating, like a Magritte painting," handkerchief-pointed pants, caftans, sheer printed organza jackets, and at-home robes. In 1970, she broke out on her own, her success hastened by a trip to New York, where *Vogue* and *Women's Wear Daily* ran appreciative reviews and Henri Bendel placed an order for her clothing. London—the British fashion press and Fortnum & Mason—followed suit. Three years after her debut as a solo designer, her clothes were chosen by Cecil Beaton for his fashion retrospective at the Victoria & Albert Museum, and the young designer's reputation was sealed.

Besides her evening dresses, Rhodes has designed a collection of day clothes under the label "Zandra Rhodes II," knitted sweaters, coats, and dresses for the Zandra Rhodes Knitting Studio, and created upholstery fabric, tailored coats, furs, and lingerie. She has also

Z andra Rhodes wearing her own fashion and maquillage designs.

costumed plays, both in London's West End and on Broadway, and movies. Princess Anne wore a Rhodes crinoline dress in her official engagement photograph. The couture-quality dresses, hand-made (but not made-to-order) in a factory filled to overflowing with bolts of fabric, scraps, and odds and ends, are sold in a Zandra Rhodes boutique in London's Mayfair and in department stores all over the world.

Of her prints, Rhodes has said that they are her own "particular handwriting," one of "wiggly undulating lines, strange flowers—large and small, rock landscapes, cowboy arrows, cactus and lily motifs . . . often with strange written words in handwriting, Japanese style, as part of the design." The fabrics that bear these prints include crisp organza, metal-shimmered silk, and floating chiffon, as well as, for day, viyella and chamois. In color, Rhodes favors vigorously pale shades, and her white prints are often white on white on white.

Every Rhodes collection includes crinoline dresses with their wide antebellum skirts, "little black dresses," and day clothes. Every garment illustrates the Rhodes vocabulary: squiggly prints; jagged fringes and petals of fabric; hand-rolled edges dripping pearls, sequins, beads, or feathers. Details and accessories are suggested by the collections' themes. The year of the "Medieval Pageant," the models wore wimples and snoods; colors were plucked from the English fields: shepherd's purse, corn, poppy, cornflower. In the "Flower Fairy" collection, colors were named for the fairies in Cicely Mary Baker's children's books: Cobweb, Honeysuckle, Pea Blossom, and Almond Blossom. This collection also included such renditions of fairy clothing as tulle tutu dresses embroidered with crystal dewdrops, chiffon dresses with ruffled jersey knickers, and mini-skating skirts sewn with pink pearls. The "Indian Miniature Painting" collection made use of madras plaids and raw silks in colors like jasmine, saffron, persimmon, and gold-shot kohl. India inspired lotus prints, suede and lace harem pants, and tiny mirror-set embroideries. Her controversial "Conceptual Chic" collection of 1977 parodied the street clothes then being worn by London's street punks by the use of ripped jersey pieced back together with diamanté safety pins.

Rhodes's personal style reflects her having come of age in London in the Sixties. She likes stopping traffic, and ensures that it will happen with her magenta, emerald, or turquoise coiffures. Lacking eyebrows, she paints them in (or arrows, or feathery dashes, or dots). Naturally, she wears her fantasy clothing well. More surprisingly, so do a wide variety of women. Despite her personal outrageousness, the Rhodes aesthetic is gently flattering, flamboyantly feminine, and never harsh.

LEFT:

Rhodes in 1977, the year of her Conceptual Chic Collection.

BELOW:

Jungle-trail printed chiffon evening dress.

Although clothing in the late nineteenth century was heading toward freeing women for the activities and responsibilities increasingly available to them, it wasn't until the beginning of this century that clothes actually began to be comfortable as well as look comfortable. At the heart of this progression was Gabrielle Chanel. It was Chanel's wiry, small-breasted, and hipless shape that became the century's ideal. For the first time in history fashion dispensed with having a single erogenous zone on which to concentrate and began to emphasize the entire figure, seen as an unbroken, supple line.

Anything that broke this line went out of fashion. The Teens' gigantic hats, cascading ruffles, and exaggerated curving postures gave way in the Twenties to close little turbans and cloches, waistless chemise dresses, and long strands of beads. Although Poiret helped pioneer the simpler, more boyish look, it was to facilitate an Oriental exoticism. What Chanel did was make suits and dresses that were easy to move in and that looked good on a healthy, athletic figure. Even her favorite fabric, jersey, was one that followed the body, rather than one that imposed another structure on it. Vionnet used even more supple fabrics, designing clothes for women who not only wore no corset, but no underclothing whatsoever.

As the Twenties progressed, the line lengthened. Patou and Louise-boulanger (with Mainbocher at Vogue egging them on) led the way for longer skirts. Augustabernard, Molyneux, and Valentina emphasized the silhouette's slimness by stripping it of extra decoration. Madame Grès paid homage to the classically narrow figure by draping her jerseys around it.

By the time World War II interrupted the couture, Augustabernard and Louiseboulanger had closed their doors, followed by Vionnet, Chanel,

PRECEDING PAGES: Detail of a Chanel afternoon dress neckline, ca. 1926.

and Mainbocher. But the war's end saw a rebirth of what had been happening in fashion at the end of the Thirties with the new designers experimenting with ball gowns and town suits elaborately constructed on an unnatural, exaggeratedly corsetted figure. By the time Chanel re-opened her doors in 1954, the New Look had begun to fade, helped along by her examples of easy suits that respected the uncorsetted body, and by Madame Grès, who had never stopped working in her idiom of classically draped jersey. During his New York career, begun in 1940, Mainbocher operated much as he had in Paris, prophetically making predominantly narrow little suits and evening dresses in the Fifties, and on into the Sixties and early Seventies when this aesthetic was finally shared by a majority of designers.

In the Sixties—a decade of fascination with the prepubescent body—the chemise shape turned into the waistless sheath, which gradually replaced the New Look. The fitness-conscious Seventies predominantly relied on pants to produce a narrow silhouette for every occasion. Today, two designers who got their starts in the Sixties are champions of the Purist's natural figure. Halston eschews inner construction to make clothes that are simple and have a fluid grace. Sonia Rykiel's aesthetic of narrowness combines with her medium, knits, to produce clothes that hug and do justice to the body. Capitalizing on the advent of a new generation of well-toned figures, they emulate their predecessors by making clothes that require a body to come to life, rather than the other way around.

Chanel

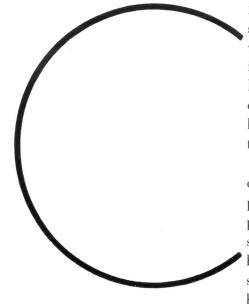

HANEL USED TO SAY THAT FASHION FADES, ONLY STYLE REMAINS THE same. It was this charismatic beauty, natural athlete, and prodigious worker that George Bernard Shaw referred to as one of the two most important women living in the world (the other being Marie Curie). Her success was greatly due to the international pertinence of her own individual style, a style and a success she credited to having been in the right place at the right time or, as she said: "I was the first to live the life of this century."

The Chanel style has everything to do with elegance but is founded on elements once considered foreign to it: comfort, ease, and practicality. It is composed of masculine elements but couldn't appear more feminine. So pervasive is this style that women who consider themselves above (or outside) fashion, all the while clad in borrowed trousers and a sweater with sleeves pushed up, are unconsciously recalling the defiance of its originator. Chanel's style, which has already outlived her, shows every indication of outliving its century, continuing to develop nuances and pertinence with every passing decade.

Chanel's most famous design—instantly recognizable in its hundreds of variations—is the suit in two and frequently three pieces. First made during World War I, it remained in style until 1939, was re-introduced in the Fifties, and is still popular today. Although Chanel borrowed many details from menswear, her suits were never imitative, like the tailleurs they replaced. Usually soft and untailored, made in jersey, velvet, silk charmeuse, or tweeds, these suits share the practical constants of boxy cardigan jackets with sleeve buttons that really button, pockets where one needs pockets, and straight knee-length skirts with walking pleats. After 1954, tweeds and braids were used, along with gold chains weighting the jacket, and brass (especially lion's-head) buttons. Chanel, who disapproved of suits that could be worn only with the jacket closed, designed jackets that looked good open, closed, or draped over a shoulder. She facilitated this by making blouses, which were an integral part of the whole, from fabrics that matched the suit's lining, were printed in corresponding colors, or made in school-girl white with immaculate collar and cuffs. So dependent are women on this look even today that it is the commercial mainstay of such designers as Adolfo, as it had been for most of Seventh Avenue in the Fifties and Sixties.

No less a Chanel trademark is the "little black dress," which she was advocating as the new uniform for both afternoon and evening as early as the mid-Teens. Deceptively simple, these dresses were wizardries of cut and proportion. She used traditional elegant materials—

lace, tulle, embroideries, or soft, weightless silks—in a newly tailored way. Worn with a cardigan of the same fabric as that of the suit on the next hanger, the little black dress made women wearing anything else seem overdressed, and during these first years of her career —the war years—overdressing was severely frowned upon.

Chanel brought the same innately practical turn of mind to every aspect of her designs. Working directly on her mannequins, she had them swing their arms and legs for hours, until she was sure how a fabric worked in motion. She put pleats in her skirts to permit women to cross their legs or get in and out of an automobile with ease. She lined these skirts' back panels so that they wouldn't "sit out." She cut armholes high and close to achieve, paradoxically, greater freedom for the arms. She dispensed with deep hems, scoffing at the delusion of clients who expected to grow further or the notion that, because it had come into fashion, a new length would be any more flattering. She avoided fabrics that looked good but didn't feel good next to the skin, and she lined her coats with suede or fur for warmth, not show. Along with this attention to practical detail, she imbued her clothes with a hidden cachet, the self-assured chic of a woman who doesn't worry about her clothes when she's wearing them.

Making clothes simple and easy to move in would not in itself constitute an immortal style. What makes Chanel's style so recognizable, along with the perfect balance of the detail, are the accessories.

Imitation jewelry had existed long before Chanel began to design clothes, but it had always been a somewhat embarrassed sham of existing modes of real jewelry, never in fashion for its own sake. Historically, the amount and quality of the jewels worn by a woman was a mark of how well she was being kept (regardless of whom that keeper was). But by the Twenties, the image of real jewelry had changed, along with the roles of the women wearing it. During the war an ostentatious display was considered vulgar and, as women began to enjoy a new-found self-reliance after the war, a rope of pearls no longer necessarily signified fetters to one's keeper or to a secure future. If costume, this same rope could be worn jokingly, a statement of bravado and independence.

Chanel made jewelry for her clients similar to that which she wore herself. Sometimes it was real, sometimes costume—and never all one or the other. Everything about her jewelry (and the way she wore it) was a break with the past. She favored masses of the stuff, mixing small and large stones, throwing in the occasional semiprecious gem with a pound or two of imitation ones, piling the whole of it atop one of her suits, and wearing it all in broad daylight. She created an

PRECEDING PAGES:
Chanel after her arrival in America on the S.S. Europa, 1935.
PAGE 121: Contemporary three-piece suit.

RIGHT:
A Horst portrait of Chanel in the Thirties.

BELOW:
This black velvet suit, from Chanel's last prewar collection, was inspired by the Watteau costume she wore to the Beaumont Ball.

unpretentious style that had nothing whatsoever to do with money, the effect of which was at once stunning and ironical.

The twentieth century's most important *couturière* was born on August 19, 1883, in the hospital of the French village of Saumur. Gabrielle (her birth certificate doesn't give a middle name of Bonheur) was only twelve when her mother died; her father, a travelling wine peddler, then took her and her sister to a convent, consigning them into the care of the nuns and disappearing to America forever.

At eighteen, Chanel left the convent to strike out on her own. She worked as an assistant at a tailoring shop but aspired to be a music hall performer (her nickname derived from her two-song repertoire of "Qu'i qua vu Coco" and "Ko-Ko-Ri-Ko").

Although small, the Auvernois town where Chanel tried to launch her singing career did have some compensations, among them a fashionable and aristocratic cavalry regiment. One of the regiment's officers, Etienne Balsan, a sportsman and horse breeder, soon noticed the young "Coco," and she became his mistress and went to live in his château at the age of twenty-five.

Balsan's home was a magnet for his numerous hunting friends and their fashionable mistresses. As she was acquiring a foothold in this grand milieu, the young Coco Chanel attracted attention, not only for her bearing on a horse and her game courage but also for her look of striking beauty paired with a defiant mien. This look seems to have arisen from her determination to set herself apart from the other mistresses and *cocottes*, an urge to flaunt the fact that she had no taste for emulating the upper classes (or hiding her peasant origins), and her conscious admiration of the casual and confident air of the men who surrounded her. By sticking to what she knew best, she achieved a style that in time would prove prophetic.

Women admired and asked for copies of the hats she made for herself. In 1908, Chanel began selling these simply decorated hats from Balsan's ground floor Paris apartment. In 1910, Boy Capel, an English polo-playing entrepreneur and a friend of Balsan (and Chanel's new lover), sensed in her a seriously ambitious nature similar to his own and set her up in a small shop on the rue Cambon. Within a couple of years, Chanel was filling orders for dresses to accompany her hats. Her first efforts included a simple navy jersey dress—Chanel circumvented her landlord's regulation that she not produce "couture" by working in an obviously noncouture fabric—and another of black velvet with a face-framing collar of white organdy petals.

During the next few years the ingénue dressmaker opened boutiques in Deauville and Biarritz, then France's premier resort towns,

Detail of a Chanel suit from the Twenties.

FOLLOWING PAGES: Chanel suit, May 1935. PAGE 127: Gloria Swanson dressed by Chanel for Tonight or Never, *1931.*

and moved into larger quarters on the rue Cambon just across the street from the Hotel Ritz. Her customers essentially came to Chanel to buy clothes like the ones she wore and that were suitable to the casual pace of seaside living: flannel blazers, straight linen skirts, sailor tops, long jersey sweaters. The suits—it was still the late Teens —had above-the-ankle skirts and three-quarter-length coats meant to be loosely belted to reveal blouses made of material that matched the coat's lining and lapels. Such simple styles reflected a general war-time sobriety observable throughout the French couture. The war effort and the participation it required of women necessitated practical clothing, and the new-found freedom of movement and of image was not about to be relinquished when the armistice came. At the heart of this revolution was Chanel, who had instinctively grasped the essence of the new epoch, an epoch that would crown her as its leader.

As her business grew, so did Chanel's social desirability and her personal legend. Liane de Pougy, a *cocotte* of the old, pre-Chanel style, described her as having "the taste of a fairy, the eyes and voice of a woman, the haircut and figure of an urchin." It was this mien that attracted Misia Sert, a doyenne of Parisian artistic and social circles,

RIGHT:
Christian Bérard designed this collar of semi-precious stones set in base metal for Chanel's personal use.

FAR RIGHT:
Lagerfeld suit for Chanel, 1983.

who likened Chanel to an uncut diamond and brought her into a group that included Diaghilev, Picasso, Cocteau, Stravinsky, Hemingway, Serge Lifar, the artist Max Jacob, and the poet Pierre Reverdy—a group whose friend and patron she would become.

Curiously, Chanel's relationship with the avant-garde had little effect on her designs. In fact, it might be said that she had a greater impact on it. The simplicity of her costumes for Cocteau's production of *Antigone* (with sets by Picasso) or the athlete-dancers' bathing suits and sports clothes for Nijinska's ballet *Le Train Bleu* proved to be as revolutionary for the theatre as it had been within the fashion milieu. Her unwillingness to participate in what she perceived as the elegance of Hollywood films limited Chanel's contribution to film costuming. She relented and did three films for Hollywood as well as Jean Renoir's *Rules of the Game* (1939) and Alain Resnais's 1963 *Last Year at Marienbad.*

Harper's Bazaar didn't know how to spell her name when, in 1915, they published the dictum that "the woman who has not at least one costume by Chenal [sic] is hopelessly out of the running in fashion," but by 1917 they were better informed and could state positively that "This season the name of Gabrielle Chanel is on the lips of every buyer."

Her first success was the immense popularity of jersey, which soon was used by everyone, and she became known for her sports clothes as well as for absolutely straight frocks, their severity tempered by ornate embroideries. In 1918 she took over 31, rue Cambon, where she piled cushions of feathers, fur, and metallic fabrics on the chaise longues in the gray and amber salons and showed increasingly simple day dress-and-coat *ensembles*, often in "biscuit" jersey (later known as beige), as well as black evening dresses in lace or jet-embroidered tulle. Chanel's early-Twenties Russian look—which has been attributed to her liaison with the Grand Duke Dmitri—consisted of tunic shapes and Slavic embroideries, and developed out of her other elaborately embroidered yet simply shaped clothing. This style also reflected the general "Russianization" of Paris that occurred after the October Revolution, when the city became home to many émigrés, both those who were willing to work as seamstresses for less money than their Parisian counterparts and those whose purchasing power briefly affected fashion.

As the Twenties progressed Chanel continued to make evening dresses notable for their exquisite simplicity. These chemises differed from their day counterparts only in their fabrics and the degree of intricate construction. In 1923, *Harper's Bazaar* described one Chanel evening frock as "little more than a breeze." This pale pink mousseline dress, worked in three scalloped tiers with floating ties at the shoulders, was a forerunner of the soft, sheer, seemingly uncomplicated dresses that Chanel was known for throughout her career.

Like most couturiers of the Twenties, Chanel designed beaded dresses, and of course, hers were different. Usually constructed in the round (as opposed to being two flat panels stitched together) they were based on the shapes of her other designs, and the patterns—if she used them—were geometric, worked in color combinations of black, beige and white, or in striking monochromatic infusions of black or white or red.

Another trademark that surfaced in the Twenties was her unorthodox combinations of fabrics: plain and patterned wool jerseys in a single outfit (horizontal stripes are particularly Chanel) or a then-surprising juxtaposition of patterned floral silks with tweeds. The ever-present Chanel perfectionism was evident in the exquisite coordination of different fabrics and prints: a floral-printed silk cut out and appliquéd to the collars and cuffs of a tweed jacket; the matching of a coat lining to the fabric of the underdress; the use of consistent colors and motifs in buttons, belts, and lapel flowers.

With the arrival of the Thirties, Chanel's evening clothes became more elongated, more feminine, and by the end of the decade, downright fantastical. For summer evening dresses she continued to surprise by contrasting scintillating touches like rhinestone straps or silver eyelet—with fabrics previously reserved for day clothes and lingerie: handkerchief linen, cotton organdy, and *broderie anglaise*. Many of these dresses came with matching gloves. One lace evening dress was shown with transparent leggings, a look Chanel revived in the Sixties. In 1937, struck by how little women looked when seated next to their escorts at the theatre, she showed a collection of head-dresses designed to lend height: confections of tulle, silk flowers, and the increasingly evident Chanel ribbon bow. Perhaps in response to the growing opinion that she had a masculine mind, the evening dresses she designed became even more romantic. Sometimes strapless, they had full skirts and boned bodices, flounces and ruffles. Chanel also showed gypsy dresses, dresses made of prints by Cocteau, and day suits worn with ruffled Pierrot collars.

Chanel, who had introduced her first costume jewelry in 1924 (a pair of pearl earrings, one black and one white), now began to elaborate this vision. The pieces grew in size and became more Byzantine, with the use of much yellow gold, baroque pearls, and rough, uncut, purposely flawed gems. Other pieces looked anything but Byzantine —collars of enamelled leaves and flowers or pearls tied with real

BELOW AND LEFT:
Two typical Chanel designs from the Fifties: a little black dress, and a tweed suit.

ribbon bows. She wore large, clunky button-type earrings and strands of beads interlaced with chains of faceted stones and they became her signature. She also experimented with real gems. In 1932 her designs included a tiara, a fringe of diamonds worn on the forehead. She was photographed in 1935 wearing her famous ivory enamelled cuff set with large, uneven stones in the shape of a Maltese cross.

As Chanel neared her sixties, her great success stood firm. She had had an affair with one English duke (Westminster) and became the good friend of another (Windsor). She had been photographed by every legendary photographer. People not only wore her clothes (many would wear no others), they went to her parties, pointed her out in restaurants, sought to be introduced. They quoted her. World War II ended all that. In 1939 Chanel closed her *maison de couture* (while continuing the production of her perfumes) and retired, living primarily in Switzerland. There she nursed her resentment of a France that could arrest her for having fallen in love with a German officer and ignore the fact that, by closing her house, she had refrained from catering to war profiteers. Paris had forgotten her. Fashion embraced Dior's highly sophisticated and artificial "New Look." This time a war had not left women pressing for freedom of movement and image: after years of deprivation, they wanted pampering and *divertissement*.

What no one could have predicted was that Coco Chanel would come back. In 1954, goaded primarily by the boredom of retirement and by a decline in perfume sales, Chanel displayed her usual sense of perfect timing. Already the impact of the New Look was waning. The stage was set for Chanel to once more liberate women from tight corsets and the foolish fripperies of male designers. The fashion press initially criticized her for bringing back the same old tweed suits and "little" dresses, but could not ignore the great numbers of women who once again clamored for wearable clothes.

Although Chanel continued to produce black or navy suits with white collars and cuffs, many of her *ensembles* were now made in subtler, more flattering pastel tweeds, muted and nubby and variegated. Her reputation as a colorist grew. She proved to be as demanding with a tint as she was with the fit of a sleeve. (Once, during a meeting with her weaver, she crushed the petals from a nearby bouquet in her hand to produce the color she was after.)

The suits had patch pockets, cuffs, lapels, and hems edged in either matching or contrasting braids; evening versions—now often featuring trousers rather than a skirt—were made in solid or patterned velvets, metallic brocades, or silks embroidered entirely with sequins. Chanel liked a suit to be so well cut that the wearer appeared to be

Chanel updated.

wearing nothing underneath, and the body underneath was likely to share Chanel's lack of breast and hip. The most prominent suit silhouette was the one most flattering to this figure, and it featured a straight jacket ending just below the waist and a straight skirt ending just below the knee. The pockets, placed in the seams of either side of the skirt's center, were perfect for achieving the famous Chanel slouch. She introduced, in a day of stiletto heels, low-heeled two-toned slingback pumps that actually facilitated walking. Her chain-handled, quilted leather shoulderbags, first shown in 1957, were dressy versions of a pocketbook that freed the arms. Chanel herself started the practical fashion of wearing boots on her jaunts across the street from the Ritz to 31, rue Cambon. She also reinstated her "fluttering breeze" chiffon frocks for evening. In a word, she continued to make the kind of clothes she always had, dressing women in a way that made them seem too content and busy to think about what they were wearing.

After her death in 1971, the House of Chanel continued to turn out clothes that deviated little if at all from her formulas. Recently new life has been brought to the house in a way Chanel herself would probably have done: by resurrecting ideas from the archives and altering them just enough to accommodate a new generation and new moods in silhouette. Karl Lagerfeld is the designer who has achieved this. Where the house had played it safe in the Seventies with the demurest of suits and dresses, Lagerfeld has dared to exaggerate proportions, colors, the use of accessories, and other Chanel details. Chanel's famous pocketbook is now embroidered in sequins and set off against a narrow black dress; the spools and dressmaking tools she used when costuming *Oedipus Rex* have become earrings and necklaces; the coromandel screens that adorned her private apartments have been translated into jewelled evening-dress bodices. As with Chanel at her comeback, Lagerfeld's new collections were criticized at first. Now journalists can hardly wait to photograph and present them.

Thus the legend not only persists—it lives. The memory of the woman who gave the world suntans and little black dresses, costume jewelry and Chanel No. 5 (she considered it her lucky number), who believed that if function came first, beauty would follow, continues to fuel fashion. This woman who grasped the allure of a quick mind, brought together looking smart and being smart. The tenets of her style, which have influenced almost every couturier since she began and which can be seen in most contemporary dress today, continue to welcome translation and reinterpretation. As Balenciaga said of her: "Chanel is an eternal bomb. None of us can defuse her."

A white charmeuse evening dress, summer 1935.

FOLLOWING PAGES:
The Chanel cabine of models backstage at an Eighties show.

Jean Patou

EAN PATOU EPITOMIZED THE JAZZ AGE. TALL AND DARK, DASHING and racy, he was equally at home playing tennis, racing automobiles, or dining, dancing, and gambling with one of his innumerable lady friends. Ever eluding marriage, he was never restricted from fully participating in the hectic international society of which he was a keen observer and sometime catalyst. As *A Shopping Guide to Paris* said of him: "He still recognizes the immediate needs—as the styles of a resort change, so do his modes; as the younger generation decides on new gods for itself, Patou follows with new ideas. He always feels the tempo of life, and adapts himself to it." His clothes were worn by tennis player Suzanne Lenglen, when competing at Wimbledon; in the sky by Ruth Elder, the aviatrix; by Bricktop at her fabled nightspot; and his model Dinarzade (Lillian Farley) was wrapped in a woolly Patou coat to witness Lindbergh's landing in France. Patou clothes could and did go anywhere, mainly because Patou saw to it that he knew where they were going.

Jean Patou was born in 1880 in Normandy to a leather tanner and his wife. After working briefly at his father's tannery he joined an uncle's fur concern, leaving for Paris in 1910 to open his own fur and dressmaking business, which failed but led to the founding of a second establishment. This proved profitable enough to finance yet a third, the successful Maison Parry, which opened in 1912 at the Rond-Point and specialized in tailleurs, dresses, and furs. Especially popular were what might be called the first "smokings," tailormades with jackets fashioned after a man's dinner jacket. One New York buyer unexpectedly came in and bought an entire collection.

Patou began to dream of a more exalted *maison de couture*. Unfortunately, just before he was to have presented his first collection under his own name, the military called and he left Paris to fight in the war as a captain in the Zouaves. It was not until his return in 1919 that the House of Patou was formally opened.

Patou, like Poiret, was a brilliant public relations man. On a visit to the United States in 1925, he was impressed by the long-legged natural strides of American women. Rather than continue to rescale Parisian fashions to suit this new breed, he advertised in New York for models who "must be smart, slender, with well-shaped feet and ankles, and refined of manner." With an illustrious panel of judges —Condé Nast, Edna Woolman Chase, Edward Steichen, and Elsie de Wolfe, all of whom were associated with *Vogue* magazine—Patou auditioned five hundred applicants before choosing six to accompany him to Paris. Predictably, they caused an uproar with the patriotic French press. In addition he pioneered the concept of the fashion

show as social event by inviting favorite friends and important press for a night-before preview of his collections, serving them a champagne supper and presenting them with perfume samples. Taking the monogram off his own shirt and placing it on bathing suits, sweaters, pocketbooks, and scarves, Patou was among the first to recognize the heady cachet of a designer's personal initials.

As a designer, Patou was a believer in the smart and the simple but was, according to *Harper's Bazaar*, "free from the hypocrisy of false simplicity." He enlivened Twenties afternoon dresses of crepe, crepe satin, or chiffon with a self-tied shoulder bow or decorative seams worked in zigzags, chevrons, or undulating curves. Evening clothes were intricately embroidered in patterns inspired by ancient textiles, coromandel screens, or modern art. Patou sports *ensembles* were designed with gradating stripes to match one of his Cubistic sweaters.

Travel and sports clothes were so important to Patou's vision that in 1925, he opened a warren of rooms on the ground floor at 7, rue Saint-Florentin, which he called *Coin des Sports* (Sports Corner). Each room was dedicated to a completely realized, and accessorized, outdoor activity; the fishing section, for instance, carried tackle as well as, presumably, the most gorgeous waders. Three years later, he introduced the Jean Patou Bag, a fourteen-piece wardrobe coordinated for one's weekend plans including sports clothes and bathing suits, evening dresses, and wraps. At the Sports Corner and the salons in Deauville and Biarritz, he sold monogrammed sweaters, bathing suits whose fabrics had been tested in boiling salt water, and an assortment of what he called *les riens*, those indispensable "nothings" like scarves, lingerie, costume jewelry, pocketbooks, and hats.

Patou is widely credited with establishing the look that signalled the close of the high-living chaotic Twenties and heralded the more sober "*après-Crash*" Thirties: the dropped hemline and raised waistline. Although legend has it that this was in reaction to Patou's having seen one too many pairs of knees bared by Chanel's *garçonnes*, he was described in the press as early as 1925 as trying to raise the waist (sometimes only in back) and devising ways to lengthen skirts with side trains and fluttering handkerchief hems.

Although it was a fairly common practice for couturiers to have fabrics made to their own specifications, Patou took the process a step further, commanding that his fabrics be dyed in the thread. Despite the extra months of labor involved, and the greatly increased costs, he believed in the importance of subtle, signature colors that could not easily be copied. At each collection he introduced two new Patou hues that became leitmotifs in almost every *ensemble*, his obsession

and skill resulting in such tints as dove's-neck gray, light oak, eggplant, dark dahlia (a red so deep as to appear black), and Patou blue (dark, but with violet, rather than navy, overtones). Patou was also obliging in making evening dresses to match a client's semiprecious jewelry.

In 1925 Patou introduced his first perfumes, a trio of scents aligned with hair colors: Amour-Amour for brunettes, Que Sais-je for blondes, and Adieu, Sagesse for redheads. In 1929 he added Le Sien, a "sports" fragrance for either sex, and in 1931, Joy, still one of the great perfumes of the world.

Jean Patou, more than many designers, was extremely fortunate in the friends and family members who worked with him and kept him in touch with *la vie parisienne.* Foremost among them was his sister Madeleine, who was seven years younger than he. As Marie had been to Worth or Denise to Poiret, Madeleine was Patou's principal source of inspiration, the embodiment of his physical ideal: the small, neat, dark, smart, active modern woman. Her husband, Georges Barbas, took over the house upon Patou's death and her grandson, Jean de Mouy, is its current president. Along with illustrator Bernard Boutet de Monvel and the architect and interior designer team Sue et Mare (who created the décor of the House of Patou), Elsa Maxwell had an important impact on the Patou image. This doyenne of Paris café society referred to Patou as having more animal magnetism than anyone she ever met and she worked with him to perfect the perfume Joy and to ensure proper attendance at his couture shows.

Patou's clientele included Louise Brooks, Lady Diana Cooper, Mrs. Harrison Williams, as well as the twin Dolly sisters, who, on their tour of America in the mid-Twenties, travelled with over two hundred changes of clothing, all by Patou. The designer always had a strong following in the United States. Irene Mayer Selznick writes in her recent memoirs, A *Private View,* of her first visit to France and the promise by her Hollywood-producer father of Paris dresses for her sister and herself. After much research, they settled on the perfect tailoring and liveliness of Patou, but unfortunately their father's promise did not allow for an extra week of fittings, and they had to make do with Poiret, the only couturier who could guarantee immediate delivery.

Patou, colorist, perfectionist and brilliant businessman, profitted from his ability to combine the traditional requirements of luxury and quality with the increasing stylishness of sport and fun. After his rather early death in 1936, his philosophy was carried on by his family, as devoted to luxurious simplicity as he, and by a series of young designers including Marc Bohan, Gérard Pipart, Karl Lagerfeld, Michel Goma, Angelo Tarlazzi and Christian La Croix.

LEFT:

Suit from the autumn 1983 couture collection, designed by Christian LaCroix.

BELOW:

Baby-doll dress from the Sixties.

Molyneux

EDWARD MOLYNEUX, AN IRISHMAN OF HUGUENOT ANCESTRY, EMULATED the success of the great Charles Frederick Worth on a somewhat more limited scale by bringing a Briton's sense of restraint and propriety to the world of Paris fashion. Never falling prey to exaggeration, he continually maintained sight of the elegant, even extravagant, heights to which the couture could soar. Molyneux was the designer to whom a fashionable woman would turn if she wanted to be absolutely "right" without being utterly predictable in the Twenties and Thirties.

Very much a part of *les Années Folles*, Molyneux consorted with both the aristocracy and café society of between-the-wars Paris, and thus gained tremendous insight into the wants and needs of women in this era of change and freedom. As a result, he had the surest of hands, whether dressing Gertrude Lawrence for the stage or Princess Marina of Greece for her much-publicized wedding to the Duke of Kent. H. W. Yoxall honored Molyneux by saying that "he always remained a designer for ladies, when some of his competitors had—shall we say—broadened their appeal." Having briefly been married to Muriel Dunsmuir, he realized that the mores of his day no longer considered divorce taboo, if handled elegantly, and thus ended his 1928 collection with two wedding dresses: one for a blushing bride, the other for "today's divorcée." The repeat bride was provided with a slim dress of lemon silk and a veil of peach-pink tulle.

Born in London in 1891, Molyneux's first ambition was to be a painter. It was while studying art that his sketch for an evening dress won a contest sponsored by Lucile (Lady Duff Gordon), who subsequently hired him, first as a sketch artist travelling with her in America, then as a designer in her Paris branch. All this was interrupted by World War I, in the course of which Captain Molyneux was wounded three times, costing him the sight of one eye.

After the war Molyneux moved to Paris, where he opened his *maison de couture* at 14, rue Royale with the help of such financial backers as Lord Derby, British ambassador to France, and newspaper magnate Lord Northcliffe. From the beginning his style was characterized by extreme simplicity and "perfect" taste, a style formed, at least in part, in reaction to the endless embellishing that he had witnessed during his years with Lucile.

Molyneux did not have to wait long for success. Almost immediately he was obliged to expand into larger quarters across the street. Here, like Lucile, he decorated his salons in shades of gray, furnished them with crystal chandeliers and Louis XVI funiture, and fitted out his *vendeuses* in pleated gray crepe de Chine dresses. Soon there were more expansions: branches in Monte Carlo, Cannes, and

RIGHT:
Molyneux evening dress,
ca. 1950.

BELOW:
Molyneux going over telegrams from well-wishers after showing a 1936 collection.

of course, his native London. He designed furs, lingerie, hats, and perfume, most notably his Numéro Cinq (he shared Chanel's superstition of the good fortune in the number five). He even entered into partnership with social doyenne Elsa Maxwell—ownership of a pair of nightclubs. Anita Loos once recalled that one of these was "the most elegant place in which to greet the Paris dawn."

Just before Paris fell to the Germans during World War II, Molyneux escaped to England on a coal barge. In 1952, *Vogue* would recount the perhaps apocryphal anecdote that "In the midst of the coiled confusion, the terror, and the soft soot came Molyneux's former batman, his butler for twenty years, the dry, thin, efficient Pawson, in a white jacket, carrying a tray with glasses and a shaker of Martinis." Once in England, Molyneux worked to benefit the Allied war effort. He determined that the Paris house would remain open, thereby providing income for its staff, while the proceeds from the London branch went to the British Defense Budget. With his own funds he operated international canteens in both Paris and London, as well as a school for couture workers and a camp for war victims, both in France. In England, he chaired the Incorporated Society of London Fashion Designers, which designed prototypes of clothes for mass production that met all the frugal requirements of the "Making of Clothes (Restrictions) Orders."

In 1945, Molyneux returned to Paris and began again on the rue Royale. But it was not the same. Not only were his greatest colleagues and competitors gone—Chanel and Vionnet in retirement, Patou dead —but his health, particularly his eyesight, had begun to fail. On December 31, 1950, he closed both his Paris and London establishments (Jacques Griffe inherited the rue Royale premises and much of its clientele) and retired to Jamaica, where he built a house near that of his good friend Noel Coward. Now was a time for what a career and two World Wars had prevented Molyneux from doing: he travelled broadly and resumed his painting. His subtly colored landscapes were shown to considerable acclaim in both New York and Paris. A second collection of paintings, ones that he had collected, was shown at the Museum of Modern Art and the National Gallery (including works by Cézanne, Van Gogh, Manet, Gauguin, Degas, Renoir, Bonnard, and Vuillard). His health gradually returned to him, and, in 1965, he collaborated with his nephew, John Tullis, on a ready-to-wear operation called Studio Molyneux, which mass-produced clothes for both the French and American markets. He died in 1974.

At his peak, Molyneux was known for conservative clothes that were never staid or matronly. The typical Molyneux client was likely to be tall, reedy, intelligent, and in her thirties, much as Noel Coward's

PRECEDING PAGES:
Molyneux pre–New Look evening dress, 1946.
PAGE 147: evening dress, ca. 1930.

BELOW:
Molyneux evening dress and sport coat from 1927.

Amanda is characterized in *Private Lives*: "pretty and sleek . . . her hands were long and slim, and her legs were long and slim, and she danced like an angel." In fact it was Molyneux who designed the costumes for this part in 1930 for his client Gertrude Lawrence. One of the designs became a veritable symbol of Thirties elegance: a streamlined, backless white satin evening dress, with several silver-fox furs tossed over one shoulder.

He was perhaps best known for his consummate handling of navy blue and black, whether in an easy, pleated skirt-suit or a sliplike evening dress, fastened at shoulder or hip with a couple of silk gardenias. A Molyneux *ensemble* differed from one by Chanel or Vionnet by its rejection of the details of dressmaking; he preferred the simplest lapel, the least complicated color scheme.

Only in the Thirties did the pure Molyneux look fully emerge. His soft velvet evening coats fell to the floor in a single unbroken line; his dresses with matching three-quarter-length coats had a graceful fluidity. Visually simple, many of his clothes were designed with the intent of making social life more efficient: a motoring dress of white crepe could be worn with any number of different colored jackets and hats; just by omitting the jacket, a long dinner dress could be worn for a more formal occasion.

However, just as the man himself glided gracefully from his restrained *salon en grisaille* to any one of a dozen Paris nightclubs, his clothes sometimes veered away from this minimal purity toward a display of strong, even unconventional effect. He might enliven a suit by fashioning its jacket from canary kidskin. Embroideries of iris, flamingoes in lotus ponds, or coral fishes swimming in and out of crystal-beaded waves on his 1923 beaded chemises outshone those of all other couturiers. He experimented with ostrich and coq feathers used in lieu of fur, and playfully chose buttons resembling cigarette butts or lipsticks. No one designed more beautiful evening pajamas.

Molyneux could be trend-setting. In 1933 his costumes for the French production of *The Barretts of Wimpole Street*, the most Edwardian of designs, led other couturiers to graft ruffles and modified bustles onto the decade's slim silhouette. And by the end of the Thirties Molyneux, like the others, had begun to experiment with a newly narrowed waist, one that would have to wait for Dior's "New Look" to truly become the fashion. Although he proved adept at designing in the postwar giddy mode, his early retirement ensured that he will be remembered for his streamlined Thirties designs, clothing from a decade whose look he helped shape.

*M*olyneux hats from 1926.

Grès

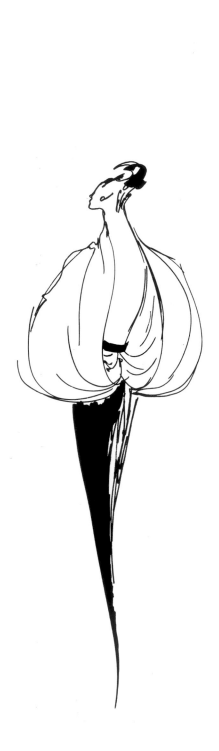

A GREAT RARITY IS THE COUTURIER WHO CAN REMAIN TRUE TO A PERsonal vision, ignoring outside influences. Rarer still is the couturier who sustains such aesthetic integrity and clarity for more than half a century while carrying on a business of international proportion. Mme. Grès is such a *couturière*, one who steadfastly refused to make clothes for Everywoman and concentrated instead on designing clothes for a select and extremely appreciative clientele. So timeless are her designs that clients treasure wearing a favorite Grès from even twenty years ago, flaunting their vintage (their provenance is obvious).

Née Germaine Barton, early in this century, Grès was reared by her well-educated bourgeois Parisian family. She was indulged in her "ladylike" interests in music, dance and art, especially sculpture, but when she announced her intention of becoming a sculptor, her family balked. It was her introduction by a family friend to a clothing buyer who praised her fine artwork that caused Grès to begin to wonder if the couture might not provide a congenial creative atmosphere acceptable to both her and her family. She apprenticed herself to Premet, a couture house known for decorating its day, sport, and evening frocks with geometric patterns in appliqué, beading, or fringe, and it was here that Grès learned her dressmaking skills.

Eventually Grès struck out on her own. She made *toiles* (muslin patterns) for loose coats, which she cut, basted, stitched, and sold to buyers from premises in the rue Miromesnil. Her new enterprise provided the young designer with an excuse to change her hated first name to Alix. Soon bored with simply turning out *toiles*, she began experimenting with other types of simple clothing, especially jersey day dresses. In 1934 she advertised that Alix Barton Couture was moving to 83, rue du Faubourg Saint-Honoré, where the house bore her new first name, Alix. Though part owner of the firm, she had difficulties with her silent partners and left six years later, leaving the name Alix, to which someone else owned the copyright. She adopted the *nom de brosse* of her husband, Serge Czerefkov, who signed his paintings with a partial anagram of his first name: "Grès."

The House of Grès opened in 1942 at 1, rue de la Paix during the Occupation of Paris. The first collection proved so offensive to the Germans (it was conceived around the colors of the French flag) that they closed the house for a year. Today, the House of Grès is still located on the rue de la Paix.

Mme. Grès ("Mademoiselle" to her staff) still works 365 days a year, producing nearly 350 models. Her method has never changed: she works alone with a live model, making a pattern directly on the figure. She cuts, pins, and bastes the *toile* herself, then passes it to

her staff. These assistants, most of whom have been with her for decades, understand her every nuance and produce just the coat or dress that Mademoiselle had in mind.

Grès's early training in sculpture is obvious from the classical "Grecian" draping and her use of the female figure as both inspiration and as anchor. She once stated: "I have always respected the body structure and the natural movement of a given material. I limit the number of seams in order to give a better impression of freedom, of suppleness of the silhouette. I like to make a body look beautiful, to enhance its qualities, to make a waist look thinner, a bust higher; I want people to guess about the shape underneath." Although her intention is to enhance the woman, the silhouette of a dress remains true to that woman's figure.

The labels—first Alix, now Grès—stand for an ideal of beauty and a rigor of handwork now nearly obsolete. Her sculptural dresses, most often made in matte-finish jersey but also in silk crepe or mousseline de soie, were described as being like Gothic statuary in 1934 when they first appeared. Having directed the flow of the folds with her hands, she then has the unpressed pleats stitched into place, making these pleated areas appear to be woven into each other. The fabric falls from them to the floor in graceful folds. Grès has also designed bias-cut, away-from-the-body (bias is usually used to follow the body) dresses and caftans in bright gilt brocades, failles, linen, silk satin, and organdy. From thin, stiff paper taffeta she manages a variety of puff, drapery, pannier, and bustle and has, paradoxically, also made exquisitely simple use of it in togas that fall in a triangle from the neck to the floor. Her dresses are most frequently monochromatic, but for pattern, she uses cut rather than a print, combining different colors of the same fabric in a patchwork. Her day clothes of leather, soft wool, tweeds, and blanket plaids are hooded, batwing-sleeved, shaped like kimonos, and then caped. The silhouette has changed little in half a century, for current mode has seldom guided Grès in the placement of a waistline or choice of skirt length.

Sometimes Grès designs hats or other accessories to supplement a specific collection. Now that the house has been sold, her prêt-à-porter collections will be extended. But licensing activities are limited to scarves and neckties, the jewelry she designs for Cartier, and her perfumes: Cabochard, whose name translates as "pig-headed," introduced in 1959, Grès pour Homme, and Quiproquo. This single-mindedness in today's fashion marketplace with its designer bed linens, chocolates, and sunglasses, is but one of the trademarks of this woman whose very concept of fashion depends on an aesthetic purity.

RIGHT:

Alix draped jersey dress *from 1938.*

BELOW:

Alix dress and coat from *1935.*

Augustabernard

LOUISEBOULANGER'S REPUTATION RESTS ON A DRAMATIC AND UP-TO-the-moment personal style; Augustabernard did not care that her salon at 3, rue du Faubourg Saint-Honoré was furnished unfashionably, or that her clients frequently found her on her knees, scrutinizing the last detail of the dresses *The New Yorker* called "grand simple affairs."

When she opened her house in 1919, Mlle. Bernard linked her first and last names, presumably to avoid confusion with Bernard et Cie. and Alice Bernard, two other Paris houses. She need not have worried, for by 1930 her reputation handily eclipsed those of the other two when the Marquise de Paris, one of the best-dressed women in France, won the Concours d'Elégance in St. Moritz wearing a décolleté Augustabernard gown of molten silver lamé. Two years later *Vogue* proclaimed her dresses the most beautiful of the season.

Augustabernard favored pale, moonlit colors; her clients, many of them from the Americas, came for her simple dresses in these shades as well as in black or white. The notion was that nothing was as exquisite a backdrop for one's jewels as an Augustabernard evening dress.

In keeping with the period, her evening gowns were slim, bias-cut, and long. Decoration was achieved by the material with itself: scarves floating at the shoulder or hip, flounces, scalloped tiers, or tucks applied in a neck-to-hem spiral. "Long lines, slim hip and not a centimetre of fullness allowed anywhere above the pelvis," was the description of her evening clothes by *The New Yorker* fashion reporter in 1930. Mlle. Bernard tended to avoid elaborate embroidery favored by other couturiers; a dress might, at most, be a sea of monochromatic square paillettes.

Lillian Farley, Mainbocher's assistant at Paris *Vogue* (and who, as Dinarzade, had modelled for Lucile and Patou), recalls that "Augustabernard came from one of the country provinces and her demeanor was that of a young country woman even to the natural color in her cheeks. Her curly brown hair was combed back in a knot and she invariably wore one of her simple, unadorned tailored suits." What she wore, and what she designed, were simple day clothes, often of rough tweed; a tweed suit might have a vest-cut blouse with V-neck and pointed waist as its third piece. Afternoon dresses of soft crepe or wool jersey were completed with attached scarves. Here too decoration was sparing and prints were almost never used.

As the Depression of the Thirties continued, her clients did not refrain from ordering from her, but often did refrain from paying their bills. Though there was no visible decline in either the amount of business or the quality of design, her house slid out of business as the decade progressed.

Simple-but-complicated Augustabernard creations from 1932.

Louiseboulanger

A PARIS GUIDEBOOK OF THE TWENTIES EXPLAINED THAT "WOMEN WHO dare to wear clothes that are strikingly individual and about three seasons ahead of the style naturally gravitate toward Louiseboulanger." The first couturier to have her portrait made in lacquer by the brilliant Dunand, she was also the first to have her *maison de couture* decorated in the modern style, a fitting background for her innovative designs.

Mme. Boulanger began her career as a workroom apprentice at the age of thirteen. Within a few years she was able to absorb nearly every aspect of dressmaking and tailoring. She was later hired as a designer by the House of Chéruit, where her talent was guided by the frequently daring taste of Mme. Chéruit. Shortly after Chéruit's retirement, Louise Boulanger ran her names together and opened her own house at 3, rue de Berri. She resumed her own business in late 1934, following her short-lived liaison with the House of Callot. Seeing her black and gold lacquered screens with their bold diagonals, Baron Adolph De Meyer noted that he was in the presence of a sensibility "decidedly modern: its designs . . . young, fresh, and vigorous." Of these designs, at least two will always be noteworthy: the "pouf" silhouette, for which she won her greatest acclaim, and the uneven hemline, an idea that has been repeatedly revived by designers for half a century.

The "pouf" evening dress was fitted close around the torso, then elaborately draped, layered, or fan-pleated at the back of the hips in what was almost a bustle, providing an effect of explosive bouffant fullness. The uneven hemline resulted when an evening dress, most often of printed chiffon, was cut to the knees in front but allowed to trail in the back or at the sides.

Louiseboulanger used warm roses, apricots, and oranges as well as icy blues and sapphire. For patterns Louiseboulanger favored figured textiles rather than the more usual embroidery. She became known for her use of flowered taffeta, painted chiffon, or printed crepe. Her fabric sense was both assured and innovative, and in the mid-Twenties, she pioneered the use of moirés and organdies as well as employing both the "right" and "wrong" sides of satin in the folds of a "pouf," thereby scattering light from every fold.

Her designs appealed to the aristocratic, soignée client who was not averse to being noticed. One client, Marlene Dietrich, was described by Bettina Ballard as "leaning insolently against a wall in a Louiseboulanger green velvet tunic richly bordered in sable."

But in 1939, as World War II bore down on Paris, she closed her *maison de couture*. Her era had come to a close. As she remarked, "the day tennis came in, the demimondaine went out, and fashion went with her."

Louiseboulanger evening dress of black tulle with gray and pink tulle corsage.

Vionnet

"T HE DIRECTION OF THE MATERIAL, THE WEAVE, ON THE ONE HAND; precision, cut, proportion, balance, on the other. That is what I oppose to the term fashion, which is an empty word and meaningless to a true dressmaker." This statement provides insight into why Madeleine Vionnet is considered by many to be the greatest, most consistently innovative, and, perhaps, most intellectual *couturière* of all time.

It was Vionnet who first approached fabric in a "modern" way. Working with the natural body—the figure of the twentieth century—she molded the dress to the woman, rather than the woman into the dress. Poiret claimed to have banished the corset but he merely made dresses that fell in folds from a gathered waistband. Vionnet took her mannequins out of their corsets, then took the intricate cut of the past and made equally elaborate dresses that seemed like a molten second skin. The advent of this "bias-cut" in fashion meant that a Vionnet dress could be slipped over the head and simply worn, without fastenings and underpinnings. Indeed, the first nipple ever shown in the pages of *Vogue* was through the bias-cut white satin of a Vionnet design in 1932—a hint at her modernity and the impact she would have on a whole century.

Madeleine Vionnet was born on June 22, 1876, across the Swiss border from Lake Geneva. As a child she showed considerable prowess at mathematics, but quit school at twelve to work for a Parisian dressmaker. Like Jeanne Lanvin, she started at the bottom of her profession, and like her she would marry and divorce before she was twenty. She worked in couture houses in both London and Paris, then served as assistant to Mme. Gerber at Callot Soeurs, where it was her job to reproduce the *toiles*.

This was followed by a five-year stint as designer with Jacques Doucet. There she quickly dispensed with the delicately wired high collars then in style and tried out her ideas for cut in her lingerie designs. By 1912 Vionnet had built up sufficient capital, and a sufficient clientele, to set up her own house at 222, rue de Rivoli, which she closed during World War I and re-opened in 1919. In 1922, she moved to 50, avenue Montaigne.

For Vionnet, it was the figure of the client for whom she was designing a given dress that was of paramount importance. At the time, most dresses were chemises that were identical front and back. Vionnet's were conceived in the round on a miniature model, then given to a *modéliste* to enlarge into a pattern. Vionnet strongly believed that designing by drawing would have shackled her and prevented her from ever discovering the bias cut. Because she worked in the round, she could visualize the garment as a whole.

Vionnet evening dress.

18

et

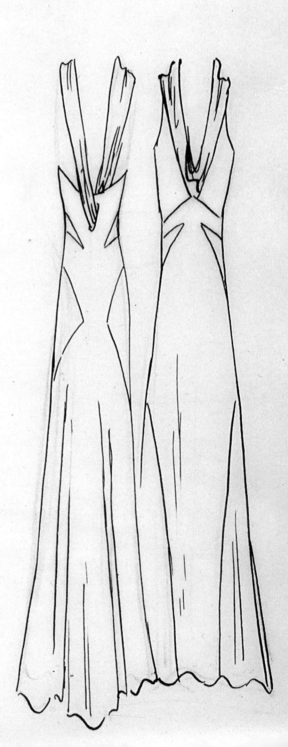

The result of these techniques was a dress that looked bad in the hand and good on the body. It is sometimes impossible to understand how a dress works until it is put on, to see that a particular asymmetric panel molds the hip or that a scarf can be tied to show both sides of the fabric at once.

Her knowledge of how a fabric moves and hangs and her experience with cut provided Vionnet with the ability to achieve extraordinary results with fabrics previously rejected for intricate patterns, especially supple silks and jersey. Her materials were made in two-metre widths to her specifications to accommodate the bias-cutting. Her favorites included crepe romain, crepe de Chine, mousseline de soie, charmeuse.

Vionnet was known for her pale, subtle palette, colors that were "non-colors": whites imbued with the slightest of tints. She experimented with every shade of flesh, rose, and pink, as well as with mauve, lichen, banana, and cactus. She made striking black clothing. Because the intricacy of construction was a form of decoration in itself, Vionnet rarely used printed fabrics; in fact, her small-scale floral silks, when made into dresses and nightgowns, looked curiously and uncharacteristically dowdy. Although she occasionally used beading and embroidery, always with great expertise, her most stunning clothes are left unadorned in the usual sense of the word.

Vionnet was called the Euclid of fashion, and geometric shapes predominate in all her collections as decorative and functional devices. Triangular underarm gussets allow for ease in a sleeve that is not set into the dress. Triangles appear at the neck and become the essence of Vionnet's cowl or halter necklines. Vionnet planned a pattern of stars, interlocking circles, connected hexagons, or stylized circular flowers to taper a dress at the waist, allowing it to widen again at the bust and the hips. She worked these elements out in pintucks, cutouts, and appliqués. She frequently used knots, both as a decorative element in a pattern of pintucked trompe l'oeil knotted lengths of fabric, or actually tied into the fabric itself.

Vionnet's clothes were masterpieces of the art of dressmaking. Her clients—from the Queen of the Belgians to such prominent socialites as Mrs. William K. Vanderbilt and Elsie de Wolfe—were sophisticated and individualistic in their attitude toward dressing; intelligent women who chose not to dress either by formula or fad. Vionnet, like Chanel, closed her doors in 1939; unlike Chanel, she would never reopen them, although until her death in 1975 at the age of 99, she continued to monitor and comment upon the haute couture, whose artistry she had done so much to upgrade.

Rather than merely sewing on a bow, Vionnet built this 1936 blouse around a bow formed from the fabric.

FOLLOWING PAGES: Detail of the bodice of a Twenties chemise dress. INSETS: A 1928 afternoon dress (left), and a 1923 dress made in tiers.

Mainbocher

A S A COUTURIER, MAINBOCHER—THE ONLY AMERICAN TO CARRY ON a successful business based in Paris—found an immediate edge in his nationality. Not everyone having clothes made in Paris was Parisian, and not everyone making them was, either. Mainbocher, like Molyneux, benefitted from émigré status. The British couturier dressed many members of his country's aristocracy, women in the public eye for whom dressing in Paris might not otherwise have been considered patriotic. Mainbocher was able to attract as his clients members of the American upper class, an Old Guard who wanted, and could afford, to look elegant but who also manifested a peculiarly puritanical mistrust of "newness" in fashion.

His was the place to go for clothes that were perfectly appropriate. Sally Kirkland, the former fashion editor for *Life*, summed up his approach when she said, "he not only made a woman look like a lady, but as if her mother had been a lady, too." When a Mainbocher mannequin appeared on the runway, she was sure to be wearing spotless white gloves, strings of pearls, and a hairband with a flat bow; discreet accessories that perfectly complemented one of his dressmaker suits or subdued evening dresses. These were clothes that projected elegance and confidence, that would brook criticism of neither themselves nor their wearer. Mainbocher's sure sense of propriety made him the obvious couturier to design the classically simple, pale grayed-blue dress worn by the American-born Mrs. Wallis Simpson at her 1937 marriage to the former King of England.

Main Bocher (his first name derived from his mother's Scottish maiden name, his surname was of French Huguenot origin, pronounced as if spelt "Bocker") was born on the West Side of Chicago in 1890. As a child he was encouraged to study both drawing and music and these interests fueled his instinctive desire to leave his hometown in 1909. He first studied at the Art Student's League in New York, and ultimately in Munich and Paris. He had already had drawings selected for inclusion in a Paris Salon des Décorateurs exhibition and was selling fashion sketches to earn extra money, when his voice failed him during an audition and he abandoned interest in an operatic career.

Mainbocher's career in fashion started to take shape. He began with an illustrator's job in the Paris office of *Harper's Bazaar*, and by 1922 he was the Paris fashion editor for French *Vogue*. By the time he left the magazine in 1929, having been turned down for a substantial raise, he was its editor-in-chief, and had learned all there was to learn about scrutinizing fashion, isolating the essential and omitting the extraneous. He had initiated the "Eyeview" section, coined the phrases "off-white" and "spectator-sports-clothes"; had been the first

M ainbocher evening dress of black net trimmed with geranium ribbons and silk flowers, 1936.

champion of a longer, more feminine mode and, at a dinner party at her house, had "discovered" Schiaparelli, asking if he could have a drawing made of her unusual sweater for the pages of *Vogue*. His editorial talents, as well as a loyal following of press colleagues, would prove invaluable in 1930 when, almost on a whim, he set about opening his own *maison de couture* at 12, avenue Georges V.

From the start, he drew on his observations as editor to shape a prestigious and exclusive image for his house. In homage to two of his favorite couturiers, Augustabernard and Louiseboulanger, he ran his first and last names together to produce the French-sounding Mainbocher. He invited only the top magazines and newspapers to attend his collections. Knowing what a profileration of cheap copies could do to a reputation, he limited the number of buyers and manufacturers who came to his salons by imposing an admission fee equal to the least expensive dress in any given collection.

His salons were exquisite, decorated with zebra skin rugs, mirrors, porcelains, and fresh flowers. In these elegant surroundings, Mainbocher insisted that his collections were not mere social occasions, a point he emphasized by having his butler serve ice water rather than champagne. His first customers included such fellow American émigrées as Elsie de Wolfe and above all, Mrs. Simpson, whose obsession with alloying propriety with high individuality would serve Mainbocher as inspiration and object lesson.

The Thirties passed quickly, and as the war neared, Mainbocher decided to close his Paris house and return to America where, he assumed, he would be able to duplicate his success since in 1940 the New York fashion world revolved around the French couture. Stores such as Lord & Taylor, Bergdorf Goodman, Henri Bendel, and Hattie Carnegie all offered originals from the top Paris houses as well as their own adaptations of French styles. The couture collections were also avidly watched by the Seventh Avenue ready-to-wear manufacturers looking for ideas to copy and ways to translate cachet into cash.

Mainbocher soon established himself on 57th Street, adjoining Tiffany, just east of Fifth Avenue, in rooms that reproduced as exactly as possible the décor of his Paris apartment and the ambience of exclusivity that had characterized his Paris couture house. (In 1960 he moved to 609 Fifth Avenue, where he re-installed the chocolate-brown banquettes, the trompe l'oeil "sky" ceilings, the mirrors, and the masses of white hyacinths.)

He never built any other branches, or had boutiques in any of the department stores. Feeling that his clothes should be worn with good jewelry and simple, well-made shoes, he never ventured into any li-

B*lack net, sequin-embroidered evening dress with apron, 1936.*

RIGHT:
A 1936 air-travel ensemble: *rose wool coat and jacket with a black wool skirt.*

BELOW:
C harmeuse evening dress *sewn with silk flowers, 1935.*

PARIS
LYON
MARSEILLE
CANNES

censing agreements. His sole non-clothing offering was his perfume, White Garden, and that was only available at his salon. Mainbocher became something to aspire to—for women who longed one day to afford one of his dresses, and for clothing manufacturers as New York became a center of better-quality design.

Mainbocher worked by making sketches, using the fabrics that he had chosen as a starting point and imagining the role a particular design might play in a client's life. "Suitability," he said, "is half the secret of being well dressed," and he had that ability to combine restraint and practicality with the most magnificent of materials. His first collections contained narrow, bias-cut slip dresses made in all white or all black patterned silks and, later, printed taffetas or crepes. In 1932 he produced a collection of cotton evening dresses, astonishing Paris with his use of checked gingham. He used men's shirtings, linen towelling, and cotton piqué for floor-length dresses with cutaway halter necklines, or evening coats cut like blazers.

He is remembered for his 1934 introduction of the first strapless evening dress, which he showed in black satin. Viewed as an oddity because of its old-fashioned "boning," it did not catch on until later in the decade, when all fashions had become more constructed and most couturiers were showing some version of a corsetted, décolleté bodice. By the late Thirties, Mainbocher was experimenting with the "femme fatale" curvy silhouette, with its all-out feminine details of gigot sleeves, ruffles, and trains, while never abandoning the less formal mode in which he excelled of covered-up dinner dresses, long-skirted evening suits, and tailored evening wraps executed in such lively materials as gold kidskin or pailletted blanket stripes. In the last of the prewar collections (1940), he presented the cinched-in "wasp" waist.

During the war, Mainbocher's natural restraint and the slimness of his chosen silhouette worked to his advantage. He solved one American fabric rationing problem by making short evening dresses; his beaded evening sweater, a cozy cashmere cardigan sewn at the neck with clusters of beads, was appropriate for dressing up in a country undergoing fuel shortages. He designed uniforms for the WAVES, the Marine Women's Corps, the American Red Cross, and the Girl Scouts, the last of which are still in use.

During the 1950s his style became fastidious to the point of sometimes seeming dowdy. The dressmaker suits featured straight knee-grazing skirts and short jackets in soft wools and non-bulky tweeds, and shell blouses trimmed with matching self-tabs, scrollery, his favorite flat bows, and Peter Pan collars. His theatre versions were not very different, though their jackets might be lined in ermine or mink and open to reveal décolleté bodices glowing with sequins. Dinner suits were short or long slip or sleeveless dresses with matching jackets. For these after-hours tailored *ensembles*, Mainbocher chose glittering brocades, muted velvets, and flowered or checkered silks. Bouffant evening dresses, shown in the fashion magazines on such clients as Mrs. Vincent Astor, were made up in glorious damask, velvet-voided-to-satin, or a new Mainbocher favorite: sari silk.

The Thirties classicism resurfaced in the stark, almost arid coats that Mainbocher made in the Sixties, as well as in his high-waisted, cowl- or halter-necked evening gowns. A new suggestion for dinner dresses was apron skirts worn with almost modish shorts or long pants and sleeveless Peter Pan collared blouses. Notable, in a decade of elaborate jewelled embroideries, was Mainbocher's lack of them.

Mainbocher's clothes were always shown in their own section of *Vogue* and *Harper's Bazaar*, a separation from other designers that became more and more pronounced as the Sixties wore on. Described as chaste, pure, serene, or classic, they began to have less and less validity in an increasingly youth-oriented society. Despite his department, *La Galerie*, where clothes were made to size rather than to order, saving a few steps and dollars along the way, Mainbocher was still the most expensive clothier in the country, with a suit and blouse costing, according to Marylin Bender in *The Beautiful People*, "as much as half a year's tuition and board at Harvard." The demand for expensive clothes that redeemed themselves by staying in fashion (or slightly outside it) was on the wane. Novelty for its own sake, Mainbocher's bête noire, had become the prevailing standard of quality.

It was only an American Old Guard who would feel the loss when Mainbocher retired. They have remained faithful to him by continuing to wear his designs (or similar replacements). Mainbocher had filled country clubs with women wearing pretty evening sweaters, sleeveless dresses with matching jackets, Peter Pan collared dressmaker suits, long skirts with simple tops for informal dinners, and even the plain kid belt with gilded seashell buckle that he first showed in 1933.

By his retirement in 1971, the fashion world had changed. Chanel died that year; Norell and Balenciaga, the last of the Old Masters, died the next. Mainbocher and his friends, including some of the great former fashion editors, mourned the death of the couture, and admired the wise decision of their colleague, Diana Vreeland, to follow the couture into a museum.

After announcing his retirement, Mainbocher lived in Europe—the Old World—until his death in 1976.

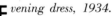

Evening dress, 1934.

Valentina

H EADS TURNED WHEN VALENTINA FIRST WORE ONE OF HER DRESSES TO an opening at New York's Metropolitan Opera in the mid-Twenties, her imperious beauty and her simple elegance set in *haut-relief* against a sea of *garçonnes* clad, as she put it, in "appalling paillettes . . . [their] waistbands at their derrières." Her own dress, which she had created from three yards of soft black velvet, was high at the neck and fell in a slender column to the floor. That she was so familiar with her own style was half Valentina's success; her ability to attract others to her vision and then design for them as brilliantly as she did for herself was the other half. For the nearly thirty-year duration of her New York couture house she designed all the clothes, showed her customers how to wear them, and appeared as her own model in fashion magazines.

Valentina Nicholaevna Sanina was born in Kiev on May Day 1904, and grew up studying drama and ballet. Her training was interrupted by the Russian Revolution, however, and in 1919 she fled her native land with her new husband, George Schlee, first to Greece and then to Paris. There they were the force behind a popular revue, "Russe," and Valentina made her film debut as an angel, a role she won by dint of her waist-length blonde hair. They subsequently accompanied a theatrical troupe to New York and, when it disbanded, decided to stay on. "New York was so beautiful," Valentina has recalled, "the skies and the river so exciting." She lives in New York today, high above the East River.

A brief stint as a mannequin for a Seventh Avenue manufacturer lasted until a salesman pinched her and she gave notice. Her next post, at an exclusive Madison Avenue dress shop called Sonia's, proved more fortuitous, for it was there that the clothes she made for herself first attracted notice. Encouraged, she and her husband opened Valentina Gowns, Inc. in 1928, initially on West 30th Street, but soon relocating to a handsome townhouse on East 67th Street. During her three decades in business, Valentina's only outside affiliation would be the annual collection she designed, briefly, for I. Magnin and, equally briefly, a perfume called My Own. Otherwise her clothes were strictly made to order and available only at Valentina, Inc. where her exalted hand-picked clientele consisted of personalities from the theatre, opera, and the movies, as well as from society. Her fame grew in proportion to the acclaim she received for her theatrical costumes and for a full five years after the opening of the play *The Philadelphia Story*, orders poured in from around the country for clothes like those she had designed for the character played by Katharine Hepburn.

Valentina's day clothes were simple, functional, and occasionally incorporated peasant influences. Among them were capes, skirts, and

Valentina wearing an evening dress of moiré with dotted organdy, and a coif of net.

blouses, including her biggest seller: a Byron blouse of ruffled linen, touted as practical because it could be washed and ironed in less than an hour and was priced at $300. Valentina pioneered the practical idea of travelling light, promoting a limited palette of black, white, brown, and beige and a limited group of interlocking pieces. Fashion editor Bettina Ballard has described a fashion show in which Valentina modelled her suggested weekend wardrobe: "She would do an amusing striptease, starting with a handsome Valentina shirt and skirt 'for arrive by car,' then off would come the blouse, underneath which was a bare top 'for sun on terrace,' then off would come the skirt to show matching shorts 'for beach with hat,' and the Russian woman in the wings would throw her a pointed coolie hat that tied with a scarf under the chin. Then 'for dinner in moonlight,' the Russian would hand her a long skirt that she would add to the bare top and she would knot the scarf smartly around her waist."

At night Valentina recommended a dramatic severity. Urging her customers not to trim themselves like Christmas trees, she set an example by wearing her stark black dresses with a triple strand of pearls or a Maltese cross. Her evening capes and dresses were frequently cut on the bias, providing a soft, body-hugging feeling. Her palette was restricted to warm earthtones—all the shades of wine, yellows ranging from chartreuse to ochre, olive browns, and greens —plus black. She preferred supple fabrics with a matte finish such as crepes (including wool and satin), chiffons, mousselines de soie, damasks, failles. Disdaining prints, she put flowers "where they belong—in the hair." She made use of variations on the halter neckline. Working with the fuller skirts popular in the late Forties and Fifties, Valentina often showed them in ballerina length with ballet slippers. Sometimes she reverted to a peasant look, as with her aproned evening dresses. Evidence of her Russian-Oriental background would also emerge in such forms as a Mandarin coat or an obi sash.

Valentina retired in 1957 as a result of the conspiracy of escalating labor costs, the ensuing high prices, and a dwindling interest in quality workmanship. One of America's few resident couturiers— perhaps the only one who can be mentioned in the same breath with Mainbocher and Charles James—she is remembered for her sense of theatre, her commitment to a severity worthy of the theatre, and at least one line she herself loved to deliver, over and over. "Mink is for football," she would say, "ermine is for bathrobes," and much later, "children are for suburbs."

Valentina sporting a day ensemble of her own design.

Halston

ALSTON BEGAN MAKING CLOTHES AT A TIME WHEN IT WAS NO LONGER fashionable to appear rich. The new social climate was one in which Park Avenue and Sutton Place matrons consigned their "important" jewels to vaults rather than lose them to muggers; when cultural impresarios were throwing parties for Black Panthers and waging war on the stuffy, the traditional, and the formal. Perhaps it is because his sensibility matured during this period of "radical chic" that Halston has rejected most vestiges of formal dressmaking. Halston makes clothes without zippers or pockets, ruffles or notched lapels, practically without seams. Luxury is present in the choice of fabric and such understated indulgences as hand-hemmed slip linings and monochromatic hand-beading. With almost devastating simplicity Halston remains true to the natural contours of the female body. Columnar, his dresses fall straight from the shoulder or are bloused gently at the waist with a tie-belt. The result is a narrow, elongated, elegant silhouette.

Roy Halston Frowick, born in 1932, grew up in Evansville, Indiana. He studied art at Indiana University and the Art Institute of Chicago, then took up millinery, first in Chicago, then in New York. Here he worked as an assistant to Charles James and in the salon of the milliner Lilly Daché. In 1958 Halston joined the design staff at Bergdorf Goodman as its "name" hatmaker, where he joined in bringing about the demise of the hat as it had been known, and the rise of "hatless" hats: the scarf hat, the fur hat, and the pillbox hat.

Halston's cachet grew throughout the Sixties. (It helped that *Vogue* and *Bazaar* sold more issues when the model on the cover was wearing Halston's red poppies, silver foil cubes, or one of his extravaganzas in pearl and gold beads on her head.) By 1966, Bergdorf's had offered him a chance to design clothes, and *Vogue* was quick to report: "Everyone knows his hand with a hat, now is the time to see how he shapes, constructs, architects a dress, a snow- or country-suit, a raincoat, an evening dress. Halston has a lot to do with this boutique—lots of his sure, bravura feeling everywhere—in the things to buy, the décor... and it's no accident that the boutique melds into his *haut chapeau* domain."

In 1968, he left Bergdorf's to open Halston Limited in a sleek, modernistic building at Madison Avenue and 68th Street, where he offered made-to-measure clothes and accessories, showing his first collection in 1969. Again, the venture was an almost immediate success. In 1972 he added a ground floor boutique to the Madison Avenue salon where one could buy off the rack; the new ready-to-wear operation, meanwhile, was headquartered on Seventh Avenue and was soon national in scope. In 1973 Norton Simon incorporated Halston's

RIGHT:
A *Halston signature look in shimmering white.*

FOLLOWING PAGES:
B *lack chiffon evening pyjamas embroidered with gold sequins.*

business for $12 million and named this new division of its conglomerate Halston Enterprises, Inc. Five years later Halston moved all his operations to the Olympic Towers building, where he shows his pared-down collections in a minimalist environment, assisted by a staff clad primarily in black cashmere.

Halston wears black cashmere too. When he designs, he adds to that favorite color beige, white, red, brown, and purple, most often as solid hues. Like his early teacher Charles James, he has little interest in prints. Cashmere shows up in simple day dresses, capes, floor-length evening gowns, and especially in the twin cashmere sweater set, one of Halston's many revivals of an old favorite, the cardigan tied around the shoulders in this incarnation. As much a Halston signature is the shirtwaist dress of Ultrasuede, a status symbol among older women despite, or more accurately because of, its utter plainness. As Halston has declared, "high style is finished for day."

Other signature looks from Halston include the one-shouldered evening gown, caftan dresses with asymmetric necklines, layered chiffon dresses reminiscent of togas and shown over silk slip dresses (first made in specially tie-dyed effects), tunics over pajamas, and the strapless columnar dress tied in a knot at the breasts. Many of his designs are made with an older or less-than-perfect figure in mind, with their one shoulder, single lapel, and layers of chiffon cut away inch by inch tending to elongate the body. His client list includes women active in the arts and society, many of whom Halston considers good friends.

Halston's activities have diversified over the years. In addition to cosmetics for Max Factor and luggage (in Ultrasuede, of course) for Hartmann, there are his Halston IV loungewear, Halston V and VI sportswear, and most recently, his line of low-priced clothing for J. C. Penney. This last move was an especially controversial one; Bergdorf's, for instance, closed its Halston boutique in its wake. Although all he has done is provide clothes in an affordable price range to a public who otherwise might have had to make do with more elaborate, and less well-made, styles, he has received the same sort of criticism that he did when he first began making clothes. As Kennedy Fraser put it, "[people who were] locked up in their respect for hidden facings and unseen linings could only shake their heads enviously at the popularity of Halston dresses with no more tricks about them than there are about a cashmere sweater or a chiffon scarf." In short, he continues to make strides for the simplification of American life.

Halston evening dresses.

Sonia Rykiel

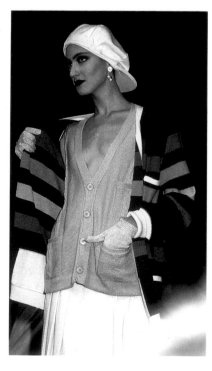

THE WOMAN I AM INTERESTED IN IS *LA VRAIE FEMME*. PUT THAT WITH a capital 'F'!" Sonia Rykiel, hidden behind her cloud of clay-red hair, told British *Vogue* a few years ago. Born in the 1930s, Rykiel is a member of the first generation of Paris ready-to-wear designers—those talented young iconoclasts who rose from the boutiques of the Sixties—who took her habitual self-introspection and turned it into clothing that allows other women to express their own personalities. Unlike her colleagues, she did not accomplish this by designing clothes that from first glance shout of an anti-Establishment independence, but by making clothes that, rather than present a façade to society, peel it away, quietly revealing the woman and her true thoughts.

Rykiel produces intensely personal, beautifully worked out collections of lean, knitted components that fit together like words in a haiku. The individual garments, though known as separates (sweaters and trousers, skirts and body stockings), are remarkably unified, with only slight contrasts in color and texture. The true Rykiel addict not only creates combinations from within a given collection, she also takes this season's new item and integrates it into a previous favorite Rykiel outfit.

Rykiel's first designs were born of necessity. In 1962, pregnant and repelled by the dowdy, childish, or timid maternity clothes then available, she knit herself huge sweaters that clung to and emphasized the swell of her abdomen. After the birth of her baby, she made new sweaters, tiny, skinny pullovers of fuzzy rabbit hair, and sold them at her husband's Paris boutique Laura. Although manufacturers derided these sweaters (one called them "obviously for twelve-year-olds"), they achieved an immense success and were worn by, among others, Audrey Hepburn, Virna Lisi, and Catherine Deneuve. By 1968 her clientele had grown enormously and Rykiel opened a store, this time called Sonia Rykiel, at 6, rue de Grenelle on the Left Bank. Today she presides over three stores in Paris, others in London and New York, and Sonia Rykiel boutiques in more than a hundred department stores around the world. She has recently begun to produce leather goods and a licensed collection of lower-priced Sonia Rykiel Knitwear, as well as a perfume, Septième Sens (Seventh Sense).

Her own image is one of sensuality and it is perpetuated in the clothes she designs for others; clothing that clings to the body in such soft-to-the-touch materials as velour, suede, knitted wool, and simple cotton tee-shirting. The coloration is languorous, made up mainly of misted shades of ivory, slate blue, charcoal, brick red, earth brown, and peach. Rykiel trademarks include flat bows and ties, fluted collars, contrasting bands and borders, visible outside seams, and no linings

ABOVE AND RIGHT:
Rykiel stripes from the
Eighties.

FAR RIGHT:
Rykiel renders her
sweater look distinctive
by baring the breasts.

or hems. She experiments most with proportion, and her pants and divided skirts may stop anywhere from the top of the knee to the ankle; her cardigans can be waist-, hip-, or knee-length. Versatility is an overriding concern and has given rise to such ideas as knitted scarves that wrap around waist, hips or head, sweaters that can be worn under or over their mates, or elements of clothing (sleeveless blazers and skirts and pants) that look as good worn inside as right-side out.

Such versatility, she feels, enables a woman to express herself within the comforting framework of a consistent vocabulary of elements, and saves the many hours that she would otherwise spend shopping and thinking about what to wear. The focus *chez* Rykiel is on working and relaxing. Although she claims that "there are no longer clothes for one occasion, one specific place, for one time, one hour: dressing is a matter of addition and subtraction (through separates and accessories)," she does design some things that are frankly evening pieces inset with lace, point d'esprit, or rhinestones.

Occasionally, if only to keep the press attentive, she resorts to gimmickry: an otherwise wearable sweater with a word picked out in glitter, or runway models wearing decorated inner tubes over their Rykiel bodystockings. But such gimmickry is in the service of ease, practicality, and a certain continuity. As Kennedy Fraser states in *The Fashionable Mind*: "Sonia Rykiel echoes the denunciation of fashion that depends on constant acts of unfaithfulness to last season's favorites, and prefers to think of her clothes lasting for years as a comfortable, neutral frame for the individuality of the wearer." Thus she allows for *la vraie femme* to shine through.

RIGHT:
Body-hugging jersey dresses.

THE ENTE

RTAINERS

There are those women who insist on being impeccably dressed, either absolutely in line with the prevailing taste or so imperceptibly ahead of it that no one can fault them. In general these women, while often possessed of enormous sophistication, wish to be noticed, but not by standing out from the crowd. It is to these women that Worth and Doucet first appealed and whom Molyneux, Mainbocher, and Chanel dressed. More recent counterparts have patronized Norell, Hardy Amies, Givenchy.

And then there are those women for whom subtlety has no charm, who enjoy mocking elegance, showing that they have taste but prefer not to be enslaved by it. The designers for these individuals understand the capabilities of the couture and choose not to perfect something that has gone before. Instead they find in it an inherent wit and drama, or references to the literary and artistic. These are clothes made for parties and grand entrances, as well as town and country: wearable in a variety of circumstances but deriving from a fancy-dress tradition.

Costume parties, long a favorite pastime, allowed those who would otherwise never step out of an image to play—to dress as one of the opposite sex for an evening, to emerge from a famous painting, or to pretend for a few hours to be living in another century. One of the many services Worth provided to his clientele was the concoction of suitably amusing fancy dress for the grandest of theme parties. Poiret, quite fond of such fêtes, developed many of his most important looks from the ones he had devised for his Oriental extravaganzas.

Schiaparelli was the first designer to apply the appeal of costume dressing to regular clothes. Her first design, a sweater, was unlike anything ever seen before. With its trompe l'oeil bow-tie, it was witty, amusing, and *casual; and it couldn't have been more different from one of Chanel's "little black suits" or Molyneux's simple ensembles.*

The same playfulness eventually led to entire collections based on such themes as the circus or the rites of spring. Schiaparelli made accessories out of everyday objects and, at the other end of the scale, embroideries from fine artists' drawings. Adrian, working in America, drew from a different source of fantasy and drama—his background as Hollywood costumer was manifested in almost every design. Marcel Rochas's flights of fancy led to whole (stuffed) birds cascading down the front of his evening dresses. Maggy Rouff brought her intellectual nature to her designs, often making use of wry references to the couture itself.

The Entertainers share an interest in finding beauty in the most humble source, and then juxtaposing the ordinary with the most rarefied. Adrian printed silk taffeta with naïve American quilt patterns, then used the fabric for ball gowns. He appliquéd dignified town suits with gingham tulip patchwork. Rouff designed an evening dress out of furnishing chintz, spotlighting the fabric's origins by using upholstery tassels in lieu of buttons. Karl Lagerfeld has used wrenches and scissors as motifs, and has hand-embroidered them in sequins across dresses. Schiaparelli, of course, made her famous hat out of a lambchop.

By examining how fabric has traditionally been used and then finding new ways to work with it, by making jokes with their designs, by exaggerating color and silhouette, by indulging all-out drama and entrancemaking flair, these designers have all set out to provoke. Characterized by boldness and intelligence, their clothes rarely depend on mere prettiness or tastefulness for their appeal.

Schiaparelli

RIGHT:
Zsa Zsa Gabor dressed by Schiaparelli for Moulin Rouge, 1952.

BELOW:
Elsa Schiaparelli in her Directoire-inspired dress and coiffure, 1932.

CHIAPARELLI AND CHANEL WERE THE TWO STARS OF THE COUTURE IN the Thirties and were its great innovators. Because they each had such strong personalities (rivalling only Poiret for the ability to attract attention), and because they both had such great impact on their era, the contrast between them is all the more intriguing. Both were sought-after celebrities, lionized by the press for their comments on the passing scene. And, even though both made the clothes that best suited their own looks, they were appreciated by many of the same clients.

Their clothes were as different as night and day and yet, representing the two extremes of the couture, fit perfectly into the life of their times. Chanel made a fashion out of anti-fashion, using the couture to promote the best of a personality-revealing kind of dressing-down. Schiaparelli, whose vibrant and sometimes outlandish designs emphasized her own *belle-laide* looks, introduced a new role to the couture, that of forum for trends in art, as well as humor. Balenciaga summed up their relationship: "Coco had very little taste, but it was good. Schiap, on the other hand, had lots of it, but it was bad." With Schiaparelli, the couture that began with Worth came full circle. Worth had made a career out of dressing the newly rich in appropriate, tasteful luxury. Now there was a *couturière* for the daring.

Elsa Schiaparelli was born in Rome in 1896. Her childhood, as she recounts it in her autobiography, *Shocking Life*, was a colorful one. Her free spirit was evident early on when she planted seeds in her throat, mouth, and ears in the hopes of transforming her "ugly duckling" self into a beautiful flower garden. A few years later, she published (with the aid of a cousin) a book of adolescent, and very torrid, love poetry. It was this that prompted her family to send the "shocking" Elsa off to convent school.

After ninety-nine days she was released from that school and returned to Rome, where she continued searching for ways to express herself. Ostensibly en route to London with friends of her family, Schiaparelli stopped over in Paris and decided she must stay. Here she made her first fashion impression when she attended a fancy-dress ball costumed in four yards of navy crepe de Chine and two of orange—the former simply wrapped around her body, the latter forming sash and turban. As she would do so often, Schiaparelli caused a sensation—not least when her *ensemble* began to unravel.

Her life story is also poignant. Schiaparelli married a theosopher and followed him as he drifted around Europe and eventually ended up in America, where he abandoned her soon after the birth of their daughter. Schiaparelli returned to Paris to face the reality that she was a young woman with a child to support.

ABOVE:

*Horst portrait of
Schiaparelli in 1936.*

LEFT:

*chiaparelli suit and hat
decorated with leaf
fronds, mid-Thirties.*

There were ups and downs for the young Schiaparelli. Poiret was so impressed with her sense of style that he made presents of his designs to her. Maggy Rouff's assistant, however, told her that she'd be better off planting potatoes when she applied for a job.

Then, in 1928, she made her first real mark in the fashion world with a pullover sweater in black and white wool, knitted with a trompe l'oeil bow-tie at the neck. Mainbocher admired it and had it drawn for reproduction in the pages of French *Vogue*. Anita Loos, the author of *Gentlemen Prefer Blondes*, was the first to purchase one, and a buyer for a New York department store placed an order for forty of them, stipulating that they be accompanied by simple knit skirts.

"Schiap" was in business. She rented an upper-floor studio at 4, rue de la Paix and hired a covey of Armenian knitters. Downstairs, at street level, she hung out her shingle: *Schiaparelli—Pour le Sport*. More sweaters followed. She made clothes for golf and tennis, skiing and swimming. By 1929 she was devising all sorts of reversible, practical, and convenient clothes that were defiantly uncouture: blouses that buttoned at their hems; six-piece suits, the pieces of which could constitute an entire day wardrobe. As ingenious were her wraparound beach dresses, each composed of four apron-tied half-dresses, sewn together and slipped through slits in the waistband, available in many different color combinations, and wearable in several different ways.

But Schiaparelli didn't restrict herself to sportswear. In 1930 she moved downstairs to the first floor of her building on the rue de la Paix, and added *pour la ville, pour le nuit* to her shingle. Most of her early evening dresses were simple, décolleté, and black, in ribbed, crinkled, or otherwise highly textured fabrics. Her first departures from sports clothing gave rise to the use of unusual dress materials including white mourning crepe and the first of the Schiaparelli prints. She also experimented with accessories, such as a necklace, bracelet, and earrings of silver latticework studded with exotic dark woods.

In the Thirties, as Schiaparelli became a more accomplished *couturière* and fashion inclined toward more construction and sophistication, her focus shifted from her chemises and sweater *ensembles* to intricately fitted suits and day dresses, evening suits, and evening dresses. In these, Schiaparelli's imagination manifested itself most in her use of fastenings. She is justly famous for her buttons, which included bullets, cupids, clowns, rabbit's feet, drums, and astrological symbols. When limited to a plain, round button, she used it in diminishing sizes. Her whimsical accessories often borrowed from non-clothing forms: hats shaped like inkpots, or her renowned lambchop; a pocketbook called "the Big Apple," whose sections were made of vivid red suede. When she wasn't being frivolous, she was being practical: if there was a way to hang everything a woman might need during the day from a bracelet or a belt, Schiaparelli found it.

Some collections had themes that tied together their various buttons, fabrics, shapes, and accessories. The 1937 spring collection was dedicated to "the things all around us" and accordingly featured bees, butterflies, pineapples and other fruits, as well as many different flowers. For her 1938 *païen* (heathen) collection, the wood nymph's necklaces were ivy leaves entwined with pearls, purses came in milk cow shapes, and the embroideries were inspired by Botticelli's *Primavera*.

The Thirties decade is remembered as a period of narrow, sinuous clothes, a silhouette with which Schiaparelli worked while also experimenting with Empire lines as well as bustle-backed silhouettes. She became famous for her dinner suits and in 1947 *Vogue* described one as "a sort of summary of her designing tradition. First because it is a dinner suit, an idea she has always championed, second because the black has more than a flick of shocking pink, and third because it is bustled and embroidered, takes a long or short skirt."

Like Chanel, Schiaparelli knew the artists and intellectuals of Paris in the Thirties, but unlike her rival, she had them collaborate actively in her work. It was Salvador Dali who designed a bureau-drawer-pull pocket and who painted a lobster on an evening dress garnishing it with parsley sprigs. Besides the Cocteau head profile—with hair streaming down the arm of an evening jacket—there is Christian Bérard's Medusa drawn on the back of a cape, embroidered in sequins. The poet Louis Aragon and his wife contributed a necklace that looked like a string of aspirins. Sculptress Leonor Fini devised the perfume bottle for Schiaparelli's famous perfume Shocking, and Jean Schlumberger, the legendary jeweler, got his start working *chez* Schiaparelli. It is one of the few times that artists and fashion designers have actually (and happily) collaborated.

Schiaparelli loved color and had a way with unusual tints. These could be subtle, or they could be piquant when used in eccentric combinations: turquoise linen with grape velvet piping, or purple and olive combined with dark red. A simple black dress became dramatic when set off by a fleecy lime green coat or fire-engine-red stockings. Most famous of all was her "shocking pink," a bright magenta, less a brand new shade than a catchy new name. Her allegiance to this color was so great that she named her best-known perfume after it, titled her autobiography *Shocking Life*, and was buried wearing an antique Chinese robe of the purest shocking pink.

Diana Vreeland, in her infamous *Harper's Bazaar* column wrote:

vening jacket from the Circus collection, 1938.

"Why don't you realize that this wonderfully creative woman is expressing our life and times in her little suits and dresses and in her unique materials?" In her use of fabrics, Schiaparelli was as innovative as ever. Pioneering the use of man-made materials, she especially delighted in fabrics that bore no resemblance to natural ones: "glass" material, which looked like cellophane, lastex, and a crinkly substance called "treebark." She had a fabric made up that was nothing more than a collage of her newspaper press clippings. Another was quilted with miniature musical notes.

The Thirties was "Schiap's" decade. In 1934 she opened a branch in London at 36 Upper Grosvenor Street and moved her Paris house into grander quarters at 21, Place Vendôme. There she installed a boutique featuring her life-size stuffed pink bear and a sofa in the shape of a pair of lips, both the handiwork of Dali. The window displays were likewise outré, something to see on the way to and from the Hôtel Ritz, which was nearby. She made costumes for the movies, and dressed stars such as Dietrich, Mae West, Gloria Swanson, and Tallulah Bankhead. Her clothes were also worn by the most fashionable clotheshorses, including Millicent Rogers, Lady Mendl, and Wallis Simpson. It is said that Daisy Fellowes, Schiaparelli's most publicized customer, even managed to carry off the lambchop hat.

The House of Schiaparelli closed down during the war and reopened in 1945. But "Schiap's" moment was over. In 1954 Schiaparelli discontinued the couture part of her business; she limited her designing to licensed items: sunglasses, swimsuits, stockings, costume jewelry, men's ties, and toward the Seventies, wigs. The house itself, having been sold twice, is still on the Place Vendôme.

Just as the Dadaists mocked the notion of good art, Schiaparelli mocked the notion of good taste, knowing that as women became increasingly confident, rules about propriety and taste could be more effective if broken. Undeniably creative, she proved that innovation in fashion need not be limited to the reformation of silhouette or explorations of dressmaking techniques. She cast a net all around her, bringing in myriad influences to bear on her designs. Aware that things are not always what they seem, she presented suits and dresses that pretended to look like a piece of furniture, an artist's drawing or a *plat du jour*. Both her actual creations and the way she worked have been widely imitated: by Yves Saint Laurent, Perry Ellis, at some time or other by practically everybody. Today her appeal is no less immediate or provoking—and no more akin to Chanel's relevance—than it was during Schiaparelli's heyday.

Adrian

ADRIAN IS REMEMBERED AS HOLLYWOOD'S MOST PROMINENT AND influential costume designer during the Thirties. It was his active mind that conjured up Garbo's crinolines in *Camille*, Harlow's bugle-beaded chemises for *Dinner at Eight*, and Garland's blue-and-white gingham in the *Wizard of Oz* and that provided Crawford with those imposing square-shouldered suits that became the trademark of them both. He designed all four thousand costumes for the historical spectacle *Marie Antoinette*, created the elegant "Parisian" *ensembles* for *The Women*, and devised the girl-next-door look for Hepburn in *The Philadelphia Story*. As the popularity of period extravaganzas began to wane, however, Adrian turned his attention to the women who had been in the audience, scrutinizing his designs, and clamoring for copies of his Letty Lynton dress, or Garbo's cloche hat.

He loathed the idea of the housewife dressing herself like a starlet, telling *Time* magazine that: "the average woman should limit herself to the costumes worn by the heroines of light comedies laid in moderate-sized towns." What Adrian, Ltd. provided this woman were not peignoirs dripping with beads and maribou, or dresses sporting six-foot-wide panniers, but sophisticated suits as wearable as those sported by actresses when they portrayed working women; long, skinny dinner dresses embroidered with bits of glitter that framed the face like those he provided for the stars' close-ups; and ingénue dresses festooned with flowers that would be at home at any country club dance.

Gilbert Adrian, né Adrian Adolph Greenburg, was born in Naugatuck, Connecticut, in 1903. His mother was a painter, and his father ran his in-laws' millinery business. A creative family to grow up in, it also included Adrian's uncle, a theatrical designer, and his sister, who was training to be a dancer.

As a boy Adrian sketched and drew, his style becoming more and more sophisticated, and it soon became obvious that he too was headed for a career in the arts. Indeed, his family gave up the idea of sending him to law school, and in 1921, he enrolled at New York's Parsons School of Design. At Parsons, where his lack of discipline was as evident as his talent, his teachers felt that he would be more stimulated at the school's Paris branch and plans were made for him to transfer. While working at a summer theatre just prior to his first Paris term, Greenburg decided to drop his surname, and to be known from hence forward simply as Adrian.

He had been in Paris barely four months when he got lucky. Irving Berlin noticed the costume he designed for a classmate for one of the biggest and merriest of the costume balls that then obsessed Paris, and invited the young student back to New York to work for his Music

Box Theatre revues. Adrian jumped at the chance and spent the next few years designing costumes not only for Berlin's revues but also for the *Greenwich Village Follies* and George White's *Scandals*. His work came to the attention of Natacha Rambova, the exotic (and entrepreneurial) wife of Rudolph Valentino, who asked him to come to Hollywood and design for her husband's next film, *The Hooded Falcon*. Although never released, it signalled the beginning of Adrian's Hollywood career. He next worked on several films for Cecil B. De Mille, the most famous of which is the 1927 *King of Kings*. Adrian accompanied the legendary director when he moved to Metro-Goldwyn-Mayer, and remained there long after De Mille himself had moved on.

This was a prosperous time in Hollywood, and Adrian was given free rein in using embroideries, French silks and laces, feathers, and jewels. Nowhere was he more elaborate, and more attentive to perfection in detail, as when he worked on such period films as *Queen Christina*, *Anna Karenina*, *Mata Hari*, and *Marie Antoinette*, but he was equally adept at costuming the sophisticated contemporary comedy or drama.

When the movies began to change, Adrian realized that his role would change too. He abruptly switched gears. With the help of Woody Feurt—a former manager of Bullock's Wiltshire, the California department store—he formed Adrian, Ltd. in 1941. From its base in Beverly Hills, the new firm provided both ready-to-wear and custom-designed clothes to stores around the country.

In 1942 he showed his first collection in his new salon and was a success within the season. Although he had been advised that beginning a fashion business in wartime would be pure madness, it became clear that instead it was an astute move. America was cut off from Paris and had to rely on its own fashion resources, and Adrian's clothes were popular. The major American fashion magazines ignored him whenever they could, using his clothes only as examples of what was happening on the West Coast. Yet Adrian's silhouette, designed originally to camouflage by exaggerating Joan Crawford's shoulders, became the most prevalent look of the Forties.

Adrian had been in business only ten years when, in spring 1952, he had a heart attack while working on that year's fall collection. He closed Adrian, Ltd. and retired to Brazil with his wife, actress Janet Gaynor. Adrian amused himself with painting and limited his designing to a collection of men's shirts and ties and some costuming for the theatre. He had just finished work on the stage costumes for the debut of Lerner and Loewe's *Camelot* in September 1959, when he suffered another heart attack and died.

PRECEDING PAGES:
Adrian *film designs for* Joan Crawford. *When* Ladies Meet, *1941.*
PAGE 207: No More Ladies, *1935.*

LEFT:
Columnar evening dress embroidered with gold bead Greek key bands, *1945.*

As a designer, Adrian was at his best when working within the restrictions of a theme, a habit and discipline he had acquired costuming period films. During the course of its existence, Adrian, Ltd. presented a Greek collection that featured columnar white dresses embroidered with Greek key motifs, and a Persian collection composed largely of dark clothing lavishly encrusted with gilt embroidery. His Gothic collection centered on dresses of jersey, with almoner's pockets and trailing medieval sleeves; his Spanish styles relied on the extensive use of black, jet, and braid. His Americana group included Dolley Madison ballgowns made in organdy patterned with patchwork quilt designs. It also featured the use of gingham and Pennsylvania Dutch motifs.

For his coats and suits, Adrian made creative use of fabrics by Pola Stout such as woolens woven in blocks and stripes of color. These he would typically cut into triangular panels and resew into facing patches at the shoulders, sleeves, and pockets of a suit jacket, as well as across the skirt. Adrian was fond of combining similar versions of a fabric in a single *ensemble*, for example, a short topcoat in a large plaid would be worn over a suit of a smaller plaid and decorated with appliqués of an even tinier check. A typical Adrian suit consisted of a long jacket with little or no collar or lapel, a single-button front closure at the waist, wide shoulders with long fitted sleeves sporting two darts at each elbow, and a straight skirt with kick pleat. His dinner and theatre suits were either of dark wool with dramatic touches of velvet or embroidery, or patterned silk brocades and failles.

He was fond of large-scaled, dramatic prints—those that incorporated his favorite animals, gigantic playing cards, palm leaves, or Etruscan figures—for his long dinner dresses, which were usually made in fluid fabrics and characterized by a use of asymmetric drapery. He also designed long dresses composed of abstract patchwork of solid colors known as "Picasso" or "Braque" dresses. More formal evening looks included his full-skirted ball gowns of filmy tulle or watercolored taffetas. His only forays into non-clothing items were his hats, and his Saint and Sinner perfumes and lipsticks.

Adrian is not the only fashion designer to have originated a career in Hollywood—certainly Irene of California, Bonnie Cashin, and Helen Rose successfully made the leap from costume to fashion design. But it is Adrian who brought to his "civilian" efforts an uncanny ability to depict the height of fashion without being in fashion, who proved that America could have its own style and that it didn't have to evolve from sportswear but could emanate from Hollywood, bypassing Paris altogether.

A *1947 Adrian suit, with gingham appliqué.*

Maggy Rouff

RIGHT:

Three Maggy Rouff
dresses for the races,
illustrated in Art, Gout,
Beauté, *1932.*

BELOW:

Maggy Rouff dress,
1939.

NOT MANY FASHION DESIGNERS ARE ABLE TO BE DESCRIBED AS INTELlectual, but Maggy Rouff was. Determined to become a surgeon during her adolescence, it was with hesitation that she focused her interest on the couture. Her designs, perhaps because they are tempered by this tendency toward the intellectual, are inventive without being strident. They are at once feminine, imaginative, and elegant.

Born in 1896, Maggy Besançon de Wagner was the daughter of the Viennese couple who founded the Paris House of Drecoll. Abandoning medicine, Maggy followed her mother into the business as sportswear designer, and was a director of Drecoll by 1928. The following year Drecoll merged with the House of Beer, moving into its headquarters, and Maggy, newly married, took over Drecoll's former premises and formed an affiliation with the established House of Rouff. Calling the new house Maggy Rouff, she installed her husband as financial director and she became its designer. (Curiously, her husband came to be known as Monsieur, or Pierre, B. de Wagner and Maggy as Mme. B. de Wagner.) Records on the house's history are incomplete but it is clear that she remained sole designer until the late Forties, when the House moved from 136, avenue des Champs Elysées to the avenue Matignon, where it remained until its 1965 move to the avenue Marceau. Maggy Rouff was closed by the time of her death in 1971.

Rouff's early designs were influenced by her experience with sportswear. Jaunty and fresh, this sharply tailored clothing was advertised in the late Twenties as a "peep into the future." Many of her day clothes were made of crepe romain or wool crepe, both matte-finished fabrics, and featured collars made of shawls or scarves. Another favorite design featured the piecing together of different kinds of fabric in one color. Monograms were often embroidered on her scarves and jacket pockets, not only in the Twenties, when they were a popular graphic device, but on into the Fifties. Maggy Rouff made coats with triangular cape collars and matching gloves, and fitted her Thirties dresses close to the body through shirring and drapery. There is also the occasional witty touch: a cupid applied to a belt, a bird's-head brooch on a shoulder, or jewelled arrows sewn to a bodice. Sportswear innovations included jersey "plus fours" in the mid-Thirties, and beach skirts with matching brassières in the Balinese style.

Her feminine evening dresses in the early Thirties were close to the body and sewn with airy, slanting tiers of ruffles. Later she worked with a fuller-skirted silhouette and appliquéd dresses with contrasting fabrics at the yoke and hem, often in a geometric pattern. A particularly innovative dress of 1936 was made of English country-

house chintz, with three furniture upholstery tassels sewn at the bodice. Organdies were prevalent throughout her work, as were other feminine details such as fichu collars, puffed sleeves, "bustle"-draped skirts, bows, and bow motifs.

Color intrigued Maggy and she felt that different textures and weights of fabrics called for different, appropriate hues, stressing that a crude wool looked best in a bright tone, a soft velvet in a somber tone, while a pliant silk should have a delicate tint. She sought to banish the prejudice that blondes, brunettes, or redheads should favor certain preordained colors. Her color innovations included the much-heralded purple-blues, a copper color called cauldron, and a family of colors dubbed "wearable" grays.

Her published works include *America Seen through a Microscope*, a study of a trip to the United States, and a volume entitled *The Philosophy of Elegance.* Fashion historians agree that the latter—filled with such maxims as "Style is like love, it can happen in a flash or develop over a long period"—is a subject on which she was well qualified to comment.

LEFT:

E legantly simple Maggy Rouff dress, 1936.

RIGHT:

R ouge satin blouse with bow-knot appliqué, 1937.

Karl Lagerfeld

ACTING FOR ALL THE WORLD LIKE A SPOILED ARISTOCRAT, FREE TO follow any interest, above rules when it comes to breaking them but not when it comes to etching them in stone, Karl Lagerfeld has managed to restore the belief that quality is not in the label, but in the dress. All of his clothes and labels are different, and practically all of them are the best in their class. As a personality he is awesome, as a designer he is a virtuoso.

Karl Lagerfeld was born in Hamburg, Germany in 1938, the son of a Scandinavian dairy magnate and his Westphalian wife. Early on he displayed a penchant for art, languages, history, and connoisseurship. His imperious nature also manifested itself at an early age. One story has it that he demanded, and was denied, a valet as a present for his fourth birthday. Supposedly one of his earliest memories was instructing this same (nonexistent) valet in the technique of ironing a shirt collar. Fashion became one of his many interests when the family moved to Paris, and, while studying at the Lycée Montaigne, he accompanied his mother on her rounds to the couturiers.

In 1954, at age sixteen, he won the top prize for his woman's coat design in the contest sponsored by the International Wool Secretariat. (Another sixteen-year-old, Yves Saint Laurent, took first prize in the dress category.) Pierre Balmain put Lagerfeld's coat design into production and made the teenager an assistant on his design staff. After three-and-a-half years, Lagerfeld had become bored and moved on to the position of chief designer for the House of Patou. This time he felt stifled after only a year.

Lagerfeld's first post-couture affiliation was with a relatively new house called Chloé, founded in 1952 with the forward-looking aim of combining the elegance of the haute couture with the immediacy of the prêt-à-porter. By 1970 Lagerfeld had put the house on the map and for the next decade both would be known for a look of lightness. Year after year, Lagerfeld made clothes out of crepe de Chine with no linings, unnecessary seams, or extraneous details. His *ensembles*, constructed of several lightweight, airy layers, included camisoles, shirt-jackets, and sleeveless *dalmatique* jackets, used in different ways. The colors were as ethereal as the thin silk itself and Lagerfeld experimented with appropriate forms of decoration—painting silk in patterns rather than using embroideries or beads, using inserts of lace. A lingerie derivation was most obvious in his choice of colors, in the narrow bands of lace, and in the construction style of the garments: "bathrobe" coats, evening *ensembles* consisting of "teddys" and matching wrappers, or slip dresses. He tied silk blouses around the waist, cardigan-style, wrapped scarves around the hip, waist, and even

tourniquet-like around the upper arm, as well as around high collars in a look that was called Byronesque.

Although most of the clothes were hailed for their simplicity and modern femininity, there was an exuberant side to Lagerfeldian design: one-button gloves appliquéd with playing-card motifs, prints that resembled blackboard mathematical equations, silk fans and parasols printed to match very contemporary dresses, and d'Artagnan *ensembles* composed of tunics over short skirts over stovepipe trousers tucked into boots. More recent are embroideries of diamanté guitars, gushing faucets, wrenches and hammers, and even the beaded Chloé-labelled top swinging from its hanger embroidered on a plain black dress.

Lagerfeld's "boy wonder" reputation has a great deal to do with his extraordinary versatility, and with his longtime determination to remain a freelancer. He steadfastly refused until 1984 the lure of his own label, preferring instead to be able to have a go at whatever stood a chance of amusing, and stretching, him.

In 1983 he took over as artistic director for the long-slumbering House of Chanel, designing first its couture and later its ready-to-wear. There his work has been a tour de force, expressing both a reverence for Chanel's brilliance and an irreverence for her clichés. He has revived ideas from her best period, that of before World War II, and subtly (and not so subtly) played with proportion while retaining what has become an idiom. His experience with lightweight fabrics, and with what is known as *flou*, has proven indispensable. Probably no other designer could have taken her "little nothing" dresses and made them look so fresh as to effectively banish the appeal of the "important" dress.

In a sense it is Chanel and Schiaparelli all over again. Although it is Lagerfeld's most obvious rival, Yves Saint Laurent, who has admitted to being guided by an allegiance to these two great Thirties *couturières*, Lagerfeld is the one who has revived their dueling points of view and who singlehandedly argues both sides. During the Seventies, while working with an almost low-key, easy, and modern look, he was occasionally given over to Schiaparelliesque flights of fancy. It was when he assumed Chanel's mantle that this side of him truly flowered— it is Schiaparelli, not Chanel, who would have applauded embroidering the Chanel chain-handled bag across the Chanel little black dress. While he claims to disparage any notion of fashion as an art, his work supports the view that it is a form of mastery worthy of scrutiny. However, the clothes themselves must provide the forum for this debate, and must do so now, not in a future museum retrospective. His best jokes are the ones about fashion itself.

PRECEDING PAGES:
Lagerfeld with model (top); fireworks embroidery (bottom). *PAGE 217: Patterned lamé turnout by Lagerfeld for Chloé, 1982.*

RIGHT:
Paloma Picasso wearing a Lagerfeld design for Chloé.

FOLLOWING PAGES:
Bejewelled guitar and violin dresses by Lagerfeld for Chloé, 1984.

Marcel Rochas

THE CAREER OF MARCEL ROCHAS STRETCHED FROM THE MID-TWENTIES to the mid-Fifties and was marked by prophetic innovations. In 1932, for example, he introduced a gray flannel trouser suit to be worn on city streets that required neither beach nor boudoir for its legitimacy. (Rochas claimed that he coined the word "slacks.") In 1937 he opened a New York branch on East 67th Street for the retail and made-to-order sale of his Parisian designs. In 1942 he invented a new corset, dubbed the *guêpière* (from the French for "wasp"), which cinched the waist and foreshadowed the more feminine silhouette of the postwar era. And eventually, when he began to sense that the importance of the couture was dwindling, he turned his attention to his boutique—to accessories and separates.

While there has been much speculation as to whether Rochas, Adrian, or Schiaparelli was the first to launch the broad-shouldered silhouette in the early Thirties, Rochas was at least able to trace his version to an event: at the 1931 Exposition Coloniale, Javanese and Balinese dancers' costumes inspired his *robe Bali*, a dress of black silk with a wide band of white piqué extending across the neckline to form squared, turned-down epaulets.

Marcel Rochas was born in Paris in 1902. His father is reputed to have been an artist from Avignon and his grandfather a Burgundian shepherd. He was pursuing a law career when, as the story goes, he decided that the only way he could provide his beautiful young wife with appropriately beautiful clothes was to open his own couture house, which he did on the Place Beauvau off the rue du Faubourg Saint-Honoré. By 1930, after just a few years, he was apparently a great success. A much-told story of that date recounts how eight elegant women all wore the same Rochas dress to a smart party, causing a bit of an outrage. True or not, the Rochas motto—*"Jeunesse, Simplicité* and *Personalité"*—caught on, and in 1931 he was able to move the house into a *hôtel particulier* at 12, avenue Matignon, where he was fond of arranging the windows himself, and accenting his dresses with objects he'd found in the flea markets and antique shops of Paris.

The Rochas output is characterized by a calculated originality. The Twenties saw such ideas as his *tailleurs* with blouses and scarves pieced in geometric patterns, blouses meant to be worn with men's neckties, evening dresses with triangular skirts that fell in folds of varying lengths, and beach pajamas with *godets* of pleats inset at the knees. In the Thirties, his coats and suits were like wool sculptures, their seams stitched wide to make them stand out in relief. He showed a tweed coat with an Empire waist and, unexpectedly, authentic Empire sleeves, long and tight and puffed high at the shoulder. (Sleeves

Evening coat embroidered with abstract motif, 1936.

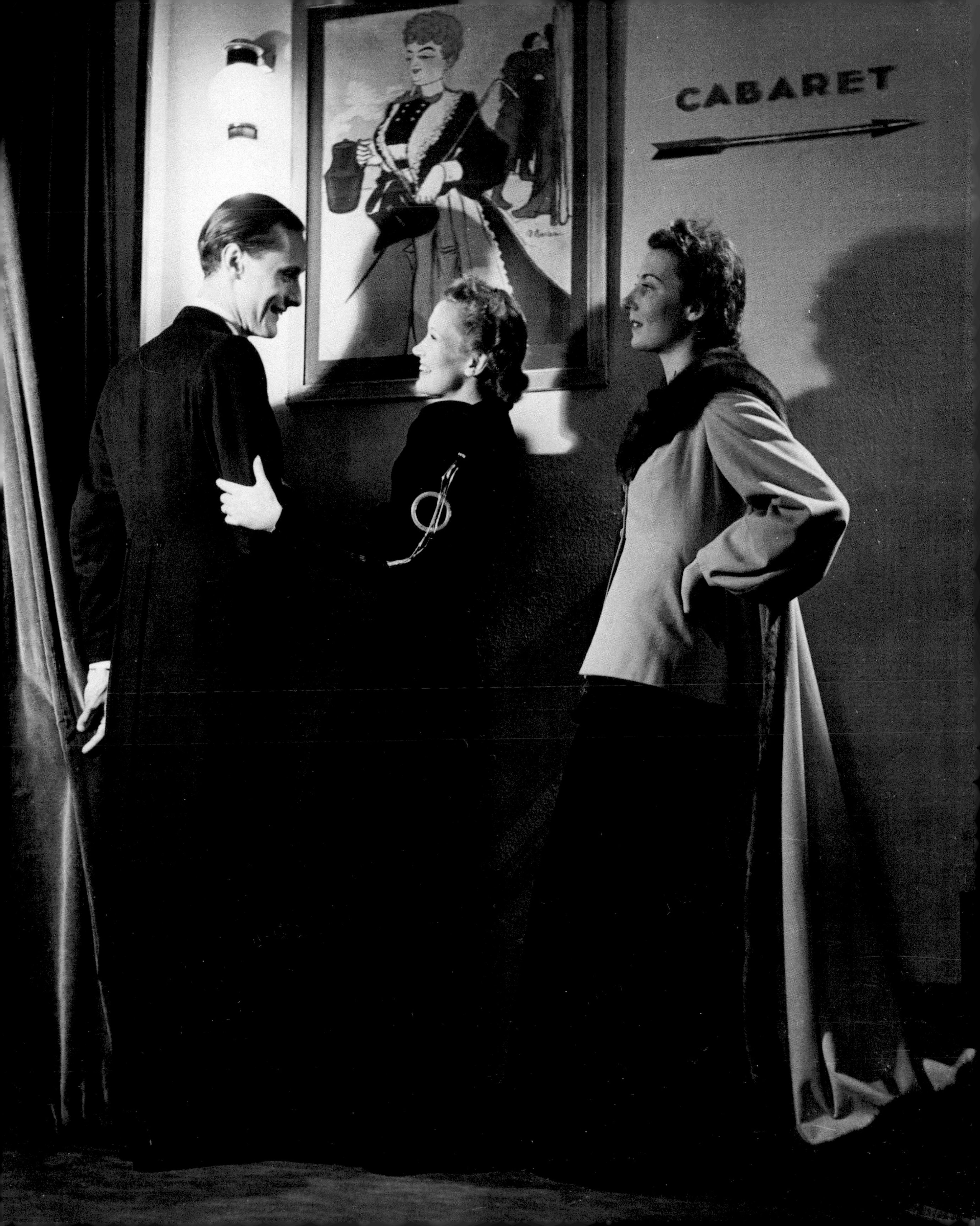
CABARET

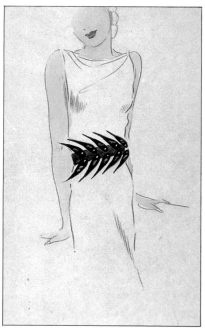

were important to Rochas—those of his "Cambodian" coat were stitched to resemble a dragon's tail.) He was consistently imaginative with furs, using exotic types like panther and leopard, and dyeing others unusual colors.

Drama came to be expected of him. Rochas sewed silk calla lilies to necklines, taxidermists' bluebirds on shoulders, and realistic seagulls on bosoms. He twisted cornucopias in spirals down the fronts of long dresses. Other curiosities included beach shorts made out of see-through crochet, cloth printed to mimic burlap or tortoiseshell, cloqué silk woven to resemble anthracite in both texture and shimmer, glass-like materials, and phosphorescent lamé. His prints and ornaments were unusual and frequently witty: a dress of silk printed with tiny open books featured a linen jabot pleated in "pages." His buttons included lipsticks, large fleurs-de-lis, royal medals, red smoking pipes, butterflies, and keyholes. Appliqués took the form of life-size pineapples on pockets and arabesques in patent leather or metallic kid sewn to silk or wool.

Rochas had a strong graphic sense too. He repeatedly used stripes to form geometric patterns on wool suits and coats—stripes formed with ribbons sewn to lace for evening dresses. For color contrasts he appliquéd wavy lines down the surplice front of a dark dress, and white scallops on the "revers" and sleeves of another dark suit. Every seam of an evening coat of sheer black silk, cut like a long blazer, was emphasized by white piping. A 1931 dress with a heart shape cut out at the neckline looks for all the world like an idea from the Sixties.

Rochas lived a life that, like his designs, was active, even hectic. He designed clothes for Sartre's play *Huis Clos* with Simone Simon, and for the movies, most notably Cocteau's 1943 *L'Eternal Retour*; in Jacques Becker's 1944 *Falbalas* he even made a screen appearance as a Bluebeard who hangs all the women he's loved in a shop window—in the dresses he'd made for them.

It was to his third wife, Hélène, one of the most beautiful women in the world, who today controls the Rochas perfume empire, that he dedicated his perfume Femme as a wedding present in 1944. It was packaged in Lalique crystal bottles and the black Chantilly lace of his *guêpière*. In 1950 he published *25 Years of Elegance*, practically a scrapbook of all the important events in fashion, the arts, and society for the previous two-and-a-half decades. It is, in fact, one of the first such chronicles to combine cultural, social, and fashionable influences, pinpointing their interrelationships. In 1953 he closed his house. Until his death the following year, he continued to follow fashion, choosing Hélène's clothing himself, but at Chanel and Givenchy.

A fternoon and sports clothes from the Thirties.

T H E   E X T R

A V A G A N T S

When the Daily Mail *of London polled its mid-World War II readers as to which wartime hardship they minded most, the answer surprised everyone: "women in uniform" topped the list. But while civilians might not have appreciated the uniforms, the women who wore them did, for they were able to wear beautifully simple uniforms by Hartnell or Mainbocher.*

As soon as the war was over couturiers wasted no time in returning to what they had been designing in the late Thirties: elaborate, pretty, extravagant clothes. These first collections were met with criticism: the rationing of clothing had not ended with the war, and it was deemed an insult to tempt women with what they could not afford, or not even afford to copy.

Christian Dior was able to convince the world that women were ready for, indeed needed, a change. He proved that what women wanted was distraction, not only through the actual clothes, but through the fun of following and thinking about the latest modes. With his nipped-in waists, floral hues, and swishing skirts, Dior brought back femininity. He also ushered in the era in which change would be the only constant.

Dior, however, was not entirely responsible for the way women would want to look in the Fifties. A new generation of couturiers came of age, including Pierre Balmain, Jacques Fath, Jacques Griffe, and Jean Dessès. Others such as Jacques Heim and Nina Ricci had been active in their own houses before World War II. All joined in purveying the luxury and quality that had disappeared in the Forties. In England, Norman Hartnell's commissions for Queen Elizabeth were increased, and no one's clothes were more lavish, extravagant, and unabashedly luxurious.

It was an exciting time. Perfumes, brocades and laces, braids and

PRECEDING PAGES:
Galanos chiffon dress,
1961.

ribbons, silk flowers and embroideries—all of the satellite businesses of the couture grew. Having trained in the Paris couture, Yves Saint Laurent, Hubert de Givenchy, Valentino (in Rome), and Galanos (in California) opened their own businesses.

Dior's death in 1957 came just as changes were beginning to be felt. The younger designers had new, younger clients who wanted what their peers were wearing, couture or not, and the couture found itself ill-equipped to downgrade into making clothes that would appeal to teenagers.

Some couturiers simply went out of business. Others took to supporting themselves with what had once been mere sideline ventures: cosmetics, leather goods, swimwear, and especially prêt-à-porter.

Yves Saint Laurent led the way, concentrating on his Rive Gauche line. Meanwhile in the United States a new breed of designers developed. These designers dispensed with the notion of clothes made to order, but they called their designs couture because of their quality. Galanos, Bill Blass, and Oscar de la Renta built careers on the making of clothing that, while sold off-the-peg, has a rarefied feel of luxury.

When one considers that the couture was, for the most part, actually closed down during World War II and stagnating in the Seventies, its recent comeback is dramatic. Realizing that the couture is its own entity, and that it cannot be meant to dress everyone, the couturiers and couture-calibre designers have resumed seeking to divert, to dazzle. In their use of all that is available to them, as well as their appreciation of femininity, the Extravagants can be credited with keeping all the artistry of fashion alive.

Dior

HAT SETS THE BRILLIANT COUTURIER APART FROM THE TALENTED one is prescience. Christian Dior was so cognizant of his own changing epoch that he adjusted his creativity to meet the demands of the society, ready to go into high gear, that emerged from World War II. More than anyone else, he comprehended that fashion had become a matter of months rather than years, pointing out that "the world has changed its pace and fashion has changed with it [and therefore] novelty is the very essence of the fashion trade."

Dior, like Worth, became a dictator of styles, perhaps the last great one. But whereas Worth and many other of Dior's predecessors had been able to claim the invention of a particular silhouette or the accomplishment of an evolution in style, Dior, in perhaps the briefest career of any, introduced a new silhouette twice a year. Opening his couture house at the perfect moment and showing a first collection that exquisitely captured the secret desires of women, he stopped the presses around the world. Then, when no one thought he could top the impact of his inaugural collection, he continued to surprise by being able to do so. Trading on novelty, he set out every six months to provide his audiences with the new "spirit" of fashion, accompanying his designs with a description of his intentions. As it turns out, his controversial first collection was less shocking than many subsequent ones.

Perhaps his single most famous design was one from that first 1947 collection: an *ensemble* with the simple name of Bar. This suit featured a natural silk pongee jacket closely fitted to a corsetted waist and padded below the waist at the hips like a peplum. The jacket was worn with a wide, pleated black skirt and, as *Vogue* put it, "your own shoulders." The skirt was long and everything else about this *ensemble* seemed radical. As is always pointed out, Dior did not invent this silhouette, which came to be called the New Look. Many couturiers had experimented with the miniscule waist and crinolined skirt for lavish evening dresses in the late 1930s and even occasionally during the war. Otherwise, the formula of severe, broad-shouldered day suits and subdued, covered-up *ensembles* for dinner and other less-than-grand events had held sway. Dior's versions, therefore, were not new. What *was* new was that he was showing them for day, thereby affecting any vaguely fashionable woman by automatically making her look démodé in skimpy, tight holdovers from the war. In some countries rationing was still in force, cried one group of protestors. Others could not believe that the new active woman would stand for being laced into her clothes again. However, in its way, the New Look was less constricting than the ill-fitting clothes it replaced, clothes that had been as hard to wear spiritually as physically.

A 1947 cotton tulle ball gown trimmed with pale satin and silk flowers.

FOLLOWING PAGES: Dior adjusting his design for Ava Gardner, The Little Hut, 1956. PAGE 235: "New Look" gown photographed on the House of Dior staircase.

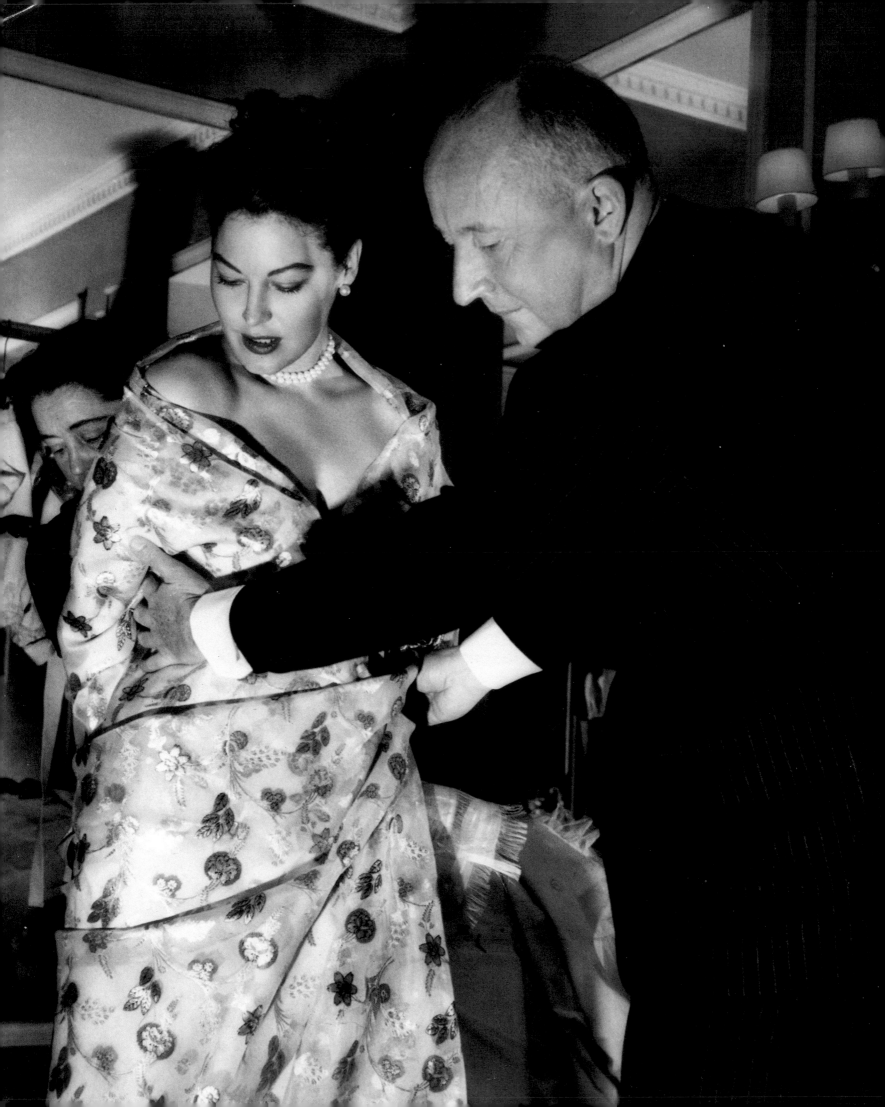

*F*eminine afternoon dress, 1949 (top); black silk crepe afternoon dress from the Cupola, an autumn/winter line of 1953.

Dior deliberately set out to evoke a happier time, drawing on his childhood memories of the scented, rustling goodnight kiss of his Edwardian-garbed mother. Instinctively realizing that what the war had banished was the ceremony of dressing, he reinstated the importance of the fashionable whole, from specially ruffled corsets to fill out a blouse, to the perfect hat, gloves, shoes, pin, and scarf.

It is appropriate that he is thought of not for a specific article of clothing but for an entire look that, once introduced, shaped the prettiness of the Fifties. He is remembered most for his afternoon dresses, sometimes called "five o'clocks," with feminine covered-up or revealing décolletés, ballerina-length skirts in muted velvets, printed taffeta or some black fabric; these were worn with cartwheel hats, opera gloves, high-heeled pumps, and silk flowers. Dior said that "fashion comes from a dream and the dream is an escape from reality." If the reality was that a woman worked hard or her life was dreary, her dream was that she didn't show it, and Dior helped fulfill that dream.

Born in 1905 in the coastal Normandy town of Granville, Dior had a happy, carefree childhood. His father was a manufacturer of chemical fertilizers, and his family was well-to-do and secure. In 1919 the Diors moved to Paris, where the young Christian studied a little and amused himself a great deal at the ballet, at the cinema, and at concerts. The Paris artistic life as then lived held great allure for the boy who, when the choice of a career couldn't be deferred any longer, proposed architecture, which his parents vetoed. Christian instead enrolled in the Ecole des Sciences Politiques, a school for diplomats-to-be.

In 1927 Dior returned from military service and dismayed his parents by opening a small art gallery with his friend Jacques Bonjean in a cul-de-sac off the rue de la Boëtie. Here they showed the works of such avant-garde painters as Christian Bérard, Salvador Dali, Jean Cocteau, and Max Jacob (numbering among their many friends). Things went well at first, for there was a great generalized public interest in art, and a great deal of cash ready to indulge that interest.

Three years later, however, Dior's world was falling apart. The 1929 stock market crash in America had strongly affected Europe, and his father, who had all his capital invested in real estate, was faced with bankruptcy and forced to sell off all his properties. The gallery soon failed as well, and its inventory was sold for less than its market value. Meanwhile, Dior's mother had died and his brother had become incurably ill. In 1934 Dior himself fell sick and left Paris for a year to recuperate.

When he returned to Paris, to share an apartment with his friend Jean Ozenne, a designer, Dior had his first formal contact with the

Dior's models displaying a complete wardrobe from his tenth anniversary collection, spring/summer 1957.

world of fashion. Following Ozenne's lead, he began to experiment with fashion sketches, selling those for hats to Mme. Agnès, one of the best known Paris milliners, and showing the others around to various designers. Several were purchased by couturier Robert Piguet who, known as editor rather than instigator of ideas, recognized talent when he saw it and, in 1938, offered Dior a job as his designer.

At Piguet, Dior's designs were both applauded and purchased. Now able to move into an apartment of his own, he quickly redecorated it in his own brand of Belle Epoque—just in time for his second major dislocation. Drafted into the French army, he spent most of World War II in a small town in central France. Afterward he joined his father and sister in the south of France, where they subsisted on what they could grow in their garden, until his return to Paris when his luck changed and he began work at the house of Lucien Lelong, a man who, like Piguet, was not much of a designer himself. At Lelong, Dior could relax. More or less free to design as he wished, he was also able to remain in the background where his shyness was no impediment. But the arrangement was a short-lived one—this time for pleasant reasons.

An old friend from Granville had put him in touch with the cotton entrepreneur Marcel Boussac, who was looking for a designer to revitalize his exhausted couture operation, an old Paris house called Gaston et Philippe. Dior resisted at first but was encouraged by the example set by his former fellow designer at Lelong—a young man named Pierre Balmain. He finally agreed, but only on condition that Boussac was willing to start a new house altogether.

Dior's favorite building, at 30, avenue Montaigne, was available. It was leased, painted in shades of pearl gray and white, and embellished in Dior's 1910 version of Louis XVI. A staff was assembled from childhood friends and colleagues from Lelong and other established houses. Boussac poured millions into it, and, while it is said that the voracious appetite for fabric in the New Look was derived in part from an intent to sell more Boussac textiles, it cannot be denied that Dior's backer was not only a cunning businessman but an indulgent patron.

Success was so immediate and orders so overwhelming that more space had to be found, more staff hired, and more cloth purchased. It was all the result of the excitement generated by a single collection in which Dior's intention was quite specific: to make clothes that would suggest an upturned flower, a feminine image that would pay homage to the beloved women's clothing of his youth. He executed these intentions with embroideries like those that had decorated his parents' house and the colors that had been popular in clothing and interior

RIGHT:
Entrance-making ball gown from 1948.

BELOW:
Dior spring/summer 1951 Oval line. This photograph bore the caption: "Oval of face, oval of bust, oval of hips."

dress or coat underneath was actually narrow. Also featured were attention-getting tricks like wide lapels and collars, which made the bust seem wider. For the 1949–50 winter Dior bloused the top of dresses to make them look two-piece. He lengthened the appearance of the body with his Vertical collection (spring 1950) by using long, narrow lapels, vertical tucks and pleating, and showing boxy suits with pleated skirts. By autumn of that year, his Oblique collection made use of slanted lines, with wide scarves run diagonally through the belts of suits, and the single-breasted front closure of the jackets starting at one shoulder and continuing to the opposite hip.

And so it went, through the Oval line of spring 1951, with curves predominating in collarless, cutaway jackets and used to connect faux-Empire and natural waistlines. The fall Long line, renamed the Princesse line, did away with the intensely bifurcated waist. In the Sinuous 1952 spring line, also called the Open Tulip, supple fabrics were crushed about the midriff and curved upward toward the bust in soft and blurry colors. Contrasting with this was that fall's Profile line with its emphasis on the hips accomplished by using stiff fabrics, manipulated by cut rather than by gathering or draping. Wide rounded necklines sliding off the shoulders provided the focal point for the spring 1953 Tulip line, while the shorter, narrow skirts of the fall 1953 Cupola line caused a writer for *The New Yorker* to complain that "the latest installment in the Dior thriller entitled 'Are Women Sheep?' was causing a lot of males to bellow." The spring 1954 Lily-of-the-Valley line—named after Dior's favorite flower—was light and springlike; what the press called relaxed.

At this point it is possible to sense a major change in Dior's thinking (and, indeed of the whole direction of fashion): the waistline was now freed and an era of loose-fitting shapes, which would peak with the 1958 Trapeze dress by the young Yves Saint Laurent, began its evolution into the Sixties' sheath. In autumn 1954, Dior introduced his H-line, with its elongated torso molded from hipbone to bust, which *Time* magazine called "The Second Look." The idea was not to make the bust flatter as was first thought, but to make it higher and therefore more youthful as well as less pointed. Then came the A-line of spring 1955, possibly Dior's most famous collection after the New Look, with its narrow shoulders crowning the triangular shape. That fall he inverted the A for his Y-line of broadened shoulders and higher waistlines. 1956 brought the Arrow line, which was described as having a Directoire feeling, then the *Aimant* fall line; both featured Empire waists and V-necklines that almost met. Spring 1957 saw the *Libre* collection, harbinger of the looser lines to come, with suits,

RIGHT:

E vening look from Dior prêt-à-porter, autumn/ winter 1983.

BELOW:

D ior evening dress with "zig-zag" skirt, 1948, shown with Dior's rose-laden cartwheel.

jackets, and skirts that were described as having "ease and walkability." For the *Fuseau*, or Spindle, line of fall 1957, chemises dominated, and some skirts even tapered in at the hem in an exact spindle shape.

The *Fuseau* collection was to be Dior's last. He died suddenly, of a stroke, that October, only a little older than fifty. The fashion world was stunned, and, in that December's *Harper's Bazaar*, Carmel Snow wrote: "To him, there was nothing frivolous about the haute couture. In a machine age, he saw it as one of the last refuges of the purely human—that is, the inimitable—and as an important manifestation of the great civilization to which he belonged. The continuing life and energy of the haute couture is vital to France. Christian Dior was vital to the couture. His death at the height of his powers will present it with one of its greatest challenges in its history."

In a way, she needn't have worried—for the House of Dior or for France. The Dior empire was enormous (the *New York Times* called it "the General Motors of the Paris haute couture"), the result of a particularly shrewd policy of multiple divisions such as furs, perfumes, hats, shoes, and jewelry. In addition, foreign branches and licensing arrangements such as the immensely successful Christian Dior–New York, begun in 1948, were all in place. The house employed over twelve hundred employees, spread among twenty-eight workrooms, plus a police force to prevent pirating.

Beyond that though, Christian Dior employed at his death two young designers who would ensure the future of France as capital of fashion as well as the future of the House of Dior. The first was Yves Saint Laurent, Dior's designated successor, whose spring 1958 Trapeze collection was hailed as brilliant, but who was called away after only a few collections to serve his compulsory stint in the army.

His replacement, whose first collection, the Slim line, received no less favorable notice than Saint Laurent's had, was Marc Bohan, who has been designing for the house ever since. Bohan has performed the difficult task of maintaining another couturier's image with great subtlety and ingenuity. The Bohan-for-Dior image is youthful, embodied by such clients as the princesses Caroline and Stephanie of Monaco. Somehow the Parisian magic in the name Dior is something everyone understands the world over, and under Bohan's aegis, the house on the avenue Montaigne has become the Paris monument that Worth on the rue de la Paix had been one hundred years ago.

Nina Ricci

THE HOUSE OF RICCI SUMMONS UP IMAGES OF PARISIAN GLAMOR AT ITS most intoxicatingly feminine. Curiously it has been the *couturière's* son, Robert, an expert perfumer as well as businessman, who has steadfastly pursued ambitious plans for the house and, by an astute choice of couturiers, has transformed it into an empire the size of which his mother might never have dreamed. The house he has built is a monument to his mother and reflects her intensely feminine personality almost more than her own work ever did.

Nina Ricci was born Marie Nielli in Turin in 1883. She moved with her family to France when she was twelve, and as a child was fascinated by fashion. At thirteen she was apprenticed to a dressmaker, at eighteen was head of the atelier, and at 22, its chief designer.

She and her husband, jeweler Louis Ricci, had one son, Robert. In 1932 she decided to stop selling her designs to other houses and opened her own to which she lured her son from his promising advertising career. Together they opened the House of Ricci in a single room at 20, boulevard des Capucines. Mme. Ricci created the clothes and Robert was in charge of running and promoting the business. The house grew rapidly through the Thirties and, by the war's outbreak, occupied eleven floors in three buildings on the same street as their original one-room *maison de couture*. Robert went off to fight, returning in 1945 to become the official director.

Nina Ricci saw dress design as a series of problems to be solved, problems to which she brought her "feminine intuition." Working directly with the fabric on a mannequin, she sought to discover in the

FAR RIGHT:
Nina Ricci wearing an evening coat of her own design, 1935.

RIGHT:
Nina Ricci at her work table in the Fifties.

RIGHT:

Contemporary evening dress exhibiting the typical Ricci romanticism.

BELOW:

Christian Bérard drawing for the Ricci perfume Coeur de joie, from the Fifties.

cloth the answer to what the dress would be. In describing a dress of 1935, she spoke of several aims: to achieve the maximum lightness so that the dress would be perfect for dancing; to give the dress a "*grand sobriété*" that, in her mind, would render it most appealing to the youthful; and to find just that elegant detail that would make the dress be a client's favorite.

She was skilled at making the most of a print, cutting a plaid for an evening dress on the bias, echoing the X-cross in the skirt pattern in the surplice, crossed-over treatment of the bodice. Confronted with a black silk material printed with a floral border, she cut one dress so that the flowers marched across the bust, with the rest of the dress a long, black column. Another dress, given the name *Jeux Dangereux* (Dangerous Games), featured a rather daring décolleté for 1937, its halter neck open between the breasts from neck to waist. Day and evening dresses alike drew attention to the figure, by being fitted to below the waist and featuring much shirring and drapery.

By the early Fifties, Mme. Ricci had ceased to take an active role in the business, and, although she continued to keep a watchful eye on it, Robert Ricci brought in a new head designer in 1954, the Belgian Jules-François Crahay, whose first collection, designed in reaction to the then prevalent chemise silhouette, made the front page of the *New York Times*. Carrie Donovan wrote: "What has brought the house out of semi-anonymity was a collection that was feminine in the extreme —beautiful of coloring and fabric, unbizarre and elegant." Under Crahay's direction, the house took a stand for the plain, get-through-the-day suit and the knockout, unabashedly luxurious evening gown. When Crahay left Ricci in 1963 to go to Lanvin, he was replaced by Gérard Pipart, who had previously worked at Balmain, Fath, and Patou. Today Pipart, a Frenchman, remains in charge of both the couture and the many boutique collections, making use of the most beautiful laces and appliquéd fabrics and turning out typically Ricci evening dresses along with silk day dresses, often based on the chemise, as well as more tailored clothes that are feminine versions of a *garçonne* look.

Nina Ricci died in 1970. Robert continued to run the house they founded together, including its many divisions and licensees (sunglasses alone were, in the late Seventies, grossing six million dollars a year), and perfumes, the best-seller being the classic L'Air du Temps, first introduced in 1951. In 1979 he realized a dream of two decades when he bought the former Kodak mansion at the corner of the avenue Montaigne and the rue François Premier, just across the street from another *maison de couture* that has taken up from where its founder left off and continued to soar—the House of Dior.

S atin evening dress by Gérard Pipart for the House of Ricci, summer 1980.

Balmain

TWO YEARS BEFORE CHRISTIAN DIOR ROCKED THE WORLD WITH THE New Look, Pierre Balmain opened his doors to the public, showing a delightful collection of easily pretty designs that were called "cool," "picturesque," and "gentle," at the same time they were dubbed "feline" and "dragonlady-like." Though sometimes criticized for not creating avant-garde sensations (Dariaux wrote in *Elégance* that Balmain's clothes were as "unexciting as they were flattering"), there was an immediate and grateful audience for the newly ornamental fashions. Alice B. Toklas, writing an introduction for his 1948 collection, remarked how ugly and utilitarian much of twentieth-century clothing had been until "one day last September Pierre Balmain showed his first collection and suddenly there was the awakening to the new understanding of what mode really was, the embellishment and the intensification of women's form and charm. A dress was no longer to serve as a more or less decorated usefulness but to once more become a thing of beauty, to express elegance, grace and delicacy in silk and wool, in lace, feathers and flowers."

Well read and an articulate lecturer, Balmain was fond of recognizing the relationship between architecture and the couture, not only in his own work (he had trained as an architect), but throughout history. In his talks he would point out that both the architect and the couturier worked to beautify the world, but that "one constructs in stone, the other in mousseline." As the comparison continued, the couturier gained the edge, for Balmain felt that an architect's work is finished when the plan is executed, but a couturier's drawing is just the beginning when one considers that a dress can change remarkably during its creation, and again when brought to life on the figure. Both choose the appropriate material for the job at hand; the architect must consider the site just as the couturier does the human body. Whereas architecture is concerned with the static, the couture, in Balmain's favorite phrase, is "the architecture of movement."

Pierre Balmain was born in 1904 in a small village not far from Aix-les-Bains, a fashionable resort in the Savoy mountains. His father ran the largest wholesale fabric business in the area. Françoise, his mother, had worked at a boutique managed by her two sisters before she married. When his father died Balmain was seven, and his relationship with his mother and aunts became quite insular. His happiest childhood memories were of their shop, to which his mother had returned, where he played with the fabrics and admired the dresses of the women who came to browse. Although his mother entertained the hope that he would one day be a naval surgeon, the boy's heart was already set on becoming a couturier.

Balmain fur-trimmed suit, 1952.

*For his 1951 spring cou-
ture collection, Balmain
chose some outrageous
accessories; models
appeared in cellophane
wigs, and this one
carried a dyed-to-match
purple poodle.*

BELOW:

*A 1958–59 wool suit in
a typically tender shade
of violet.*

Balmain became acquainted with the daughter of Mme. Premet
and with the *directrice* of the House of Bernard et Cie., both reputable Parisian houses. Entranced with their stories of the fashionable
world but afraid to tell his mother why he really wanted to go to Paris,
he informed her instead that he had decided to become an architect
and intended to study at the Ecole des Beaux Arts. His interest in
architecture was considerably diminished by the hazing he received
from the older students and the mundanity of his assignments. Increasingly his notebooks came to hold fashion sketches, not blueprints.

He eventually took a few formal fashion drawings to show Robert
Piguet, who bought three. Next he was offered a job as junior designer by Molyneux, who agreed to give him a month's trial, explain-
ing that after four weeks he would be able to tell him which to give up:
architecture or dress designing. Architecture went.

In 1936, when he was called up for military service, Balmain had
been employed by Molyneux for two years. Molyneux gave him five
hundred francs for a first-rate uniform and the promise that while he
was wearing it he would remain on the payroll. The young soldier was
subsequently transferred to Paris where he spent more time working
at Molyneux than he did in the barracks. After his discharge, the
realization that he was unlikely to be given more responsibility prompted
him to give notice. In 1939 he began work at Lucien Lelong. When
war broke out he returned to Aix-les-Bains where he helped his mother
with her newly opened dress shop. It was here that he first encoun-
tered and dressed Gertrude Stein and Alice B. Toklas.

In 1941, Lucien Lelong reopened his house and summoned Balmain
back to Paris with the enticement that he, along with another young
designer (Christian Dior), would have complete control over the
collections. For the next few years Balmain and Dior worked happily
side by side, exchanging ideas and editing each other's work to such
a degree that, by the time a dress entered the collection, it was hard
to tell which of them had designed it. They even began to talk of
opening a house together, but this was not to be. In 1945 Balmain
opened his own house at 44, rue François Premier.

On October 14, he showed a small first collection made up of trouser *ensembles* with homespun jackets, kimonos zippered at the shoulder,
evening tailleurs, narrow, taffeta-swathed evening dresses, and foamy,
full-skirted ball gowns trimmed simply with artificial cherries and
leaves or with elaborate silver embroidery and *strass.* Stein and Toklas
brought their poodle, Basket, and a friend, Cecil Beaton, and it was
this collection about which Stein would write—for *Vogue*—her only
fashion article.

Pierre Balmain was a sketcher, not a draper of fabric or a tailor. Beginning with simple drawings, he elaborated on them over the course of building a collection, allowing ideas to jell and motifs to assert themselves. Besides his simple day clothes and his elaborately embroidered evening dresses, Balmain made much use of fur, especially as an accent: mink to bind an ethereal tulle evening dress, leopard for the hem and muff of a long, skinny black satin dress, an ermine ascot, or a necklace of astrakhan sewn with pearls. The embroideries often were combinations of gold or bronze on white, the palest gray or the iciest blue, usually in scroll-like patterns. Day clothes, such as chintz shirtwaists, or the suits *Vogue* described as having "eventful skirts, a Balmain specialty," were often in soft colors, with mauve, daffodil, and pale almond predominating. His Sixties evening dresses were often made out of organdy, appliquéd with guipure lace or pale silk flowers. In every collection there was sure to be, in homage to the Duchess of Windsor, an *ensemble* in blue and black, once considered a radical color combination. More recently, the haute couture collections included simple wool suits enveloped in huge, matching stoles and long narrow evening dresses spiraled all around in ruffles.

An extrovert, Balmain loved parties and was seen everywhere. His passion for architecture showed itself in his collection of houses. Besides his Paris apartment, there were residences in Normandy and Morocco. Perhaps his most extravagant dwelling was the house on the island of Elba that he had shipped over piece by piece from Thailand and then reconstructed. He enjoyed designing for the theatre and the cinema and was involved in costuming over one hundred productions, dressing Brigitte Bardot, Marlene Dietrich, and Katharine Hepburn. Many of his clients were ambassadors' wives and royalty including Queen Sirikit of Thailand.

Balmain was also a good and ambitious businessman. In 1947 he opened his first boutique in Paris: Jolie Madame, named after his most famous silhouette. Others followed in Venezuela, Brazil, and New York, the latter becoming home of a ready-to-wear line while his sportswear line, called Elbalmain, was produced in Elba. He introduced a perfume in 1947, Elysées 64–83 (his telephone number). Then came his better known scents: Vent-Vert, Jolie Madame, and Ivoire.

Since Balmain's death in 1982, his house, with its many divisions and licensees, continues to operate under the direction of Erik Mortensen, a Dane and formerly Balmain's right-hand man, who has said that for him—as it was for the man whose empire he now shapes—the "supreme test of elegance is the greatest simplicity."

Every year someone declares "hats are back." This is from the autumn/winter prêt-à-porter collection, 1983.

Jacques Heim

THE HOUSE OF HEIM, THE OLDEST PARIS HOUSE THAT IS STILL RUN by family members in direct descendency, is noted for its somewhat incongruous combination of excellent designs for fur, beachwear, and for young ladies' debut and wedding dresses, and is still very much a part of the Paris fashion establishment. Begun in 1898 by Isidore and Jeanne Heim, the house supplied the aristocracy of Europe with the most luxurious of sable and ermine evening wraps, only experimenting with the more humble furs at the instigation of Mme. Heim.

Jacques Heim was born to the couple in 1899, and by the time he joined his parents in the business, in 1925, the ostentation of the Belle Epoque had been chased off by the rigors of World War I. The house began to reassess both its purpose and its market, leading young Jacques to initiate a couture department for coats, suits, and evening dresses, in which fur played a prominent, but not exclusive, part. Although this claim is made for many designers, Jacques Heim truly worked with fur as if it were a fabric.

His first collection featured a tailleur consisting entirely of triangular patches of caracul (Persian lamb) and matte black wool. This geometric piecing, as well as his use of contrasting textures, demonstrates his interest in contemporary art, especially Cubism. Other designs included day dresses and coats made in interesting conglomerations of black and white fabrics. Heim interpreted the by then standard evening wrap in silver and white lamé with silver fox collar. For afternoon he created a white wool coat pieced together in T-squares with a collar of black fox fur.

RIGHT:
Jacques Heim creating an evening dress on a mannequin.

BELOW:
Portrait of Jeanne Heim wearing one of her house's specialties: a velvet evening coat trimmed with white fox.

BELOW RIGHT:
The House of Jacques Heim in the Fifties.

The couture venture proved so successful that, in 1934, the house moved to 50, avenue des Champs-Elysées and, a few years later, to even larger quarters at 15, avenue Matignon, spawning branches in Biarritz and Cannes at the same time. Though Heim was forced to leave France during the Nazi Occupation, he returned to expand the house even further after the war. He became the official dressmaker to Mme. Charles de Gaulle and, from 1958 to 1962, was president of the Chambre Syndicale de la Couture Parisienne. At his death in 1967, he left the business to his son, Philippe Jacques, who presides over it today.

Heim was an innovator by nature, and when he introduced the first sarong-style bathing suit, inspired by the Tahitian exhibits in the Paris Colonial Exhibition of 1931, the fact that it was not knit but made of cotton and was draped created what *Harper's Bazaar* called "an international style furore." The Pareo, as it was called, gave way to all sorts of beachdress: coats, skirts, and bloomers in vivid Aztec colors. In 1950, his Atome two-piece suit, called the "most petite bathing suit ever," spawned versions that led to the bikini. In the Fifties his beachwear included such items as halter-necked piqué aprons worn over knee-length madras shorts, one- and two-piece bathing suits with all manner of lunch and cocktail-time cover-ups.

In 1937 he launched the *Jacques Heim Jeunes Filles* line, designed specifically for teenaged girls and often including long dinner dresses with tucked, lace-trimmed blouse-like bodices, day dresses made like jumpers with shirts underneath, and dancing dresses with puffed sleeves, sweetheart necklines, and accents resembling panniers or aprons outlined with ruffles. For these designs his colors were softer than his usual warm browns, sunset orange, fuchsia, or apricot. The *Jeunes Filles* wedding dresses were always greeted with applause.

In 1947 he sponsored a perfume called Alambic, and in 1950 *Heim Actualité*, a ready-to-wear line with an even larger boutique market as its audience, made its debut. Also in the Fifties, the *Revue Heim*, a fashion newspaper that began as the house organ, and the Jacques Heim Design Contest, from which the winning design was made up and manufactured under the *Jacques Heim Jeunes Filles* label, were initiated. Today, Philippe Heim is busy with plans to revive the couture operations of the house.

The fringed shawl of this 1947 white satin evening dress, "Château de Madrid," covers a bodice cut with one shoulder strap.

LEFT:

A *bevy of mannequins wearing 1952 evening dresses.*

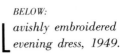

BELOW:

L *avishly embroidered evening dress, 1949.*

LEFT:

S *ixties coat in the colors of the French flag.*

D *inner dress, ca. 1949, complete with an evening hat.*

Jacques Fath

OR THOSE WOMEN OF STYLE WHO FOUND "DIOR TOO BOURGEOIS, Balmain too discreet, or Balenciaga too formidable," as Prudence Glyn said, Jacques Fath "presented an alternative." Like Dior, he named his collections for a distinguishing characteristic, but in his case this might be, as it was in 1949, something as indefinable as its flash. He designed discreet clothes but when a Fath dress was discreet, it was discreet to the hilt. If Balenciaga's clothes had their monumental, architectural bearing, Fath's were imbued with movement. For a decade and a half Fath designed flirtatious evening dresses, jaunty day clothes, and accessories that were at once witty and sexy.

All of these were worn to the greatest effect by his wife, Geneviève de la Bruyère, an actress and former secretary to Chanel. The Faths became known for their entertaining, and parties at their château were sumptuous but rarely formal, such as the famous square-dancing fête staged after Fath's trip to Texas. At these events, Fath could upstage even his wife with his sparkling eyes, flashing white teeth, and blond good looks offset by tartan dinner jackets or gold-buttoned red blazers.

Jacques Fath was born outside Paris in 1912 to an insurance agent of Flemish and Alsatian extraction and his partly British wife. Jacques's grandfather, René Fath, whose mother had been a *couturière* to the Empress Eugénie, was a well-known landscape painter. Despite such ancestors, Fath's parents sought to curb their young son's obvious artistic leanings, and packed him off to business school where he studied bookkeeping. This training led to a job in a stockbroker's office, then to military service. Only after his discharge did Fath begin to indulge his artistic bent, first by attending drama school, then by designing for the theatre.

A life in fashion seemed inevitable. In 1937 Fath opened his atelier in two rooms at 32, rue de la Boëtie, where the quarters were so tiny that customers and mannequins alike spilled out onto a courtyard. His first collection consisted of a mere twenty models. But in just two years he was acknowledged as one of the most promising of the young designers. After fighting in World War II he returned to Paris and reopened in more spacious quarters in the rue Francois Premier. In 1944 he made his final move to a luxurious *hôtel particulier* at 39, avenue Pierre Premier de Serbie.

Thanks to his financial training and to his adventurous nature, Fath was not just a good businessman, he was a creative one. He understood that Paris had a market of enormous and largely untapped potential in America. In 1948 he contracted with the Seventh Avenue ready-to-wear manufacturer Joseph Halpert, to design two annual collections of dresses and suits. Besides the obvious advan-

6232
Fath

68

tages of profits and name recognition, this arrangement helped Fath understand the capacities and the limitations of the ready-to-wear in a way that had eluded the French, whose attention seemed single-mindedly limited to a tradition of one-of-a-kind hand workmanship. When he entered into an arrangement with the textile magnate Jean Provoust to produce a ready-to-wear line called *Fath Université*, he imported American cutters and workers, as well as American sewing machines. Fath's recognition and utilization of the American system, unhampered as it was by the example of the haute couture, paved the way for the establishment of a French deluxe prêt-à-porter industry that would run parallel to, rather than somewhere below, the couture. The same acumen led him into the less novel, but nonetheless lucrative, avenues of the perfume business and a boutique accessories line.

The New Yorker said of Fath that he was "sometimes very, very good and sometimes very, very out-of-line." Although written earlier, this comment aptly describes his Playboy-Bunny look of 1950: evening dresses showing nothing but skin and cleavage between a strapless décolletage and a wing-collared choker. Teetering on the brink of the risqué, his best work had a flair and a raciness that appealed to a younger, highly sophisticated clientele. His fin-tailed, skintight dresses, diamond snake armlets, and black lace-topped stockings summon up visions of the Fifties at their most glamorous, perhaps best embodied by his client Rita Hayworth, for whose marriage to the Aly Khan he made both wedding dress and trousseau.

Because he worked directly with the fabric, draping it on a mannequin (or himself) with a team of workers watching to transform his efforts into sketches, Fath's clothes are masterpieces in the display of movement. Diagonal lines, sometimes accented by a profusion of buttons, cut across his suits and dresses. Angled collars and pockets, slanting or zig-zagging skirts and tunics, plunging V-necklines, bustles or fans or swags jutting out from skintight dresses; these as well as a plethora of tucks, tiers, and knife-sharp pleats all contribute to the kinetic quality of his clothes. Even decorative devices had a projectile feel: sheaves of wheat, darts, ferns, dashes, and quills. Although known as a superb and inventive colorist, his shades of silvered amethyst, gray-pink, pale green, ruby, grapefruit, and marron glacé contrast somewhat with the swagger of his cut.

Jacques Fath died at the height of activity in 1954. Geneviève took charge of the Fath-trained staff of design assistants and *Vogue* wrote of her first collection that "the tradition of feminine, flattering clothes goes on." But his widow found herself lost without her husband's direction and closed the house in 1957.

PRECEDING PAGES:
Jacques Fath suit from 1951, cut with his usual swagger. PAGE 265: 1949 evening dress in precious- and semiprecious-jewel tones.

RIGHT:
Fath trying out a dress idea on his wife, Geneviève, 1946.

BELOW:
Fath evening dresses and mantles photographed at Versailles, 1951.

This tunic suit of beige rep jacket and narrow black skirt was one of the hits of 1951.

RIGHT:
Bettina Ballard, Vogue's fashion editor, filling in as stylist for a shoot of Fath pale taffeta shantung afternoon dresses, spring 1951.

Jacques Griffe

N FRENCH, THE WORD *GRIFFE* LITERALLY MEANS "CLAW MARK," BUT it has come to infer one's "thumbprint," a special mark or signature —and it is also the word used for label. In placing a stylized thumbprint on his label, Jacques Griffe was not only acknowledging his debt to Madeleine Vionnet, whose label bore a very realistic rendering of her thumbprint, but was also cleverly incorporating the meaning of his own name.

Jacques Griffe was born in 1910 in the town of Carcassonne in southwestern France. From the beginning, his mother was a formative influence. Convinced that she might have been a great *couturière* had she not been relegated to life in a small provincial town, she transferred her passion and ambition to her small son, encouraging him to work with her until he was sixteen, when she found a position with a local tailor for him. Though he complained of the long hours and the repetitive, mundane task of assembling jackets and waistcoats, she coaxed him into persevering, which he did. He was soon apprenticed to a couturier named Mirra in nearby (and by comparison, cosmopolitan) Toulouse. Luckily, Mirra followed the Paris collections and frequently bought toiles to make up, and sometimes actual dresses to copy, in his own workrooms. Griffe, though still young, began to like his work better.

After military service, he realized his (and his mother's) dream of moving to Paris, where he found work at the house of Vionnet. He remained there from 1936 to 1939 and during those three years perfected his ability to work directly with fabric on a form or mannequin, without drawing or sketching. Of course, working in the house of this pioneer of the bias cut, he learned its mysteries and acquired what Celia Bertin would describe as a preference for the dress that has "plenty of work in it." Although at the time he had no direct access to the great *couturière*, she later took an active interest in his house, sitting in the front row at practically every collection, occasionally fingering a hem as it went by.

Griffe fought, and was taken prisoner, in World War II. He returned to Paris in 1941 to open his own *maison de couture* in the rue Gaillon. Five years later, having received financial backing from the manufacturer of the *Scandale* corset, he moved to 29, rue du Faubourg Saint-Honoré. In 1950, with Molyneux retired, he moved, yet again, to the hallowed rooms of that designer's eighteenth-century mansion at 5, rue Royale. Although he did design a boutique line whose simplicity justified its fine workmanship, he was affected by the waning of the couture in the mid-Sixties and retired at the height of the ready-to-wear revolution.

③

Griffe, like Vionnet, was a master at draping and cut, and at under-standing the relationship between fabric and the human form. Unlike Vionnet, he had an inventive way with color, and was equally adept working with a supple fabric like chiffon or with a silk broadcloth, lamé, moiré, faille, satin, or tulle. His evening dresses most often had simple halter, camisole, or "shepherdess" décolletés that acted as foils for skirts made with elaborate decoration or with his virtuosity of cut: pieced bias-cut floor-length spirals, all-over chevron shirring, or giant bows swathed at the hip.

In the early Fifties, he was among the first to make boxy, unfitted suits, superbly cut with an almost imperceptible curve indicating the waist. His narrow day and evening dresses draped at the bodice or at a hip into a knot; a scarf could magically flow down a dress or suit by Griffe, then disappear into a seam. While his peers were imposing their whalebone wills onto women's figures, his gently bloused or draped dresses presaged an attitude, forgotten since the Twenties and Thirties, that would not come back into its own until after his retirement.

LEFT:

Jacques Griffe dinner dress of silk printed with carnations, from the early Fifties.

ABOVE RIGHT:

Bow-swathed ball gown from 1954.

Jean Dessès

NOT EVERY COUTURIER'S NAME BECOMES INEXTRICABLY LINKED WITH a single, immediately identifiable article of clothing. Of course there are the Fortuny tea gowns and the Chanel suits, and there is also the intricate chiffon evening dress of Jean Dessès. Of Greek descent, Dessès managed to evoke in his clients, and the press, a sense of the classical sculpture of his ancestors by draping and entwining the supplest of fabrics over an unrelenting wire frame.

Jean Dessès was born Jean Dimitre Verginie in 1904 in Alexandria, Egypt, where he spent his childhood. He came to Paris to study law and diplomacy but, like so many other couturiers, he was more apt to fill his notebooks with sketches of dresses than notes on torts or foreign affairs. He came to realize that he could sell these sketches and, by 1925, was a designer for the Maison Jane on the rue de la Paix. He remained there until 1937 when he opened his own house at 37, avenue George V. A decade later he moved to the Hôtel Eiffel at the corner of the rue Rabelais and the avenue Matignon, the former residence of the builder of Paris's famous tower.

Although his collections were hailed by the press as being "full of ideas," time and again the showstoppers were his dresses of chiffon or mousseline de soie. For these he used *ombré* fabrics, a favorite effect since even his fur coats were shaded light to dark. His goal of dethroning black was pursued by his use of soft, hazy colors in dresses that involved much plaiting and twisting, as one or more fabrics were joined with ribbons or bands of mink. Often scarves trailed from neck to floor, and rippled like his uneven hems.

His manner with less supple fabrics was similar: tulle, faille, satin, or brocade would be twisted, then gathered up into bunches, panniers, folds, or paper pleating. A long, narrow evening dress might have a corsage composed of two different-colored fabrics, each twisted, then formed into two long stole trains. One faille wedding dress boasted side puffs at the hips which were gathered into bunches of white silk lilacs. The Dessès palette included Wedgwood blue, old rose, taupe, the deepest tones of eggplant, green, and brown, and a range of pale grays, faint pinks, and whites. His clientele included the royal family of Greece, the Duchess of Windsor, and, surprisingly, the irrepressible Elsa Maxwell.

Dessès moved in 1958 to 12, Rond-Point des Champs Elysées, where he remained until 1963, when he closed his business and retired to Greece to run the boutique he had opened there in 1955. He died in 1970.

Norman Hartnell

A S OFFICIAL DRESSMAKER TO QUEEN ELIZABETH II, THE QUEEN MOTHER, and, occasionally, Queen Mary, Sir Norman Hartnell clothed three generations of top British aristocracy. With an informal theatrical training to guide him, he brought into play his faultless tact and his ingenuity to costume spectacles at Westminster Abbey as well as royal tours to the corners of the world. Always ensuring that his clients would stand out from the crowd, he allowed them to shine in clothes that reflected their ancient status without being anachronistic.

Norman Hartnell was born in 1901. A childhood interest in sketching the actresses of the day in all their finery was revived at Cambridge when he joined the Marlowe Dramatic Society and the Footlights Dramatic Club, amateur organizations for which he designed posters, scenery, programs, and costumes. His plan to one day study architecture dissolved when he read Minnie Hogg's review of one of his productions. *The* London gossip columnist of the day had happened to catch a Footlights Dramatic Club matinee and queried in her write-up: "Is the dress genius of the future now at Cambridge?"

When young Hartnell approached her for advice, she was instrumental in securing him a job with a London dressmaker called Madame Désirée. Although this post lasted barely three months, it helped him make the important decision to quit university and become a couturier. His next two positions—at Lucile's and at a house called Esther's—proved equally short-lived and convinced him that he would be better off on his own. With his sister to help and his father providing the finances, he moved into upper-floor premises at 10 Bruton Street in 1923. Business proceeded shakily until 1934 when he moved for the final time, across the street to 26 Bruton. Painted in Hartnell green (a mixture of Veridian and Hooker greens, mid-gray, and white), and decorated with deep green banquettes, crystal chandeliers, and mirrors, Norman Hartnell, Ltd. remains today.

His early collections, which he sometimes showed in Paris, comprised the usual combination of tailored day *ensembles* and extravagant evening clothes for debutante parties. Like Lanvin, he leaned toward the design of the *robe de style*, and it was his creations of ceremonial clothing that propelled him into preeminence. His first wedding dress, fashioned from silver and gold net, was the showstopper for one of his collections. It was worn by the bride of Lord Weymouth, and described as "the eighth wonder of the world." The 1927 wedding dress he made for Barbara Cartland—long-waisted with a tiered, ruffled skirt—was only slightly less noteworthy.

What Hartnell described as the turning point in his career came in 1935 when he designed the bride's and bridesmaids' dresses for

A *portrait of Norman Hartnell.*

the wedding of Lady Alice Montagu-Douglas-Scott to the Duke of Gloucester, third son of George V and Queen Mary. Two of the brides-maids would grow up to be Queen Elizabeth II and Princess Margaret, and while their custom was still to come, his reputation as a royal dressmaker had already made its first step toward being established.

When Edward VIII abdicated, Elizabeth, Duchess of York (today the Queen Mother), became Queen Consort to George VI. Her coronation dress was designed by Handley-Seymour, but Hartnell was summoned to Buckingham Palace to discuss designs for the coronation dresses of the maids of honour. It was on this occasion that the King led him through the hall of Winterhalter portraits, giving him the inspiration for the crinoline dresses, similar to his *robes de style*, that would become the royal look for two Queens. His first commission for the Queen Consort was a wide-skirted, jewelled dress for her to wear at a state dinner honoring the Belgian monarch. This led to Hartnell's being chosen to design her wardrobe for the highly visible state visit to France.

Among Hartnell's other famous designs are the wedding and coronation dresses of Elizabeth II. The wedding dress was of Scottish satin embroidered with seed pearls and crystal used for Botticelli-inspired patterns of White York roses, ears of corn, and wheat. For Queen Elizabeth's coronation gown, Hartnell wrote an explanatory press release: the white satin dress, with its heartshaped neckline, short sleeves, and fitted bodice, was embroidered in pearls and crystal with the emblems of Great Britain including the Tudor rose of England, the leek of Wales, the thistle of Scotland, the shamrock of Ireland, as well as such Commonwealth insignia as the Canadian maple leaf, Australian wattle flower, New Zealand fern, South African protea, Indian and Ceylonese lotuses, and Pakistani cotton and jute.

In order to achieve the desired effects for his clothes, which were often outside fashion and more akin to costume, he drew inspiration from paintings, citing some of his sources in his autobiography: "The Italian Masters are for purest line, and all the French fun of Boucher, Watteau, and Madame Vigée-Lebrun; Fragonard for the *folies de grandeur*; and later Garvani, with Renoir and Tissot for a touch of chi-chi." Inspiration, however, could be found anywhere; "even common objects such as a slithering sardine or the steel-bright lines of the railway station can stimulate ideas if a silver reception gown is wanted."

Although he also designed for the theatre—for Noel Coward productions, Mistinguett, and Dietrich—and for movies, not all his attention was devoted to such monumental efforts. During the war he was responsible for the uniforms of the British Red Cross, the Women's

A *1937 sequin-embroidered evening dress.*

Royal Army Corps, and the women's division of the British Police Force. For the Queen's war wardrobe Hartnell obligingly adhered to regulations about buttons, number of seams, width of collars, and fabric yardage. He substituted his own hand-painted fabrics, since embroideries were banned, and chose muted, but not mournful, colors.

Although it is argued that Hartnell was ultimately shackled by his work for royalty, his personality was the kind that was happiest working within restrictions imposed by protocol and one that also required such a highly visible arena for his extensive creativity to keep from being stifled. He was at his best when creating to promote and protect the image of the royal family and, as a result, can take much credit for actually designing an image that is no less venerable today than it was when he first began.

Knighted in January 1977 (the first couturier to be so honored), Sir Norman Hartnell died in June 1979.

Valentino

A MONG THE ITALIAN DESIGNERS WHOSE NAMES CAN BE MENTIONED IN the same breath as Saint Laurent, Givenchy, and Lagerfeld, only Valentino has found a way of imbuing the *alta moda* with the glamor and authority of the haute couture. Pierre Bergé, Saint Laurent's right-hand man, has paid him quite a compliment, though a backhanded one, by avowing: "I don't know any other Italian designers." Implied is the attitude that it is only the couture that counts and that Valentino is the only Italian who succeeds in making meaningful couture, and ultimately it is his connection with France that makes this possible. His couture, although shown in Rome, combines French embroideries with Italian fabrics and workmanship. His ready-to-wear is manufactured in France, shown in Paris with the other prêt-à-porter collections, and even the clothes themselves testify to Valentino's distance from the Milan-based ready-to-wear movement.

Valentino Garavani was born in 1932, the son of an electrical-appliance store owner, and grew up drawing fashions and wanting to study art and design. Taking lessons in French enabled him to move to Paris when he was seventeen. After stints at the Ecole des Beaux Arts and the school of the Chambre Syndicale de la Couture Parisienne, he found apprentice jobs, first with Jean Dessès where he used to help Jacqueline de Ribes sketch her dress ideas, then with Guy Laroche. He returned to Rome in 1959 and a year later, financed by his father, opened his own small atelier on the via Condotti, moving in 1967 to the via Gregoriana at the top of the Spanish Steps. He began to be recognized in 1962, when he presented his first collection at Florence's Pitti Palace in a fashion showcase attended by foreign buyers and journalists. It became clear that he was something more than just another competent couturier in 1967, when he presented his famous no-color collection, with models and escorts dressed in various shades of white—cream, chalk, sand, ecru, and beige —and sporting what one journalist called "an aristocratic pallor, as if from in-breeding." At a time when psychedelic colors were in the ascendant, Valentino's collection astounded with its subtlety and power, provoking a binge of all-white clothing throughout fashion. In 1969 he opened his first ready-to-wear boutique in Milan and his empire has been growing steadily every since. He is now responsible for two couture and three ready-to-wear collections a year.

In the Sixties he designed suits and coats, indulging his predilection for precise tailoring through welt seams and bold lines. Evening clothes were of fairly standard shapes, including strapless columnar dresses and wide-legged palazzo pajamas, sometimes in large-scale flashy prints, enlivened by masses of feathers, jewels, or petalled

Valentino fashions in triplicate.

organza. The late Sixties saw the emergence of Valentino's gypsy, or Zarina, look with full skirts, lavish embroideries, mixed prints, and knotted fringes.

By the Seventies, Valentino had developed a turnout look to replace the suit, usually consisting of a printed knife-pleated skirt, worn with a skinny cardigan, or a floor-length coat over a pantsuit. Coats and jackets have continued to play important roles in his collections, as have prints, which he sometimes designs himself, basing them on the patterns in the paintings of Klimt or Bakst, or on chevron variations inspired by his initial "V," which he has been using as hardware detailing and in seams and pockets since the mid-Sixties.

So knowledgable, and so confident, is he about the couture that he plays with the elements of fashion, switching the roles of garments, making expressive use of contrasts and exaggeration. He can soften the edges of a razor-sharp blazer by coupling it with a ballooning skirt or a sweatshirt hood. He elevates the sweater's status by showing a plaid knitted one with a skirt of contrastingly textured lamé-figured chiffon. A tee-shirt becomes an evening dress when made up in the finest silk and studded with diamonds at the sleeves. Flowers intrigue Valentino and he has used them in prints, in silk and appliquéd to a dress, as color inspirations for his billowing ombré silk, and for petal shapes of bodices or skirts. André Leon Talley has described his fondness for bows, citing "brontosaurus—science fiction bows at the waist or perched on one shoulder."

His clientele includes Jacqueline Kennedy, who wore one of his dresses when she married Aristotle Onassis; Elizabeth Taylor, Gloria Guiness, Babe Paley, and Farah Diba, who wore a coat of his when she made her last official appearance before entering into exile. Aware that he has been fortunate in drawing such a clientele to Rome, and fully admitting that his background is in the French couture, Valentino has recently laid plans for establishing a fashion school, library, museum, and foundation—all in Italy—to ensure that future talents will not have to leave their country to pursue their dreams.

Valentino basking in the applause of his mannequins, 1972.

*V*alentino déshabillé,
1978.

Givenchy

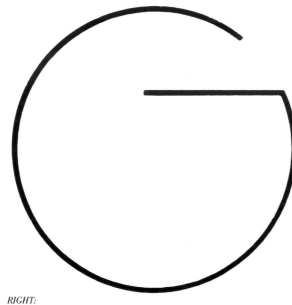

RIGHT:
Givenchy travelling costume, 1955.

BELOW:
Givenchy Watteau-backed evening dress from 1964.

IVENCHY HAS SOMETIMES BEEN MISTAKENLY ACCUSED OF NOT BEING innovative. The originality is there, but always under complete control; never could one of his dresses or *ensembles* be termed loud, overbearing, or offensive. For over thirty years Givenchy, the perfect gentleman of the couture, has dressed a clientele ranging in age from debutante to dowager in a style that has been young and mock-elegant, pure and sculptural, refreshingly ladylike as well as addictive. His clients are women for whom elegance is not an end in itself, but merely the way they do everything. For them, Givenchy is a last bastion of quality.

Hubert James Taffin de Givenchy was born in 1927 in Beauvais, France. His father was a pilot who died when the boy was two years old. He was raised by his mother and her parents, and was greatly influenced by his grandfather, who had once studied painting with Corot and had been director of the Gobelin tapestry works. Hubert was much taken with the environment of fine objects and rare textiles his grandparents had created. This interest was broadened when he was taken to see the Pavillon d'Elégance at the 1937 Paris Exposition, where he decided that his future lay in the couture. He attended college in Beauvais before moving to Paris, where he found a job with Jacques Fath in 1944. In the mornings he worked in Fath's *maison de couture* and attended the Ecole des Beaux Arts in the afternoons.

Givenchy eventually left Fath to begin working with Robert Piguet. Next came a stint at Lucien Lelong (the house from which both Balmain and Dior had launched their careers), followed by one at Schiaparelli where his bright, youthful separates designed for her boutique were much appreciated by her sophisticated clientele. Such encouragement led him to consider opening his own house, which he did in February 1952, presenting his first collection in a nineteenth-century *hôtel particulier* (formerly owned by the chocolatier Menier), at 8, rue Alfred de Vigny, near the Parc Monceau.

Business went well for Givenchy from the beginning, although economy necessitated showing every style in his first collection made up in inexpensive white cotton shirting. This seeming humility endeared him to the press and his new customers alike. His publicity was handled by Bettina Graziani, who had gotten her start at Fath and had gone on to become Paris's top model. It was for her that his first great success was named: the Bettina blouse of white cotton, with bishop sleeves ruffled in black and white broderie anglaise. Widely copied, it earned him worldwide recognition. It also furnished the paradigm for the young, bouncy clothes of his early career. It was teamed with a narrow nutmeg-colored skirt, or a wide black cotton dirndl, and flat shoes, sometimes made of woven straw.

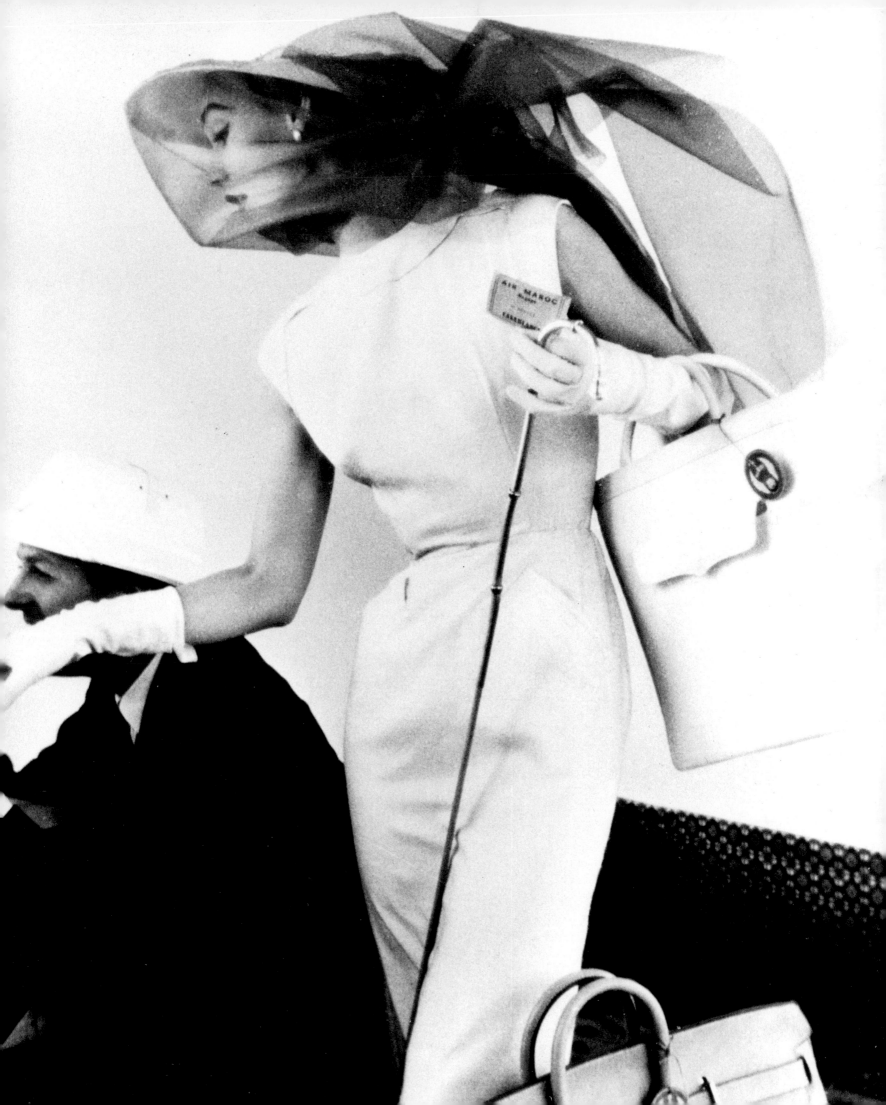

LEFT:
Tiger python on an evening suit and toque.

BELOW:
Givenchy evening dress from 1983 (top); his taste in prints tends toward the bright and cheerful.

For several years, Givenchy presented his semiannual collections of deluxe separates and simple sheath or full-skirted dresses in imaginative embroidered fabrics. Early on he showed that he was equally capable of designing for grand evenings, dressing up one white organdy ball gown with scattered amethysts and a stole of violet satin.

Around 1953 a chance meeting with Cristóbal Balenciaga, long one of Givenchy's idols, had a formative effect on the novice couturier. Their friendship burgeoned, and Balenciaga allowed Givenchy to preview his collections, Balenciaga acting as a teacher. Such a relationship, unusual in the history of couture, helped Givenchy mature as a couturier. Speaking of these informative sessions, he has said that Balenciaga "taught me it isn't necessary to put a button where it doesn't belong, or to add a flower to make a dress beautiful. It is beautiful of itself."

In 1955 Givenchy moved his *maison de couture* to 3, avenue Georges V, across the street from his mentor, and increasingly the two began to be mentioned in tandem. In 1957 both banned the press from their shows until the buyers had had a chance to place their orders without being influenced by any reviews of the collection. Their clothes therefore came to be shown together in the fashion magazines a month later than those of the other Paris collections. Side by side, the resemblance between them was even more obvious. Givenchy's clothes grew more *sobre* as he became more involved with shape and color, and he temporarily abandoned his predilection for separates and interesting patterns. He joined Balenciaga in pioneering the chemise, or sack dress, in 1955 showing a fairly straight dress with a bloused back, and in 1957 sheaths that would, as *Harper's Bazaar* announced, "barely touch, but not erase, the figure."

His clothes for day and evening became simpler, with *bateau* necklines and form-following gored panels. Their simplicity was highlighted by his characteristically cheerful palette: buttercup yellow, chili pepper red, bright pink, and brilliant purple. He made use of Balenciaga's favorite fabric, gazar, as well as his own favorites including heavy glazed linen for evening, silk broadcloth, gabardine, and cloqué-textured silks.

Two designs by Givenchy show how he was influenced, but not dominated, by Balenciaga. One was a powder blue linen suit from 1965 that was barren of detail—and it is here that one sees Balenciaga's influence—but paired with a one-shouldered top, of chocolate organza covered entirely with minute self-fabric blossoms, that is purely Givenchy. The Balenciaga influence is again apparent in the way a 1968 evening dress of purple gazar falls to a triangular point in back;

*G*ivenchy photographed at
the time of his Fashion
Institute of Technology
retrospective, with
models wearing thirty
years of his designs.

yet it is recognizably a Givenchy with its softly twisted halter neck entwined by a circlet of sparkling stones.

Throughout these times he was busy developing his boutique of accessories and "fun" articles of clothing. In 1968, the year of Balenciaga's retirement, Givenchy introduced a ready-to-wear line, *Givenchy Nouvelle Boutique.* It was under this label that he designed such youth-oriented items as leopard-printed pantsuits and brushed denim skirts with orange stitching. This was the beginning of a shaky period for the couture, and Givenchy proved himself able to adapt to the changing times.

A widespread desire for more carefree and freewheeling clothes began to pervade fashion, and Givenchy returned to his fondness for pattern—but with a difference. Whereas in the early Fifties he had shown organdies embroidered with peas in the pod or oyster shells, each sewn with a pearl, in the late Sixties he showed *coupe de velours* cut in a pattern of miniscule elephants and monkeys. In the early Seventies he designed clothes with appliqués inspired by Miró, Braque, or Rothko. He has also used handsewn kiss appliqués and zebra stripes for the length of an evening dress. Frequently, he combines suede or reptile skins with other materials, ranging from tweed suits appliquéd with suede to gilt python trenchcoats to elaborately embroidered suede jackets and skirts in jewel colors. His palette continues to tend toward bright colors, with garnet, turquoise, electric blue, purple, and yellow used alone or in combination.

Givenchy's clientele has included some of the most elegant women of the century: Jacqueline Kennedy Onassis, the Duchess of Windsor, Gloria Guiness, Bunny Mellon, Mercedes Kellogg, and actress Capucine, formerly a Givenchy model. It has been for Audrey Hepburn, however, that he has created not only one of the world's great perfumes, but dozens of his best designs. By dressing her for her roles in *Funny Face, Breakfast at Tiffany's,* and *How to Steal a Million Dollars and Live Happily Ever After,* he has influenced how generations of women the world over want to look.

BELOW AND RIGHT:
n Funny Face *(1956),*
Audrey Hepburn played
a fashion model and
Fred Astaire an Avedon-
inspired photographer.
Givenchy designed Hep-
burn's Paris wardrobe
from suits to evening
dresses . . . and finally
her wedding dress.

Galanos

ALTHOUGH JAMES GALANOS MAKES CLOTHES THAT ARE SOLD "OFF THE rack" in American department stores, among America's fashion designers he alone is considered the equal of the great Parisian couturiers. From his headquarters in Los Angeles he turns out semi-annual collections of day and evening clothes, always to much acclaim but with little of the expected accoutrements of exotic music and elaborate choreography and sets. His almost austere presentations force his abilities with intricate embroideries, thoughtful cut, and meticulous standards of construction to occupy the spotlight. The real difference between Galanos's creations and those of the couture, according to Bernadine Morris, a fashion reporter for the *New York Times*, is that "the Galanos styles are more complicated in concept and construction than the French ones."

James Galanos, who was born in Philadelphia in 1924 to a Greek-American restaurant owner named Gorgiatos and his wife, wanted to be a designer from an early age. At thirteen he won an award for designing a cheerleader's uniform; then, after high school, he went to New York to study at the Traphagen School of Design, permitting him the opportunity to try selling sketches to various Seventh Avenue manufacturers and to work briefly for Hattie Carnegie. In 1947 he travelled to Paris, where he worked briefly as an unpaid apprentice at Piguet and where he made the most of every opportunity to observe the couture scene.

He returned to New York, where he spent a few seasons working as a designer for Davidow. The work proved stifling, however, and he moved on once again, this time to California. With financial backing arranged by Jean-Louis, the couturier who held the post of head costumer at Columbia Pictures from 1944 to 1958, he founded his own house in 1951, with a staff of but one French dressmaker. Success came quickly: by 1953 the 29-year-old Galanos was bringing his collections to New York and had firmly established his name.

Galanos disdains machine sewing and the other hallmarks of mass production. His workrooms are staffed with craftspeople who learned their trade in the ateliers of Europe or the film studios of Hollywood. He is most famous for his superb embroideries, each bead sewn by hand to a fabric that has been pinned to a form, thereby assuring an in-the-round fit with contoured patterns such as a jewelled band encircling the figure like a lemon peel. Sometimes working from sketches, sometimes by draping the material directly on the mannequin, he is never finished with a design until absolutely sure that it hangs properly, believing that the fall of the fabric is everything. Toward this end, he frequently uses the bias cut. In thirty years of designing clothes, he

Galanos preparing a model for her entrance, 1961.

FAR RIGHT:
Bow-tied evening dress from Galanos, 1985, characteristically long and narrow.

RIGHT:
For this 1985 evening dress, Galanos designed an embroidery that would relate to, but not imitate, the pattern of silk.

BELOW:
An·array of Galanos dresses, 1982.

has rarely wavered from a body-close silhouette, producing lean and long dresses, at times covered up, other times barer than bare.

Acclaimed for his skill with chiffon, he obtains unusual, tailored silhouettes with it, at the same time providing an effect that has more ease than most evening looks. *Vogue* described a 1969 collection as "Just chiffon. Air. Pleats. Smocking. Tucks. Marvelous freedom." For linings, he chooses soft silks, ensuring that his designs will, as he puts it, "feel beautiful on the inside."

His clothes, so long appreciated by a select clientele, achieved nationwide prominence when Nancy Reagan wore his designs to the Inaugural Balls of 1981 and 1985. Despite having his house in Los Angeles, he shows his clothes in New York, on a schedule that completely disregards Seventh Avenue's attempts to mount a unified press and public-relations barrage. He keeps his operation small enough to enable him to oversee every detail and therefore also refrains from any licensing efforts other than perfume and furs. Confident in his own standards and those of his clients, he finds it inconsequential that his clothes don't and can't have mass appeal. His greatest pleasure seems to derive from developing a new proportion or a twist in scale that enlivens an otherwise classic design.

Oscar de la Renta

THE ADJECTIVES APPLIED TO THE DRESSES OF OSCAR DE LA RENTA rarely change: in addition to "romantic," they include "ornamental — dramatic — magical — flashy — gorgeous — dreamy — flirty." With an inherent awareness of femininity, de la Renta has never stopped making his "portrait" dresses of rustling taffeta with ruffled décolletés; "at home" clothes embroidered with gold galloon and make-believe jewels; ornate luncheon suits and afternoon dresses; and simple day clothes often based on peasant prototypes.

Oscar de la Renta was born in 1932 in the Dominican Republic. At the age of seventeen he moved to Madrid to study art; there he developed skill in fashion drawing. Some dress designs he had sketched were seen by Mrs. John Lodge, wife of the American ambassador, who commissioned him to design a debut dress for her daughter. Both dress and daughter subsequently appeared on the cover of *Life*, bringing him to the attention of Balenciaga who arranged for de la Renta to have a job. Several years later he was hired as an assistant to Antonio del Castillo at Lanvin, and two years after that moved to New York to design the couture collections for Elizabeth Arden. Another two years and he was off to design for Jane Derby. When Mrs. Derby died, he took over part of the firm, giving it his name. By 1968 he had introduced a boutique line and his name appeared alone both on the labels and in the magazines.

Throughout his career he has worked with simple silhouettes and complicated decorations to turn out evening dresses with close-fitting jewel-encrusted bodices and wide, full skirts, often in a contrasting color. His day clothes during the Sixties were almost austere by comparison: little coats with welt seaming, dresses that button down the side, suits made lavish only by the trim—of cheetah or lynx.

By 1967 his clothes had become ornate and witty parodies of those worn with imagination and abandon by the self-styled counterculture. His borrowings resulted in bejewelled hot pants worn under a silk mini-dress, and coats made of bandanna-printed denim. Djellabahs appeared around 1969, the scrolling Moroccan braid enhanced by pearls and gems. "At home" caftans were similarly made up in chiffons, psychedelic sari silks, even crushed velvet, and sometimes the caftan became a long tunic over evening pants.

By the early Seventies his day clothes had become, if not simpler than before, at least more casual. Although some of his soft chiffon evening dresses followed the prevalent silhouette, he maintained his tradition of the close-fitted waist, emphasized by a deep V-neckline or a corselet. In 1974 he showed almost the exact evening dress that would make such waves for Yves Saint Laurent two years later: a

Jerry Hall wearing one of de la Renta's elaborate lunch-in-town turnouts, this with leather jacket, 1981.

bright floor-length dirndl skirt with black puffed-sleeved, peplumed bodice. By this time, de la Renta was also working with gypsy themes, making both day and evening *ensembles* with full skirts, aprons, fringed shawls, boleros, and peasant blouses.

In recent years, de la Renta's reputation as fashion designer has almost been eclipsed by his renown as socialite, thanks in large measure to his successful marriage to the late Françoise de la Langlade, a former editor of French *Vogue* who created houses that were the equivalent of salons in which the worlds of politics, the arts, and fashion mixed headily. This just provides further proof that New York had come of age as a fashion capital, and that the designer had assumed a social significance based as much on the degree of his personal luster as on the extent of his fashion empire.

FAR RIGHT:
Adding a huge bow is a mid-Thirties trick for giving a narrow evening dress a greater presence.

RIGHT:
Antonio rendering of an evening dress.

Bill Blass

B ILL BLASS—FOR TWO DECADES THE BEST RECOGNIZED AMERICAN fashion personality—manages to meet standards of country club propriety and evoke Hollywood glamor simultaneously in his work. He believes that today's designer fulfills a different role from that of his predecessors, from Worth to Dior, whom he has called "the last of the great dictators." In his opinion, it is the contemporary designer's function to interpret the needs of his clientele and provide them with the needed clothes, made up in the finest fabrics and boasting the best available workmanship, but the client, not the designer, must ultimately be in charge. Of all designers, probably no one travels more than Blass, who is as familiar a presence at department stores around the country as he is at the greatest parties, making sure in the fitting room as well as at a gala later that his clothes will work wherever they are worn.

Blass was born in 1922 in Fort Wayne, Indiana, where his father ran the local hardware store until his death when the designer-to-be was only five. Like everyone else in Thirties America, the young Blass escaped the Depression years at the movies, watching Marlene Dietrich in her lavish Travis Banton creations, or examining Adrian's clothes on Joan Crawford or Greta Garbo. He was five or six years old when he began sketching and his drawings reflected the fantastical nature of these movies as well as those fashions being shown in magazines. He continued to draw throughout high school and eventually began sending his sketches to New York, where clothing manufacturers paid him $25 or $30 for them. At nineteen Blass left the Midwest.

Once in New York, he found work sketching for a sportswear firm, left to serve in the Army, and returned to New York, working first at Anne Klein and then at Anna Miller, Ltd. By the time Mrs. Miller retired in 1959, Blass had become her head designer and he remained with her business when it was merged with that of her brother, Maurice Rentner. By 1960 his name was on Rentner's label. The company's image more and more came to be that of Blass, and its ads, witty in a field that rarely is, ran with tag lines like: "Positively Blassfamous," and "Blass Rejects 1965." One featured an interview between the designer and Dr. Joyce Brothers. Still another demonstrated his growing intimacy with the circles in which his clientele moved, with this caption under a photograph of an elegant businessman: "How do you compete with a husband like this? Screen the galleries on 57th Street for him. Study the complexities of his Mazerati. Learn to sail before the Larchmont Regatta. Discriminate between Louis XIV and XV. Speak a third language (American and French are not enough). Hire a fencing master. Angel a hit play (Anyone can angel a

loser). Try outdressing him—make Bill Blass your designer." In 1970 he bought the company and renamed it Bill Blass, Ltd.

Working by constantly sketching his design ideas, Blass continues to turn out clothing in categories that have changed little during his career. For day his clients have always gone to him for suits made casual by the shape of safari or shirt jackets, knickered or culotted turnouts with both vest and fabric borrowed from menswear and, of course, lunch-in-town suits that often have lavish fur collars. He has always been skillful with lace, in the Sixties producing babydoll mini-evening dresses as well as the most sumptuous bathing suit ever made—a strapless, Empire-waisted, skirted suit of white re-embroidered lace. His favorite fabrics have always been "pure wool, pure cotton, pure silk, and pure linen." When choosing from these he is prone to pick clean grid plaids or bold patterns, just as he tends to work in strong, bright colors such as tomato, emerald, and citron, along with the mandatory black and white.

For evening he most often has chosen a narrow silhouette and his dresses are often tailored, such as a long navy georgette dress with bright white collar and cuffs, a black silk spaghetti-strapped dress that buttons down the front with self-covered buttons, or his recent *ensemble* of a long cashmere sweater set paired with a bouffant satin skirt. Against a relatively simple ground, his decorative effects can be whimsical, like an abstract calla lily blossoming down the front of a tubular black evening dress, or the curved blazer lapel of a cocktail suit beaded to resemble a slice of watermelon.

Today Blass harks back to his Hollywood influences when he decries the fact that movies and television are incapable of accurately depicting elegance. He appreciates, however, the fact that in real life dressing up has regained its status as an American recreation. A practical man, he would like to be remembered as the quintessentially American designer. In that sense his attitude has changed little since 1969 when he told *Life* magazine that, in his estimation, "Fashion is a craft, and an expression of a period of time, but it is not an art. It's pretentious to be in awe of it."

RIGHT:
Black re-embroidered lace evening dress, 1978.

BELOW:
Baby-doll dress of green and white lace, 1968.

Yves Saint Laurent

THE MOST CONSISTENTLY CELEBRATED AND INFLUENTIAL DESIGNER OF the past twenty-five years, Yves Saint Laurent can be credited with both spurring the couture's rise from its Sixties ashes and with finally rendering ready-to-wear reputable.

It was twenty years ago that the young became the consumers holding most sway. Suddenly barricades separated them from the old, and even those too timid to rebel in other ways adopted the clothing styles of their more outrageous peers. In fashion the couture represented the old way, and the young would have none of it. Ready-to-wear manufacturers no longer had time to cull their ideas from the couture and the public no longer wanted watered down, affordable renditions of the best clothing. They wanted to express themselves in increasingly extreme versions of the "latest thing," and the "latest thing" was what was found in the boutiques and the street.

Yves Saint Laurent attempted to reflect the trends originating in the street. For him, as for other couturiers, the couture became a figurehead, something tame that upheld the image of a house, while its ready-to-wear became its bread and butter. It was Saint Laurent who acted on the realization that the couture and the ready-to-wear each has its own distinct identity and purpose. Some ideas are too simple to work in the couture just as others require care, skills, and time not feasible for clothing that has to be made up in great volume at little expense. In renewing the couture, Saint Laurent was defending his right to experiment, his right as a talented artist not to have to suppress his creativity or stint on the raw materials available to him.

Saint Laurent owes his triumph in part to his skill as a walker of tightropes. One such tightrope extends from the past to the present, and, as he has admitted, the same spirit of eclecticism that guides him in his art collecting extends to the wealth of literary, historical, theatrical, and fashion sources constantly alluded to in his designs. The tightrope between the ready-to-wear and the couture can also be seen connecting the poles of simplicity and opulence that so many women aim to embrace in their dress today.

Yves Mathieu Saint Laurent was born in Oran, Algeria, in 1936. Though taunted at school by bigger, stronger classmates, Saint Laurent found solace at home where he became increasingly absorbed in drawing and painting, occasionally designing dresses for his mother and two sisters. The experience of seeing a topnotch production of Molière's *School for Wives*, with sets and costumes by Christian Bérard, proved to be a formative one that revealed to him a new world, one in which he immersed himself by designing miniature sets and costumes based on what he had seen.

Recognition of his talents was not long in coming. When he was seventeen he won first prize in an International Wool Secretariat contest with a design for an asymmetrically draped, one-sleeved cocktail dress. After receiving his baccalaureat, he went to Paris where Michel de Brunhoff, editor of Paris *Vogue*, gave him a job sketching coiffures for the magazine, along with the advice that he should get technical knowledge if he wanted to become a designer, and therefore should enroll in the school of the Chambre Syndicale de la Couture Parisienne. School proved primarily to be drudgery and it was only during a vacation that he was able to give full play to his imagination by designing an entire collection, from sports clothes to evening dresses. When de Brunhoff saw this portfolio he was astounded that such a young man,

Higher-waistlined evening dress in softer fabric and cut, 1984.

one not even in Paris, could be thinking along lines parallel to those planned by Christian Dior for his upcoming A-line collection. He hurriedly introduced the two and Dior engaged the boy as an assistant. Over the next couple of years, Dior came to rely on Saint Laurent more and more, incorporating his ideas into Dior collections in significant numbers, even referring to Yves as his "dauphin."

Suddenly, in October 1957, Dior, the "King of the Couture," was dead. In November, the "dauphin" ascended the vacant throne. At the age of twenty-one he was already head of the largest *maison de couture* in France.

Saint Laurent's first collection—shown in January 1958 and named, in typical Dior style, after its trapezoidal silhouette—was the "Trapeze." It was a *succès fou*, the young designer receiving cheers from the crowds when he appeared on the house's balcony afterward.

His following collections were praised for their effective combination of youthfulness and beauty, but in the spring/summer 1960 Beatnik collection, youthfulness took the upper hand. Motorcycle jackets made of alligator, mink coats with ribbed sweater sleeves, and turtlenecks under finely cut suits caused an uproar. It was generally felt that Saint Laurent, however perspicaciously he might be looking into the future, had misjudged the somewhat staid clientele of Dior. As it turned out, the collection would be his last for the house.

Saint Laurent left on compulsory military service and returned to find Marc Bohan ensconced in the head-designer position. Nor was the House of Dior displeased with this new, safer arrangement. Clearly it was time for Saint Laurent to open his own house.

In laying his plans, he had the advice of his good friend Pierre Bergé, a man who possessed great financial acumen and ability in promotion. The financing was arranged when Atlanta businessman J. Mack Robinson agreed to back it, and the new house opened in January 1962 in quarters on the rue Spontini. Robinson subsequently sold his shares to the Lanvin–Charles of the Ritz division of the Squibb Corporation, which agreed to sell everything but the perfume and cosmetics operations back to Saint Laurent in 1972.

Since founding his own house, Saint Laurent has chosen not to work in Dior's tradition of producing a new silhouette every six months. Instead, the news in any given collection tends to be derived from Saint Laurent's constantly varying allusions to a treasure trove of sources ranging from Proust to the theatre, styles of painting and, as time goes on, even references to his own work.

Just as his interest in the history of fashion reveals itself in specific pieces in a collection inspired by the fad of thrift-shop dressing, his

RIGHT:

A *Horst portrait of Saint Laurent in 1958, while Saint Laurent was the head designer at Dior.*

BELOW:

S *aint Laurent couture, autumn/winter 1983.*

love for the traditions of the couture provides references to other designers: a wedding dress appliquéd with Dior's good-luck lilies-of-the-valley; white collars, black braid trim, elaborate costume jewelry, and artificial gardenias all in tribute to Chanel; a fox head muzzled in jewelled gold, copied directly from one made by Schiaparelli, or a shocking pink jacket embroidered with lines from a Cocteau poem, a design that picks up where Schiaparelli left off. Most recent is a buttoned-midriff dress based on Mainbocher's famous design for the wedding dress of Wallis Simpson, described in Saint Laurent's program notes as being in "Windsor blue."

Saint Laurent relies on a basic vocabulary of prototypes, and it would be difficult to imagine a collection of his that doesn't contain examples of his smock, chemise, tunic, peasant blouse and dirndl, evening sweater, and "smoking" *ensemble.* Also recurring are his versions of pantsuits and narrow, draped evening dresses.

The smock, a garment that he debuted in 1962 and that remains one of his favorites, has variously recalled a Normandy peasant smock in an allusion to Balenciaga's versions, a Russian Cossack overshirt, a Chinese informal coat, a velvet artist's jacket (bow-tied like the one worn by Worth and, with its lace collar, little Lord Fauntleroy). It has been the jacket for a crisply tailored gabardine pantsuit. In printed silk crepe de Chine, cinched at the waist, with a matching skirt, it redefines the day dress. Elongated, it becomes his chemise dress, made in countless wearable versions over the past fifteen years.

Tunics take many guises, sometimes overlapping the territory of the smocks. His early "bubble" dresses for Dior, gathered into a band at the knees, were an early form of tunic. His use of ⅞-length coats or tunics over sliver-thin skirts or matching trousers appeared throughout the Sixties and Seventies. Sleeveless tunics were shown over ribbed turtlenecks for day, diamanté ones for night. Ornate re-embroidered lace or lavishly beaded tunics had narrow satin skirts, above-the-knee shorts or knickers, or wide-legged trousers as accompaniments. Softer tunic looks in the Seventies took the form of bias-ruffled overdresses topping similarly trimmed skirts. His 1982 *ensemble* of navy wool jersey tunic over skinny gold kid skirt was outstanding.

Peasant blouses first appeared in a Rive Gauche collection in bright, jungle-inspired prints and shown with gypsy skirts. Made up in every color of mousseline de soie, patterned lamé, and velvet, trimmed with tassels, jet, fur, and fringe, and teamed with rustling taffeta, moiré, and velvet skirts, they comprised his rich peasant, Dr. Zhivago, and Carmen looks of the late Seventies. As shapes interpreted in one-piece dresses, in different conglomerations of color and fabric,

they became a particular style of Yves Saint Laurent evening dress.

In the late Sixties and Seventies, when clothes became their most casual, Saint Laurent filled a need for insouciant luxury by devising evening "sweaters": cardigans and pullovers of sheer mousseline de soie covered with sparkling bead embroidery. For his "smokings" he began in 1966 to adapt the components of a man's dinner suit for women, showing tailored jackets with shorts, skirts, and long pants; with cummerbunds and ruffled shirts, no shirt at all, or one of sheer see-through silk. Saint Laurent is often given credit for rendering the pantsuit presentable. His versions, with jackets evolved from both his "smoking" and safari looks, have combined sharp, precise tailoring with the *flou* of bow-tied or scarf-sashed charmeuse blouses.

One of Saint Laurent's first evening dresses for Dior, captured in the famous Avedon photograph of Suzy Parker posed between two elephants, was long and narrow. Like his International Wool Secretariat competition-winning dress, it was trimmed with the asymmetric swag of material he still revives to define a narrow figure. For these draped, form-fitting dresses, he manipulates the play of light and dark materials, color against black, that he used in 1955.

Besides these articles of clothing, by no means his only garments, he displays other characteristics in his evocations of past and present. Day or night, he uses predominantly bright colors in striking combinations highlighted by black, stained glass style. His hand with patchwork and appliqué is always recognizable, whether paying homage to Mondrian, Pop Art, or Picasso. Beaded embroideries go beyond decoration for its own sake, resulting in Cubist profiles, Chanel-like baubles stitched at random around a dress, his favorite leopard spots, or the wood and straw that sometimes adorn African sneltpure. It is the way he uses basic shapes, decorative devices, and an idiosyncratic color sense in examining the boundaries of the couture that most frequently astounds his public.

Today he retains much of the shy, nervous, almost off-hand qualities that rendered his achievements so remarkable when he assumed Dior's mantle in 1957. Every new discovery makes its way into his clothes and the longer he works with the couture, the more he stretches its boundaries to its outermost limits. His youthfulness keeps him from being staid or formal, even when his scholarship maintains its allegiance to a métier that is age-old. "I have a kind of *angoisse* that I am the last real couturier," he has said, and it is for all of us to hope that he will leave behind, not just his already astonishing body of work, but an example that others will aim to follow, and a hope that the world will continue to foster his kind of genius.

RIGHT:

A Horst portrait of *Paloma Picasso in her 1979 Saint Laurent couture suit, with bib front in two colors of purple lamé.*

BELOW:

A 1981 *très décolleté evening dress.*

T H E   A R C

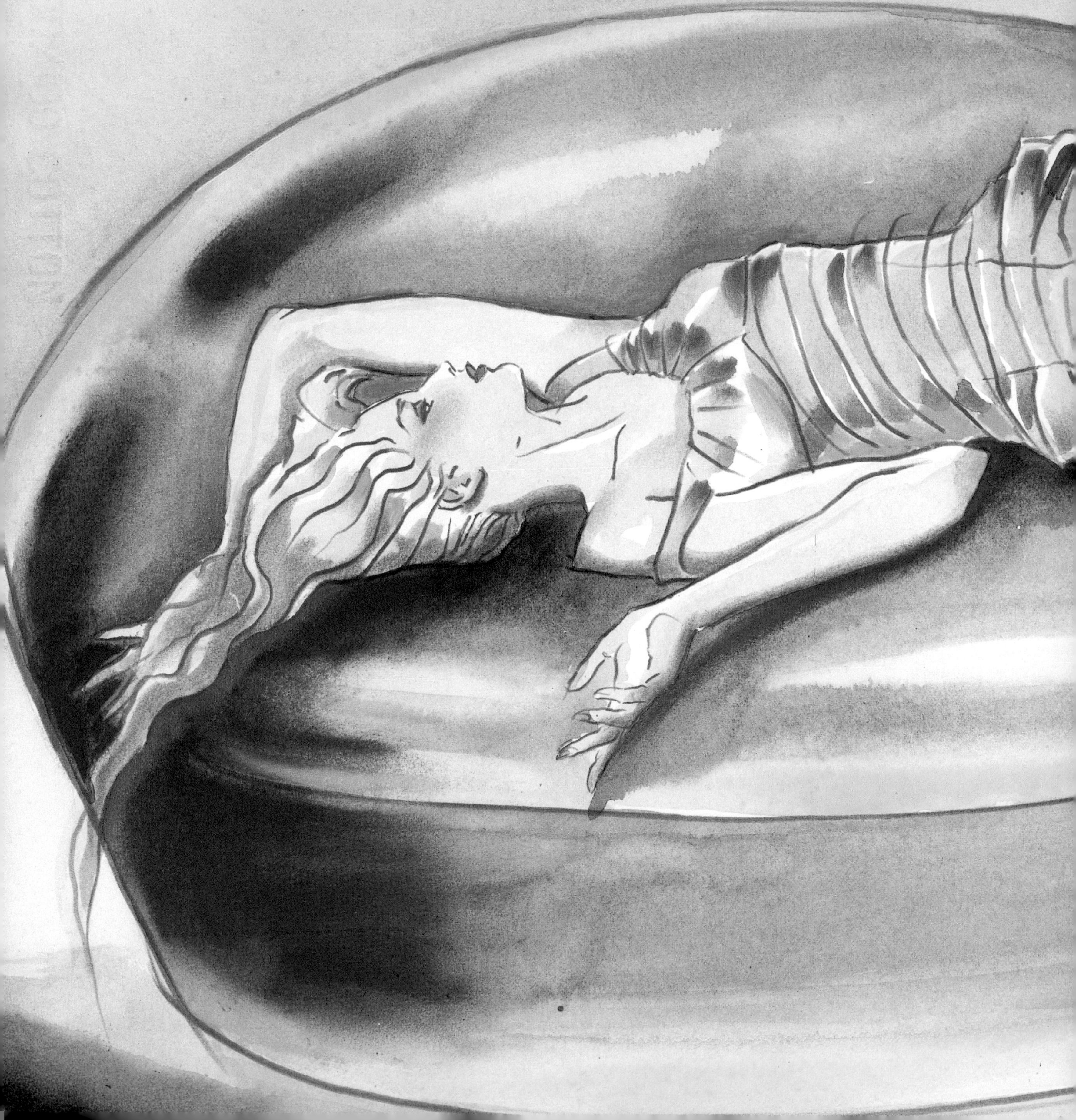

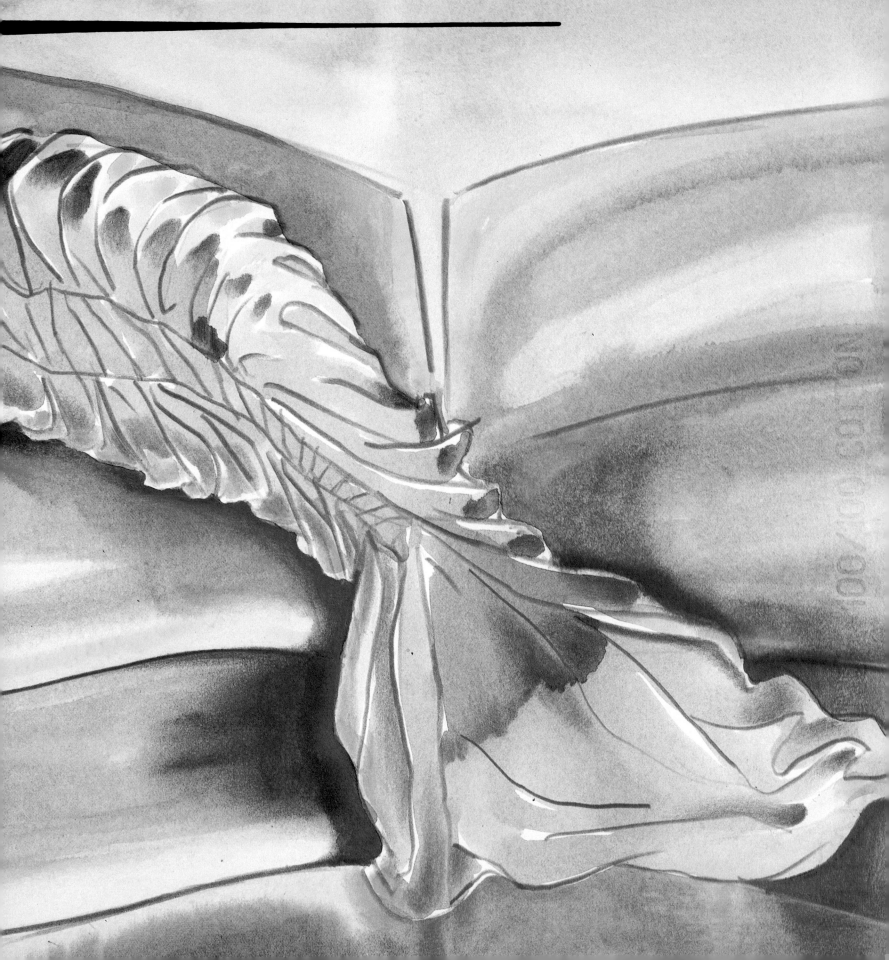

Cut and construction in the nineteenth century constituted a highly complicated problem. Bits and pieces of fabric were stitched together to make a dress, probably boned, that provided its wearer with the going silhouette. When the corset was discarded in the twentieth century, clothing began to be relatively easy and flowing, but elaborate construction did not disappear. Such couturières as Vionnet and Grès developed new techniques to make clothes seem fluid, even simple, but they designed with the live, moving body in mind. And while they may have looked like any piece of cloth off the body, they were so carefully conceived that on the body they vividly recalled classical sculpture and have been called "sculptural."

Fashions change, but precedents for quality craftsmanship and the visible presence of a creative mind at work had been set. The couture clientele had always appreciated clothes that were as beautifully made inside as out, and now, thanks to Vionnet and those like her, they also began to appreciate construction as an intellectual concept.

Balenciaga, among the greatest of couturiers, treated the bodies of his clients with sympathy. But finally, it was not the individual bodies that mattered to him—as they did to Vionnet—but his treatment of those bodies. He and Charles James used the body as a jumping-off point, abstracting its form until construction became an art in its own right. For the couturiers in this chapter, the clothes themselves have an actual shape and are more like pieces designed by an engineer or architect than the sculptural dresses with no inherent shape of their own. These clothes never look as if they happened naturally, but show what went into them. Nor do these clothes change the shape of a woman's body; they celebrate the shape without actually mirroring it. These couturiers have all worked

PRECEDING PAGES: Antonio drawing of a model wearing a Charles James creation, reclining on a lip-shaped sectional sofa, another of James's designs.

with shapes that relate to, and comment on, the female figure, whether through those organic forms found in nature—like Capucci's or James's flower-form skirts or bodices—or by contrast, geometric forms, like the spirals, squares, and circles of Cardin or Courrèges.

It is always thoughtful cut, rather than drapery, that formulates these constructions. The work methods of these couturiers have tended to dictate the use of fabrics that hold their shape: gazar, faille, satin, double-knitted and double-faced wools, even vinyl. Very rarely do they resort to printed fabrics, preferring to highlight their construction with obvious seams, the construction providing the pattern. All are masters of color, used in a single, striking blast.

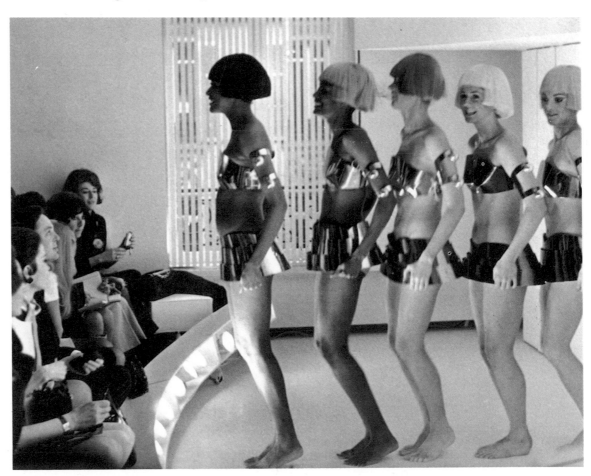

What the future looked like in 1969: rainbow-hued wigs and metal bikinis from Courrèges.

Balenciaga

THROUGHOUT BALENCIAGA'S WORK RAN WHAT *VOGUE* WOULD CALL "THE sure stimulating flame of prophecy." He was able to maintain his ability always to be several steps ahead of the other couturiers with his incredible integrity and self-allegiance, a fidelity to art as much as to craft. A couturier who made his own toiles, Balenciaga was fascinated by every seam; every part of a jacket or a bodice was perfectible, and perfection was something he aimed for. A master of color, cut, and line, Balenciaga is the hands-down favorite of the fashion purist, whether client, editor, or historian. His suits, coats, and evening dresses might, at first glance, seem difficult to wear, but for the woman sophisticated enough to appreciate—and "project"—his clothes, they guaranteed, as much as Schiaparelli's wildest efforts, the attention of every pair of eyes in any restaurant, salon, or ballroom in the world.

Balenciaga hated the fashion press and the publicity it generated, a position that, in an age of celebrity fetishism, automatically guaranteed his awe-inspiring and mysterious image. In avoiding the press, however, the goal of personal privacy was subsidiary. What Balenciaga truly hated was the idea of working to sate a voracious press that demanded newsworthy ideas from each and every collection. He just didn't work that way. Not for him the new color introduced each season at Patou, the new biannual silhouette *chez* Dior. Balenciaga's whole work was thematic, each collection growing out of the last; his collections, in fact, were more intrinsically related than those of practically any other couturier. As *Vogue* said, "With every collection the Balenciaga idea is refined, the level of excellence freshly stated, and the sense of the future sharpened." Moreover, in the presentation of his collections, which were held (after 1957) a full month after those of all the other couturiers, he went out of his way not to woo the press. At these rather austere occasions, his mannequins, the frostiest—some say the ugliest—in Paris, walked unsmilingly between the gilt chairs, bearing numbered cards in their hands (most couturiers announced their whimsically named creations with a flourish à la Lucile). The only embellishment at Balenciaga was the actual brilliance of the clothes.

Although Balenciaga is remembered for providing the well-dressed woman of the Fifties with an alternative to the highly gussied-up New Look, his real achievement was more complex. He was always carefully scrutinizing the figure as well as cut, and ever so carefully relating the two in a genuinely creative manner. In 1938 his was the place to go for dresses that, according to *Harper's Bazaar*, "fitted the figure like a wet glove," and many of his black jersey hip-draped dresses looked ahead to a prevalent Forties silhouette. For evening he showed ball gowns with skirts a "mile wide" held out "not by hoops but by

crinolines and petticoats." By the time Dior was making headlines with this very silhouette, Balenciaga, typically for him, was experimenting with a suit whose jacket was waistless, curved in toward the hip, and worn over a pencil-slim skirt. This look, again, became the norm several years later. By then, Balenciaga was playing with chemise dresses, as early as 1950 showing them bloused in gently below the hips or beltless. This garment would become the prototype of the sleeveless sheath prominent throughout the Sixties. Balenciaga then reinvented the leg as a focal point, both in his recall of the Twenties short chemise and in his uneven-hemmed evening dresses first shown in the 1950s.

Cristóbal Balenciaga was born in 1895, just over the French border, in an ancient fishing village called Guetaria in Spain's Basque country. While his father, a fisherman, was away at sea, his mother took in sewing; from an early age, the young Balenciaga was fascinated by the art of tailoring and had soon taught himself to cut and sew.

How he came to receive his first design commission is one of the most-told anecdotes in the history of the couture. In the summer, it seems, the rich and titled Casa Torres family from Madrid occupied a villa in Guetaria, and Cristóbal played with the children of the household. Their grandmother, the Marquesa de Casa Torres, was an elegant woman who, when the boy was in his early teens and already enthralled with beauty and elegance, allowed him to copy one of her Drecoll suits. From the moment he delivered his copy, the marquesa was Balenciaga's patron. With her help, he found a position in a shop in Madrid, where he learned dressmaking techniques. Soon he had a tailoring shop of his own, financed by the marquesa, then three, in Madrid, Barcelona, and San Sebastián, the last in his native Basque country. He made regular trips to Paris to buy models from the great couture houses (Chanel was a favorite), but he also did a fair amount of designing. Had it not been for the Spanish Civil War, he might never have emigrated to Paris, as he did in 1937.

Once in Paris, with minimal backing, he opened his *maison de couture* at 10, avenue Georges V. There it would remain for over thirty years, the center of the couture at its most intense and most creative. His designs instantly met with acclaim, *The New Yorker* lauding a 1938 collection for its clothes that were "quiet, with rather the same sort of simplicity and restraint that one finds at Molyneux and Mainbocher. Neat little tailored suits, plain black crepe day dresses...."

But it wasn't long before the "quiet," safe clothes gave way to those with stark, impressive drama. By the early Fifties Balenciaga had

Balenciaga late-day dress of black tissue taffeta with ballooning sash, autumn 1951.

emerged as the foremost creator among the couturiers, and it was to him that everyone looked to see the future. All along he had been building a clientele that included many of the most elegant women of the postwar years: Gloria Guiness, Mme. Arturo Lopez-Wilshaw, Mrs. Paul Mellon, the Hon. Mrs. Reginald Fellowes, Mrs. Charles Wrightsman. And he had been training younger men in his exacting and iconoclastic ways: not only Givenchy, but André Courrèges and Emanuel Ungaro would come to regard Balenciaga as their mentor. As a result of his shyness, a mystique grew up around him; as a result of the perfectionism of his work, an aura grew up around the clothes. As Ungaro once said of him, "He created a silence around him, an atmosphere of almost tangible quality."

Although he never stopped making clothes with fluid draperies fashioned out of jerseys and silk crepes, Balenciaga preferred to work with those fabrics that have the most body: gazar (a screen-wire-like transparent stiff silk), faille, slipper satin, shantung, as well as wool and silk ottomans, double-faced wools, and the thickest of double knits. His designs, then, could be architectural in their relation to the body, never adhering to it, always gently curving. Some of his evening dresses assumed nonfigural forms: a black crinkled silk dress cut like a tiered wedding cake, the strapless bodice its upmost tier; another dress constructed of two balloons of paper taffeta (the point where they narrow and connect has no relation to the body's narrowing). Even the simplest suit jacket stood away from the torso; the most basic neckline curved away from the neck.

When a woman wore Balenciaga's clothes, she felt an enchanting dichotomy between the pure, cool expanse of perfectly cut fabric and the warm animation of her skin. Often he chose to "frame" a special part of the body, creating in the process new erogenous zones. Because the Balenciaga neckline stood away from the neck, especially in back, it elongated it and drew attention to the curve of the neck —and moreover, left a place for a spectacular necklace. The three-quarter-length sleeves, one of his hallmarks, made of a woman's wrist (and gesture) a new focal point. Ever a fashion psychic, he was the first, in 1957, to bare the legs to the knee in one of his many evening dresses cut high in front and sweeping the floor in back. Always he presented a woman with the dual possibility of looking grand, elegant, and removed at a distance and yet endearing and charming when close enough to whisper to.

His richness of ornament, as often as not inspired by his native Spain, ran the gamut from black lace, black ball fringe, jet or braid passementerie, and flamenco ruffles, to flat bows that looked simple

RIGHT:

Simple, black, and sheath-like cocktail dress, late Fifties.

BELOW:

A favorite Balenciaga combination: cinnamon taffeta and black velvet. Underneath the severe jacket, the evening dress has a bare décolleté, 1939.

but were intricately constructed with interior linings of their own. The jewelry he designed consisted of heavy golden necklaces and bracelets and jet pieces, including collars made like late nineteenth-century jet mantelets.

Hats—with which he was fascinated and which his models wore perched like finials on the tops of their heads—showed the same pure construction as his clothes whether they were pillboxes (his invention), berets, derbies, bowlers, or wimple-like "coifs," as he called them, in organdy. When they weren't made of fabric to match the *ensemble*, he used kidskin, patent leather, antelope suede, along with straw, felt, fur, and lace. His shawls were circular wreaths or flower-like masses of fabric. Elisabeth de Gramont claimed that "he invented the game of the scarf," allowing women to flirt with their scarves (really more like shawls) as earlier they might have with a fan.

Balenciaga is remembered as a master of black—little black dresses, indispensable suits, and magnificent ball gowns. Next, he is remembered for his combinations of black with white; with all the browns from chocolate to nutmeg; with the palest of aquamarine; and with ice or hot pink. But what consistently elicited praise from his audience were his brilliant colors—such tints as goldenrod, peacock blue, melon orange, and teal green—and his ability to draw any color out to its most aggressive intensity. Violette LeDuc wrote for *Vogue*, "The violet in the Balenciaga collection—I would like to prolong it as an organist prolongs a note. This violet in depth was sought and discovered by Balenciaga underground, in a bulb where sounds along with colors, organs along with stained glass windows were germinating." Like all dramatic couturiers, Balenciaga made scant use of prints, occasionally choosing one with a flight of life-size birds or butterflies, strongly drawn, or a beautifully blurred warp-printed taffeta.

Because of their severity, Balenciaga's clothes were worn by women who could "carry" them. Because of the ease of the not-quite-form-fitting shapes, they were relished by women with less than perfect shapes of their own (especially women of a certain age) as well as by American manufacturers seeking always to make the greatest number of a suit that would fit the greatest number of women.

Every new fashion is a reaction to what has gone before, however, and in the late 1960s, the rigidity of highly constructed clothes began to take second place to clothes with *flou*. Balenciaga became increasingly disenchanted with the couture and, in 1968, decided to close his house. His retirement came as a vast surprise to everyone, especially to his devoted clientele. He died four years later.

Architectural coat of fuzzy wool, 1952.

Charles James

OST OFTEN RECOGNIZED AS THE FOREMOST AMONG AMERICA'S
couturiers, Charles James is always described as a great master of cut
and construction. He could (and would) work on a single dress or
suit, even a single sleeve, for years—always refining, always working
toward a moment when it would exactly embody his vision. But this
technical perfectionism did not result in rigid or contrived clothing.
His evening dresses especially look as if they were captured in the act
of unfurling. Although rigorously thought out and fixed, they capture
the essence of movement, like St. Theresa's robes "caught" in a specific
moment by Bernini. These dresses that were moments in time and
space have often been called "timeless." They existed outside contemporary fashion because James did not bother with current modes—he
didn't have time to. His lifetime's output equals that of the average
couturier's single largest season.

James's reputation might have been more widespread, his influence
more pervasive, had it not been for a personality that too often led
him to bite the hand that fed him. Maniacal and paranoid about design
plagiarism, James spent much time and money disputing with those
who supposedly had robbed him of his ideas. Unable to accept the
very basic fashion tenet that copying is a way of life, even a way of
promoting reputation and appeal, his fanaticism led him to concentrate on aspects of clothing that, to his mind, only he and a minority
could appreciate. Unfortunately for him, he was unable to run a couture house that was self-sufficient, and his efforts to find other ways
with which to support his art led him increasingly into financial and
legal trouble.

James was temperamental and artistic from an early age, traits that
caused his conservative and socially prominent family no end of
concern. He was born in London in 1904 to a Chicago-bred mother
and an English military-officer father and attended Harrow, where he
met and fell in with a set that included Evelyn Waugh and Cecil
Beaton. After his expulsion, his family thought to instill some discipline in him and sent him to Chicago to work in the architectural
design department of a utilities concern. This lasted only a short
time; so did a job on the Chicago *Herald Examiner*. In 1926, borrowing the last name of a school friend, he opened Charles Boucheron, a
hat shop, on North State Street. There followed two other small shops,
and in 1928 he moved to New York, where he opened a millinery
shop on the second floor of a carriage house once rented by Noel
Coward. He began to design dresses as well as hats.

In 1930 James moved to London and established a house at 1
Bruton Street, using the name E. Haweis James (Ernest and Haweis

RIGHT:

The center model is
*wearing a 1944 Charles
James evening dress
with stiffened, pannier-
draped skirt.*

BELOW:

A portrait of Charles
*James outside the
Chelsea Hotel.*

A 1948 Cecil Beaton
photograph of various
Charles James ball
gowns.

FOLLOWING PAGES:
Charles James's last years
were spent in this room
at the Chelsea Hotel.
He was in the process
of having his work
photographed when this
picture was taken, three
weeks before his death
in 1978.

being his father's two middle names). This venture went bankrupt almost immediately, and he began another in 1933, farther down the street. For the next few years, he showed collections in both Paris and London, leading *Vogue* to identify him first as "London's Charlie James" and second as "that itinerant designer." As early as the middle Thirties his designs were sold by Best & Co., Marshall Field, Lord & Taylor, and Bergdorf Goodman. As a result he found a favorable environment when, in 1940, he returned to the United States and opened Charles James Inc. at 63 East 57th Street. Soon he had become involved with Elizabeth Arden, for whose "Fashion Floor" he executed couture designs. The relationship ended in 1945, when he opened another of his own establishments at 699 Madison Avenue.

Soon the pattern repeated itself. James began a host of businesses, each formed to salvage something from the preceding one. There always seemed to be lawsuits, involving creditors or manufacturers to whom he had sold the rights to his designs. James was never happy with what happened to his designs when they left his possession, a dangerous attitude when, with no money to be made from his couture, he was forced to sell models to stores and manufacturers to do with what they would.

Yet throughout this chaos, James maintained ongoing relationships with a number of private clients, among them Millicent Rogers, Mrs. William Randolph Hearst, Jr., Mrs. Harrison Whitney, and Anne, countess of Rosse. Despite his constant association with these names, his actual client list was quite lengthy and included such people close to fashion as Mrs. Lucien Lelong, Mrs. Condé Nast, Elsa Peretti, Carmel Snow, Diana Vreeland, Janet Gaynor (Mrs. Adrian), Elsa Schiaparelli (who had to pay), and Coco Chanel (who didn't). All his clients had a job to do in remaining faithful to him—he was thoroughly capable of borrowing back a dress from one woman and lending it to another; selling the supposedly exclusive pattern to a manufacturer to be mass produced; not delivering the dress at all and instead, sending it to a museum; or delivering it, but only after having danced in it all night himself. That they kept coming back can be explained by his statement of what fashion meant to him: "what is rare, correctly proportioned, and, though utterly discreet, libidinous."

His evening clothes, which weighed up to fifteen pounds apiece, and which, with several petticoats, each cut differently, used up to twenty-five yards of fabric, fell so perfectly that they are said to have felt light as a feather and to have been more comfortable than any other clothes. His evening palette included celadon, celery, moss and bottle greens, stormy sky blues, chestnut and auburn browns, various

shades of rose. Most often his fabrics reflected light; he also played with texture by juxtaposing satin with tulle or velvet with starched cotton. Rather than resort to striped fabric, he made dresses and capes from millinery ribbons, which were sewn together narrowly at a bodice or shoulder, widening to form huge skirts or cape backs. (One dress made on this principle consisted of hundreds of bands of narrow gold braid densely sewn to create an entirely golden bodice, then forming rays hidden in the folds of a gray tulle skirt.) His evening dresses were often asymmetric, the fabric arranged in bunches and folds around the décolletage and throughout the skirt, so that a woman looked different from every angle. His most famous dress was called the cloverleaf or "abstract" dress, perhaps the only dress ever made with a specific view as to how it would look from above. Its skirt was formed from petalled sections of black velvet fit into white satin.

James's suits and coats were immensely structural, made of thick wool bisected into planes by geometric seams. The Arc, a favorite sleeve, was cut as part of the body of the garment. A short coat was cut like a cocoon, a skirt like a tulip with a high-boned waistband. In an age when coats were designed to fit over other clothes, his had a shape all their own, complete with inside tape that, when tied, ensured that the coat would "hang" according to his vision. The coats were often lined in satin of a contrasting (and surprising) color, sometimes in bright, large-scaled plaids.

James also made belts that, like many of his waistlines, were curved to follow the contour of the natural waist; fairly typical-looking rhinestone jewelry with an Edwardian air; feathered "palm" or nonfolding fans shaped like a bird's wings; scarves in intriguing geometric shapes; stoles that were merely clouds of tulle; and hats that were no less intricately constructed than his other clothes. A maternity collection was followed, after the birth of his son, by a line of infant's and toddler's clothes.

The James story is ultimately dominated by temperament, not talent. By the Seventies, he was unhirable, surrounded by stories about his reneging on business deals and his growing obsession with having his genius rediscovered. Unappreciative of what help he was offered, he busied himself by documenting his life's work, with the help of the illustrator Antonio, working out of his studio in New York's bohemian Chelsea Hotel. In 1978, in this same room, filled with what once had been testimony to his brilliance but by now had become debris, he died, largely unmourned and unappreciated.

A "parachute" dress of 1945, with black velvet bodice and biscuit satin pannier-draped skirt.

Roberto Capucci

RIGHT:
Several fabrics used in a single 1985 evening dress, three versions of which are shown here.

BELOW:
Capucci flower-form ball gown.

ALTHOUGH THERE HAVE ALWAYS BEEN COUTURIERS IN ITALY, IT IS ONLY since World War II that they have become well known around the world. After the war, the first real change was brought about by a Florentine businessman, the Marquese Gian Battista Giorgini, who conceived of a fashion show to be shown formally to the American press and buyers. At the end of a lavish party, as a special surprise, five creations by the young, just-beginning Roberto Capucci were to be modelled. The other couturiers, perhaps sensing that he had the ability to one-up them, did not give their permission for this segment to take place. But word leaked out, and the press clamored to see the banished dresses the next day. All of them sold, and since that time, Roberto Capucci has been included in the Pitti Palace group shows representing the finest of the Italian couture.

For ten years, Capucci contributed to the Roman fashion scene until, in 1962, he opened a couture salon in Paris in the rue Cambon. For the six years that he remained there he was well received but, missing his artistic roots, he decided to return to Rome, where he established himself anew in the via Gregoriana.

Capucci has called his work a "study of form." In his approach to the female figure he refuses to limit himself to a curved cylinder. One of his most important collections was based on the box shape: each tunic or dress had two side seams stiffened and squared away from the body. His dresses may fly out like weightless balloons after the belt is removed, or conform to the torso only to take off below the hip or at the shoulder as a butterfly wing, a fan, the petals of a flower, the fins of a fish. His most famous dress, immortalized in Cadillac ads of the Fifties, featured a skirt of nine layers, each more cutaway than the one underneath, each one more curved away from the body.

Although perfectly adept at producing an elaborately beaded, sensational, and traditional ball gown, Capucci is known for his choice of unusual mediums. For one collection, he gathered garden pebbles and applied them to stone-colored dresses; for another, he used clear plastic "quilted" with pockets of colored liquids, complete with liquid-centered buttons. Fascinated another time by ribbons, Capucci manipulated them every possible way, weaving together hand-span-wide bands to achieve miraculous harlequin dresses. Intrigued by phosphorescence, he sought to reproduce its effect in beaded embroideries.

Capucci eschews publicity—and even recognition. He doesn't even care to duplicate a dress. A client wishing to own a Capucci must arrange to purchase it out of his show, assuming, of course, that she can fit into it. For Capucci, it is the idea behind a garment, and how that idea has been worked out, that counts.

Pierre Cardin

T IS DIFFICULT TO NAME SOMETHING THAT PIERRE CARDIN HAS YET TO design or transform with his imprint. He can take credit for rethinking not only clothes, but transportation, communications, environmental design, entertainment, food, and drink. As *Time* magazine described him a decade ago, Cardin is "that shrewd fanaticist who has tacked his name onto just about anything that can be nailed, glued, backed, molded, bolted, braced, bottled, opened, shut, pushed and pulled." No other designer has his finger in as many pots (at last count 506 licensees in 93 countries). No other couturier is so well represented on the streets, in the subways, in the stores. No other couturier owns a chain of restaurants with branches in Rio, Brussels, Peking, New York, Monte Carlo, Sydney.

But Cardin *is* also a couturier. As such, he has been restlessly inventive, experimenting with the notions of abstraction, exaggeration, technique, and technology the way another designer might with buttons and bows. Always he has paid special attention to construction. Ironically, many of his most inventive structural solutions are, in fact, antique tricks of fashion: his knitted minidresses stretched over wire hoops recall both the crinolines of the age of Worth and Poiret's minaret tunics. When he is not using age-old tricks of cut to achieve his forms, he is manipulating fabrics three-dimensionally in ways no other couturier, living or dead, could ever have dreamed.

Pierre Cardin was born outside Venice in 1922, while his parents, a winemaker and his wife, were living in Italy. They returned to France soon afterward where their schoolboy son became fascinated simultaneously by costume design and architecture. He was apprenticed to a tailor at fourteen. At seventeen he was on his way to Paris when the war intervened, and he went to work for the Red Cross.

After the war Cardin found employment in Paris, first at the House of Paquin, then with Marcelle Chaumont, who had been Vionnet's assistant before setting out on her own, and finally with Schiaparelli. He later met and worked with Jean Cocteau and Christian Bérard. He remained at the House of Dior for three years, leaving to open his own *maison de couture* in 1950 in the rue Richepanse. In 1954, he opened a boutique, Eve, for women, in the rue du Faubourg Saint-Honoré, following this venture with his Adam boutique for men in 1957.

Most of Cardin's early designs were day suits and coats in simplified forms made in heavy fabrics. He designed coats with raglan sleeves, dresses that foreshadowed the sack with their front-defined waistlines and Watteau backs. Suits and dresses had tulip skirts and boxy, waist-brushing jackets with rolled or scarf-tied collars. By 1955, Cardin was making barrel coats with rolled-tweed collars or gigantic ribbed

LEFT:
Rainbow chiffon toga dress photographed on the Great Wall of China.

BELOW:
Reserved Cardin tailleur from 1984 (top); *characteristic lettuce-edged pleated ruffles on a 1984 evening dress.*

ones. In 1958, he showed a suit with a narrow skirt, its jacket gathered like a bubble into a band at the hips.

By the Sixties, Cardin's reputation had changed—and grown. Whereas before he had been known for designing simplified couture for a young clientele, now he was heralded as a most innovative designer. His clothes made references to Op Art, the trappings of science fiction, and space travel. He made dresses out of vinyl, brooches out of carpenters' nails and diamonds. The clothes shrank in size as the patterns grew. In 1965 there were minishifts, bisected (and bicolored) by huge zig-zags or a diagonal row of his favorite scallops. By 1966 he was showing women in ribbed bodysuits over cut-out tiny jumpers, men in sleeveless one-piece overalls over turtlenecks. In 1968, he designed short dresses with barrel skirts in a knitted fabric heat-manipulated into egg carton indentations. That year, he also showed wide-striped bodysuits with little skirts of flat fringes in vinyl or wool. These fringes were bound into a hem-band to form a barrel in the skirts of some of his evening dresses.

In 1970 Cardin showed longer coats with channel quilting that terminated in disc-shaped tabs. These circles at the end of a line were also seen in the discs at the end of a stove-pipe trouser leg and in dresses made of circle-tipped strips of swirling fabric worn over a bodystocking. Dresses and coats had kimono sleeves with large round cutouts through which a wide patent-leather belt was threaded. In 1973 he made his lampshade dress of stretchy knitted fabric shaped over a wire hoop. Evening dresses of the 1970s might fall from a band placed just above the breasts, have one sleeve that formed a long train, or culminate in any one of his many versions of an uneven or handkerchief hemline.

Cardin's most recognizable details include cartridge pleating and tucking; geometric cutouts and appliqués; collars of petals, hammered-metal rings, or layers of organdy; single artificial flowers; and over-sized buttons. His colors are bright and clear.

Today Cardin's diversification overshadows his work in the couture. And that, while still undeniably "Cardin," has a tame quality (almost certainly due to neglect) that harks back to his pre-1957 period. His current reputation rests more on the variety of his endeavors: on the theatrical, musical, and artistic events he sponsors at his theatre L'Espace Cardin, as well as on his undaunted efforts to dress (or somehow affect) every human being in the world. One wonders what the space-age couturier will do when other planets are made accessible to him. This is a man who surely would embrace the universe as his cocoon.

Courrèges

D URING THE SIXTIES *VOGUE* DESCRIBED COURRÈGES AS "IT." ANYONE looking back at that kaleidoscopic decade remembers fashion as nothing but miniskirts, skinny-legged hip-huggers, bare midriffs, and —these always make the list—bright white boots, AKA "go-gos." All Courrèges looks, adopted by everyone.

The Courrèges look was described, again by *Vogue*, as "refreshing as a streak of luck." His clothes were seen as pure, exact, fresh, and young, and what made them work was his amazing, much-lauded sense of proportion. Training as a civil engineer, taught everything he knew by Balenciaga, Courrèges was known as the Le Corbusier of fashion, the man celebrated for bringing modernism to clothing design by stripping away every last excess and laying bare its very construction. Underlining every point, Courrèges emphasized this streamlined construction by top-stitching, bias-banding, and welt seams. Suddenly the world was dazzled by his futuristic precision, a precision that contrasted beautifully with the innocence of his shapes, his revelation of the legs (and the arms), and his baby-like shoes and hats and gloves. Touted always as the designer for "tomorrow," he has never stopped working in the métier he perfected early on.

André Courrèges was born in Pau in France's Basque country in 1923. From early youth he was entranced by art, design, and fashion. After completing a course in civil engineering during which he was sidetracked by architecture and textile design, he found work designing boots, shoes, and men's suits for a tailor, all the while keeping up with his rugby, pelota, and mountain climbing. During World War II he served as a pilot in the French Air Force; then, in 1945, he came to Paris.

Courrèges worked briefly for a designer named Jeanne LaFaurie, then realized that he could be truly stimulated only in the employ of the man he considered to be the master of the couture. That man, of course, was Balenciaga, also from the Basque region (though of Spain) and also a kind of engineer. He waited until 1950 when a position opened up, and stayed with Balenciaga for eleven years, taking in everything he could about cut, quality, and construction.

In 1961, he opened his own house—cramped, all white, reverberating with progressive jazz—at 48, avenue Kléber. His assistant was another Balenciaga pupil named Coqueline Barrière, whom he married six years later. From these premises he began his leap into the future, taking his "ascetic scissors" and turning out clothes that were magical in their simplicity. 1964 was the first year of his brief reign over all of fashion. His first proclamation was "elongate the leg!" And for the next few years his skirts became progressively shorter and

Courrèges shoulder- and hip-yoked mini-jumpsuit, ca. 1968.

shorter—and his skinny little pants were shown with equally leg-lengthening tiny tunics and jackets.

Courrèges is credited with establishing the widespread acceptance of pants for "everywear." Unlike other couturiers, he did not design them merely to fill certain needs of a clientele otherwise interested in luxurious evening clothes and dressy town *ensembles*. Courrèges assumed his clients lived in pants, and his versions went to balls, to the theatre, and to lunch in town. His trousers were not based on men's, unlike those previously worn by women. He dispensed with the front pleats and cuffs, with side pockets and fly-fronts and even with the belt-tabbed waistband. His were stove-pipe slim, slit to fit over the foot, and they came to the top of the hipbone. Nor were they to be worn with the shirt tucked in. Courrèges pants came with slit-backed boxy tops that showed a sliver of midriff and had a no-bra back. For grand occasions he made these tops in sequins or in sheer organdy appliquéd with his own particular flowers, flat, round-petalled daisies. His famed trouser suits had chasuble tunics and doublet overdresses that were brief versions of the little dresses he also sponsored for day wear. Courrèges showed all of his clothes with chin-tied baby bonnets (or cowboy hats or baseball caps), slit-eyed opaque white sunglasses (later adorned with gigantic false eyelashes), Mary Janes, short boots and socks, and wrist-grazing white kid gloves. His clothes (sans sunglasses) were embraced as uniforms by Lee Radziwill, Margaret Trudeau, the Baroness de Rothschild, and the Princess Ira Fürstenberg. Having already bared the leg, arm, and midriff, Courrèges began in 1967 to experiment with transparency, making minidresses and jumpsuits in sheer organza appliquéd with judiciously placed vinyl or sequined flowers and circles. One pair of pants was shown with no top at all, just a pair of "flower-power" pasties.

By 1965, Courrèges's business had grown too large for his present premises. While preparing to move, he closed his doors, showing only a smallish collection to his regular clientele (no press). When he reopened in October he had reorganized his enterprise into a carefully planned three-tier structure: Prototypes (his couture division), Couture Future (deluxe ready-to-wear), and Hyperbole (inexpensive ready-to-wear for a younger clientele). From the luxurious premises at 40, avenue François Premier, he turned out variously priced versions of his clothes—in white (of which he said "It is sun and laughter . . .it's a state of mind"), pale pink, ice blue, pale turquoise, cool beige, day-glo orange, and lime green. Recognizably Courrèges were his simple grid plaids, wide stripes, and white with one other color stylized floral patterns. For his body-skimming (but not clinging) clothes,

RIGHT:
Bare-backed dinner dress in Courrèges's favorite white, ca. 1970.

BELOW:
Ice-cool pink coat.

he chose fabrics with body: gabardine, double-faced wool, cotton lace, organdy, and leather.

During the Seventies, Courrèges's popularity was limited to a clientele of resort habituées, but, fashion being what it is, his aesthetic is once again attractive, and his boutiques are now being enlarged to meet increasing demand. He has continued to design within a multilevel structure, adding levels as he has gone along. Today he has his hand in a wide variety of endeavors ranging from furs to Courrèges Homme, active sports clothes called Sport Futur to uniforms for the Olympics, and including all sorts of accessories, Empreinte and Eau de Courrèges scents, and, most recently, a design for a Courrèges camera.

LEFT:

Crinkle-patent jacket over ribbed bodystocking, ca. 1971.

BELOW:

Cosmonaut turnouts, 1968.

Even Worth designed the occasional skating or yachting costume, and almost every fashion designer since has devoted some of his or her attention to what we call "sportswear." Along with their other clothes, couturiers have supplied their clientele with the clothing called for when participating in a sport, when watching a sport, or, as the century wore on, simply when relaxing.

Even though every designer may create some sportswear, there is also a kind of designer who specializes in it. Such designers share the feeling that their clients never, or practically never, "dress up," but nonetheless need not be deprived of interesting, attractive clothes. When these designers do make formal clothes, they rely on their thoughts about informal clothes and thus do much to blur the distinction between the clothing for day and evening, and between the beautiful and the pragmatic.

Beginning with the Gibson Girl shirtwaist and the crisp, tailored skirt of the turn of the century, sportswear has been regarded as an area of American expertise, and this chapter primarily includes American designers, beginning with the innovative and unpretentious Claire McCardell, who created unique kinds of clothing for everyday wear that owed their attraction as much to being easy to maintain, to wear, and to pack as they did to their actual appearance. These attributes are also important to Bonnie Cashin and Vera Maxwell, who pay close attention to what women do, how they move, and how their lives are changing in terms of pace and responsibility, and design accordingly.

But not all innovation in sportswear has been American. In Paris, couturiers such as Jean Patou, Lanvin, Maggy Rouff, Schiaparelli, and Jacques Heim have imbued their tennis clothes, bathing suits, golf and

*PRECEDING PAGES:
Kenzo ensemble
from 1985.*

walking clothes with typically French panache. And in England Hardy Amies got his start working for LaChasse, an all-couture sportswear house that showed no evening clothes at all.

Very American, however, is the tendency to make evening clothes that match day clothes in mood, comfort, and effect. In the Forties, both Trigère and Norell, designers of high-quality ready-to-wear, made evening clothes that were both luxurious and sporty. Norell's floor-length sequined turtlenecks and Trigère's plain maillot-bare long black wool dresses are obvious examples. Geoffrey Beene is another American who uses color, material, texture, and detailing to create relaxed clothing made glamorous.

It is perhaps the borrowing of elements of male dressing for female clothing that forms sportswear's most characteristic aspect. Ralph Lauren, Hardy Amies, and Giorgio Armani remain particularly true to the vocabulary of men's clothing when designing for women. As well as their treatments of scale and shape, they use such elements as hacking jackets, shirting fabrics, wing collars, French cuffs, military detailing, a subtle mixing of patterns and, of course, trousers.

A new generation of designers—Kenzo, Perry Ellis, Norma Kamali, and Issey Miyake for example—has used the elements and traits of sportswear in experimental ways, sometimes even abandoning the traditional menswear approaches for various ethnic or pop influences.

Even at its most vivid and elaborate, the new sportswear encourages movement and activity. It is for their allegiance to women's lives and demands, and respect for their many needs, that the men and women in this chapter are called The Realists.

Claire McCardell

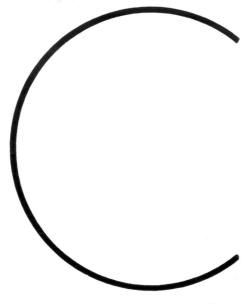

LAIRE MCCARDELL HAS OFTEN BEEN CALLED THE FIRST TRULY AMERI-can designer, originator of "The American Look." American women have always been admired for their freshness and energy, as well as their achievement of style without endless fittings and an undivided attention to wardrobes. Although she displayed an active interest in high fashion—buying up end-of-the-season Patous and Vionnets during her student days in Paris, collecting antique fashion prints and Fortunys—she did not shrink from working to perfect a garment intended for doing housework and retailing for $6.95. She didn't see why any garment, mass-produced or not, should be unattractive or uncomfortable, and she put herself and her own needs into everything she did. Her influence has been tremendous and she is far and away the designer most often mentioned as a favorite by both fashion designers and students, in the United States and abroad. But she didn't see her innovations that way; for her they were simply more expedient ways to dress, which the rest of the country soon came to see.

It was World War II that first propelled McCardell to fame. She discovered, as did Mainbocher and Adrian, that in the absence of Parisian fashion inspiration and despotism, America was free to go its own way. But McCardell didn't require the war's isolation and urgency the way her colleagues did (she even admitted that for her, working with the rationing restrictions was fun). Her penchant for innovation, combined with her conviction that clothes should fit both the individual and the occasion, and should solve problems rather than create them, would almost surely have served her well even with Paris at the height of its powers.

Claire McCardell was born in Frederick, Maryland in 1905 to a bank-president father and a southern-belle mother. Thanks to her three younger brothers, she grew up with a love of sports and games. After high school and two years of college, Claire persuaded her parents to send her to study fashion illustration at Parsons School of Design, then called the New York School of Fine and Applied Arts.

During her second year she began to blossom, for it was this year that she spent in Paris, at the Parsons branch on the Place des Vosges. Claire had been shocked in New York to learn that she would have to study art before she could study fashion. In Paris fashion was all around her. She and her friends explored the city and they were even able to buy samples from the top houses at much-reduced prices. Thus did the young McCardell begin to understand the relationship, or more aptly, the chasm, between style and comfort.

She returned to New York for her last year at Parsons, then after graduation embarked on a frustrating succession of jobs. In 1930,

Claire McCardell photographed in the Fifties.

she became an assistant to Robert Turk, a young designer just starting his own business, a venture that failed and caused Turk (and Claire) to move to Townley Frocks, an established sportswear house. Turk was drowned in a sailing accident in 1932, and it was decided that Claire would take his position and finish the collection. She remained at Townley for seven years, until the company disintegrated, and it was there that, in 1938, she scored her first commercial success: the so-called "Monastic" dress, described by McCardell as a "flowing robe-like design that the wearer shaped to her own waistline with a sash or belt." Best & Co. bought a hundred of them and they were soon notorious. Sally Kirkland, in her chapter on McCardell in *American Fashion*, tells of one Seventh Avenue reaction: "'Drop everything,'" she describes one dress manufacturer as shouting to his designer, "'There's a girl up the street making a dress with no back, no front, no waistline, and my God, no bust darts!'"

When Townley folded, McCardell spent some time working for the indomitable Hattie Carnegie, whose top-drawer house sold Parisian imports, her own copies of French fashion, and original designs. This job was doomed not to last, for McCardell's designs were too simple for Carnegie's tastes.

So, when Townley Frocks resumed their business, McCardell returned to designing for them. Her work was so successful that, at the end of the year, Townley added her name to its label and exchanged the word "frocks" for "clothes," an omen of things to come. In 1952 McCardell became a partner and a vice president. A year later she added sunglasses she called "Sunspecs," gloves, jewelry, shoes, hats, sweaters, and juniors' and children's clothes to her other designs.

In 1940, her first collection for Townley featured the then radical natural shoulder, cut in one piece with the sleeve and designed in reaction to the prevalent and over-exaggerated man-tailored silhouette. Like her obvious influences Vionnet and Grès, but unlike most sportswear designers, McCardell made few references to the tradition of men's tailoring, choosing instead to use pleating or the bias cut to achieve a comfortable and appealing fit. McCardell also evoked Chanel in that she liked "buttons that button and sashes that tie."

McCardell worked by choosing a fabric, stretching it, playing with it, then putting it away until inspiration struck. Eventually she would pull it out again, make a little stick drawing, then give fabric and drawing to her sample makers for execution. Unlike most other designers she kept favorite shapes and pieces in her collections, offering them in slightly changed form over and over.

But if she sometimes made reference to Paris and its couture, there

RIGHT:

Tube bathing suit of elasticized sand beige jersey.

BELOW:

A 1946 "at-home" ensemble.

was never any question that she designed for America. And within America she created clothing for busy women, not those she once called the "formal rich." Mass-produced, her clothes were affordable and were meant to facilitate the lives of women who would be cooking for their own dinner parties. One of her most popular designs was the "popover" dress, a wrap-around housedress she first showed in 1942, and that would never go out of production. She is also credited with such innovations as the first (non-jeans) use of double-stitching; brass hardware—including her favorite, hooks—instead of buttons, snaps, or other fastenings; the "diaper" bathing suit; and the idea of ballet shoes as street wear. In addition, she did much to popularize hoods, pedal pushers, dirndls, dancer's leotards, and the concept of "separates"—skirts, blouses, pants, and sweaters sold individually with the intention that they be combined by the wearer.

McCardell, like Vionnet, forbade her models to wear rigid underclothes when they showed her dresses. In her aesthetic, a little tummy could be attractive and for women so endowed, she made clothes that had adjustable surplice bodices or drawstring necklines. A Monastic, or full, pleated dress could be worn belted or unbelted; her string ties could be wrapped around the waist in a number of places.

McCardell used casual fabrics like denim, sailcloth, balloon cloth, corduroy, wool jersey, lingerie nylon, wool fleece, seersucker, calico, mattress ticking, and cotton velveteen. She blunted the boundaries between day and evening clothes by using these fabrics interchangeably. Thus a playsuit might be made of raw silk and an evening dress of cotton shirting. The top to accompany a pair of shorts or a bathing suit might have a formal décolleté, and a summer evening dress the demure puffed sleeves of a child's dress. She made very few ball gown-type dresses; most of her evening clothes were more likely to read as floor-length sundresses or what have come to be known as hostess gowns.

Most of McCardell's colors were warm: toast, red, brown, purple with red, or pink with orange, olive green with turquoise, as well as black and white.

When she died of cancer in 1958, McCardell was still at Townley, transforming the American experience into a profoundly American fashion aesthetic. Though her career had sadly been cut short, her legacy has proven both enormous and enduring, an antidote to all that was fussy, preening, or ephemeral.

Gray wool gabardine bathing suit shown with a Phelps leather belt, 1946.

*C*laire McCardell enjoying
a *Fifth Avenue window*
tribute to her career.

Vera Maxwell

V ERA MAXWELL HAS ALWAYS DESIGNED FOR THE KIND OF BUSY, MULTI-faceted woman who does her own hair and rushes from appointment to appointment—who has limited time for wardrobe-planning and shopping. The clothes that bear her name reflect her dancer's knowledge of how the body moves, as well as her affection for the ease and durability of men's country clothes. She has always disapproved of change for its own sake. By sticking to her guns and making classic clothes that never seem to wear out, she has seen her business go in and out of fashion in the wake of Seventh Avenue's fickleness.

Born in New York City in 1901 of Viennese parents who often took the family to Europe, she was encouraged in her ambition to be a dancer. In 1919, she joined the Metropolitan Opera Ballet, only to leave it five years later to marry Raymond J. Maxwell. She began modelling in 1929, and the clothes she wore as a mannequin, especially the riding habits, inspired her to start making clothes for herself that were truly wearable. Her first "separates" *ensemble*, consisting of a gray flannel skirt and a russet tweed jacket, was lifted from her professor-brother's weekend garb. Gradually she began making clothes for other people as well, and by 1936 was being reviewed in the fashion press. For the next few years she designed for such Seventh Avenue firms as Adler and Adler, Glenhunt, and Max Milstein, until 1947 when she incorporated as Vera Maxwell Originals.

Vera Maxwell tends to use fabrics with character, borrowed either from men's clothes or from the day-to-day clothes of different countries: rough handwoven Indian silks, camel's hair, Austrian loden cloth, Donegal and Harris tweeds. In 1940 she was admired for her skill in transforming these heavy fabrics into reed-slim silhouettes. Partially because of the materials and partially due to her preference for natural dyes, the Maxwell palette has tended to be muted: beiges and browns, autumnal reds, oranges, and ochres, olive as well as loden green, grayed blues and turquoise.

Her intense hankering after practicality was especially evident in the clothes she made during the war years. She designed a one-piece coverall for the female factory workers at Sperry Gyroscope, and was ingenious in minimizing the problems of fabric rationing. Her simple lapel-less suits with self-covered buttons and channel seaming were marvelously spare, yet gave no hint of having been stripped of their decorations. She prides herself on the timelessness of her clothes, and with reason. Many of those she designed in the Fifties and Sixties display the same simplicity of her wartime designs.

Maxwell admires Chanel above all other designers, and over the years has borrowed many of Chanel's touches for her own clothes,

RIGHT:
A *Forties sports coat.*

BELOW:
A *portrait of Vera Maxwell.*

most notably the use of a coat lining matched to the dress underneath. She has made such *ensembles* for day in tweeds and rough silks, for summer in bright plaids and striped cottons, and for evening in patterned silks combined with solid-colored silks. Her suits have included vested models (her dancer's understanding that a vest allows for greater freedom of movement coming into play), reefer suits with jacket-coats, riding-jacket suits, and suits with a dress underneath in lieu of a blouse and skirt combination.

Vera Maxwell's sensitivity to the requirements of all women, not just clotheshorses, has led her to design for those under 5'4" and those who do not have mannequin figures. For women whose jobs take them well beyond their desks she plans wardrobes in seasonless and uncrushable fabrics, with pockets for stashing a toothbrush or pair of eyeglasses on an overnight plane trip. She has also supported the introduction of man-made fabrics which, she asserts, respond to the needs of busy women. (She was the first designer to import Ultrasuede, an extremely practical material, though it is Halston who usually gets the credit.) A dress that sums up her attitude toward fashion and its importance in life is her 1974 "speedsuit." It is jersey with an elasticized waist, and is able to be pulled on in just seventeen seconds.

Bonnie Cashin

F OR BONNIE CASHIN, CREATION IS BOUND TO NATURE, AND SHE READ-ily admits that her childhood landscape—California—is an important influence. "The sea, the mountains, the flowers, the vineyards, and all the textures of nature are indelibly a part of my being." Today, despite the most urban of environments (she lives and works in a skyscraper overlooking New York's East River), she designs practical clothes that evoke a casual "country" air.

Cashin came to New York to study at the Art Student's League only to move back to the West Coast, to Hollywood, where, for six years (and dozens of films) she was a costume designer for Twentieth Century-Fox. Her favorite costumes were the "character" designs, such as those for *Laura* and *A Tree Grows in Brooklyn*. Even those early accomplishments reveal her tendency away from the tradition of entrance-making "Hollywood" clothes.

In 1949 she returned to New York and founded her own business, which to this day is as individualistic as her clothes. Cashin has never bothered to follow Paris fashion, and in thirty years she has produced a body of work remarkable for its consistency and continuing appeal.

When Cashin undertakes a design, she is "envisioning the whole person." She sets about making her clients' lives easier, giving them ample pockets, seeing that they are free to move arms and legs, ensuring that they will be warm and comfortable. Most important, she provides them with options: different pieces of clothing to be worn in different ways. She pioneered this concept of "layering," showing as early as 1950 *ensembles* whose components worked in different temperatures and situations but that could be dressed up or down, depending on the combination of pieces. Every year she designs a poncho, a "piece of material with a hole cut in the middle," and since her California days her signature sweater has been the funnel-necked pullover, its neck doubling as a hood.

Cashin's fabrics—canvas, suede, leather, alpaca, mohair, cashmere, tweeds, linens—are rugged and natural. Her palette encompasses both natural tones (peat, mushroom, wheat) and ebullient ones (canary, bright pink, red). Distinctive is her use of leather bands and pipings, as well as her brass turnlocks used as closures on coats and dresses.

Like her ideal client, "the woman with something to do," Cashin moves easily from project to project, finding time to stop and probe the very nature of creativity. Today she heads a foundation called the Innovative Design Fund, the purpose of which is to seek out "emergent creators" and provide funding for the making of prototypes for novel, utilitarian designs for living.

T urnout by Bonnie Cashin.

Norma Kamali

ANYONE CAN DESIGN A BEAUTIFUL EXPENSIVE DRESS FROM A BOLT OF fabulous French silk," Norma Kamali told André Leon Talley for *Vogue*, but only she has pulled off transforming the drabbest fabric ever made (fleece-backed gray sweatshirting) into hundreds of thousands of spirited garments that have managed to supplant the popularity of jeans once and for all. Although comfort formed, in large part, the appeal of Kamali's "sweats," not to be overlooked is the pleasure of the unexpected, something Kamali herself not only loves, but knows how to turn into clothing designs.

Born in 1945 to a candy shop owner and his wife, Norma Arraez grew up on Manhattan's Upper East Side wanting to be a painter and expressing herself through the clothes she wore: the widest of skirts (up to eight different, starched layers), the whitest of white bucks (with day's supply of powder to cover up scuff marks), and the tightest of trousers (she would sew herself into them for the evening). After graduating from the Fashion Institute of Technology, she practiced fashion illustration and, under the aegis of a job at Northwest Orient Airlines, flew to London at every available chance.

London in the Sixties was undeniably an exciting place so, when Norma and her new husband, Eddie (Mohammed Houssein) Kamali, opened a basement boutique on East 53rd Street in 1968, they stocked it with anything they could find that looked like Carnaby Street. What they didn't import, Norma designed. The clothing offered ran the

FAR RIGHT:
Exercise pants in gigantic gingham checks, 1983.

RIGHT:
Taxi-stopping ensembles, 1983.

gamut from hot pants (New York's first) to custom-made suits and evening gowns, the first sign of Kamali's extraordinary versatility. It was also during this period that her playful, anti-status sensibility emerged. She mocked formality in her designs for rhinestone-legend-emblazoned leotards and playing-dress-up strapless evening dresses with attached opera-length gloves.

In 1974 the shop moved to a bigger space on Madison Avenue. Four years later, now divorced, Norma opened OMO Norma Kamali (OMO stands for "On My Own") on West 56th Street. Since then she has signed licensing agreements for children's wear, shoes, stockings and socks, lingerie, and hats. There are also both a ready-to-wear Norma Kamali line (sold in hundreds of stores across the country) and one for "couture"—higher-priced ready-to-wear, which is available only in New York, Los Angeles, and London.

Along with the "sweats," the designs Kamali is best known for are parachute-fabric jumpsuits, evening gowns of tee-shirting encrusted with pearls, high-heeled sneakers, coats fashioned from sleeping bags, swimsuits, and cotton lace separates. She recognizes that a single client might have many moods and proceeds accordingly, juxtaposing cheerleader skirts and bobby socks with cotton flannel shirtwaists or Lurex showgirl gowns. Her shoulders are the widest, her heels the highest, and her skirts go to the extremes in length. Her colors are bright and confident, her stripes and plaids and jungle prints strong and aggressive. As a body, her work reflects an ability to see possibilities even in the banal and familiar. Her collections seem to switch channels with a frenzy, from a late Fifties sitcom to a late-late show Busby Berkeley extravaganza, then back to a Saturday morning kid's cartoon.

For someone whose work is so ebullient, Kamali herself is famously shy. The theatricality of her extremes—and even her simplest designs run to extremes of simplicity, as in her charmeuse lingerie—is simply her way of concealing that timidity. Whatever the motivation, she has restored a lot of the fun to buying and wearing clothes. And by using familiar fabrics (from L.L. Bean flannel to Hawaiian prints) she has made fantasy dressing palatable to those who may also be shy, or who may be getting up the nerve to step out of an established image for the first time.

K*amali "couture"—Raquel Welch wore one of these matte jersey dancing T-shirts to the Academy Awards, 1983.*

FOLLOWING PAGES:
K*amali's trademark snoods, shoulders, and patterns, ca. 1985.*

Norman Norell

IKE CLAIRE MCCARDELL, NORMAN NORELL CAME TO PROMINENCE DUR-
ing the war years, when America was stranded from the fashion guidance of Paris. But unlike McCardell, who worked with the democratic
determination to dress Everywoman, Norell chose to work within the
tradition of high fashion, though his clothes were technically ready-to-
wear, not couture. When one considers how a Norell looked and
moved (and what it cost), that coat, or dress, or suit was equal to
anything the Paris couture knew how to turn out. For over thirty years
Norell demonstrated to what heights American design might climb,
by producing collection after collection that was at once stunning and
practical. By shaping the very character of the ready-to-wear industry
and its capacities, he has served as role model to the younger generations of American designers.

Norell made elegant, and often very dressy, clothes, as well as simple ones, always lavishing care not only on their exteriors but on
details like linings and interfacings. Rarely did he deviate from his
vocabulary of chemises, pea jackets, trench coats, turtleneck sweater-
type tops, middy blouses, kimonos, bathrobe-wrapped coats, pajamas,
and camisole-topped dresses. Norell necklines were round and plain,
or finished with pussy-cat bows, stock-tied scarves, or small, round,
or pointed Peter Pan collars. Every button was functional, every embroidery abstract. Sleeves were either cigarette-shaped or gently cuffed
with self-covered buttons and bound, tailored buttonholes. His show-
ings were showcases for what he had perfected: a patent simplicity
and a self-assured absence of extraneous detail. In 1966, *Vogue* wrote:
"One coat is all he believes in and one coat is all he shows—and it's
enough." Earlier, *The New Yorker* had pointed out that his influence
was rivalled only by that of Balenciaga.

Another designer, limiting himself to even one perfect coat with
such a limited group of shapes and embellishments, would likely
have produced staid, conservative, or uneventful work. But Norell
was heralded as a prophet and his collections were eagerly monitored
by the press, who came to realize that what Norell showed one season
was apt to turn up in Paris the next. In 1945 he presaged the New
Look, not only by showing full-skirted, tiny-waisted dresses, but also
through his use of boning and laced-up corselets. By the time this
look had become a general predilection, his sheaths were appearing
and by 1948 Norell dresses were as narrow as could be, suit jackets
standing away from the body-topping thigh-tight skirts. He showed
culottes for day in 1960 and later in the 1960s it was his version of
the trouser turnout that yielded the standard pantsuit: a safari-type
jacket and straight pants in glen plaid teamed with a stock-tied polka-

Traina-Norell taffeta
ensembles, *1949*,
photographed by Cecil
Beaton against a back-
ground inspired by
Matisse's book Jazz.

dotted silk blouse. Yves Saint Laurent would later become known for a similar *ensemble*. As the Sixties pared away clothes, it was Norell who bared the entire midriff, not by cutouts but by slinging his long black crepe dinner skirt low on the hips and topping it with a bodice that really was just one of his favorite cape collars. At the same time, he was showing the most covered up of dresses: floor-length, long-sleeved turtlenecks pavé with sequins, or long, balloon-sleeved, middy-bloused organdy ball gowns that were anything but prim.

Norman Levinson was born in Noblesville, Indiana in 1900, to a successful haberdasher and his wife, and he grew up in Indianapolis. Young Norman wanted to be an artist and, at the age of nineteen, moved to New York to study, first at the Parsons School of Design, then at Pratt Institute. This was when he decided to design for himself a new name, one based on the first syllable of his first name and the phonetic spelling of the first letter of his last.

At Pratt he studied drawing and costume design, both of which were put to use when he became a costume designer at Paramount Pictures' Astoria Studios in Queens, where he dressed Rudolph Valentino in *The Painted Devil* and Gloria Swanson in *Zaza*. When Paramount relocated to Hollywood, he stayed in New York and carried on with costume design for such clients as the Ziegfeld Follies, the Cotton Club, and the Brooks Costume Company.

In 1924 Norell was hired by Charles Armour of Seventh Avenue, where he remained for four years. He subsequently went to work for Hattie Carnegie where, over the space of a decade and a half, he acquired both his sure hand as a designer and his unshakable commitment to quality. A disagreement with Carnegie over a dress he had designed for Gertrude Lawrence to wear in *Lady in the Dark*, which Carnegie wanted to water down and sell copies of later, led him to accept a position with the firm of Anthony Traina. Offered more money to design anonymously, and less if his name was to appear on the label, he opted for the latter. Upon Traina's retirement in 1960, both label and company became Norell's.

From the beginning in 1941, the clothes that appeared under the Traina–Norell label were handsome, simple, and luxurious. Norell's way with sequins—among the only items not rationed by wartime clothing restriction regulations, and used by many designers for flowery decorations that circled necklines and trimmed pockets—set him apart as early as 1944, when he used them for entire garments, sometimes sewn in a pattern, but usually in a solid field. Norell sequins were flat rather than concave, and were individually sewn side by side to organza-stiffened fabrics. Also frequently used were tiny round beads, pearls,

and bugle beads for borders on dresses, tunics, and trousers.

As important, Norell used the traditional sportswear elements for evening clothes. Cardigan jackets, jersey turtlenecks, trousers, and tank tops were enlivened with sequins, organdy, and faille. He liked to play the opulence of a fabric against the dress's shape, and to combine day and evening fabrics for evening clothes that were at once glamorous and sporty. The resulting *ensembles* included wool jackets embroidered with sequins, wool coats over sparkly dresses, tweeds with leg-o'-mutton sleeves, organdy with patent leather.

Norell's taste in buttons tended toward the bold and plain and his wool day suits and coats frequently featured double rows of large buttons that contrasted in color to the rest of the garment. Although he sometimes sashed his sequined dresses with a band of satin ribbon, for the most part Norell belts were wide with self-covered rectangular buckles.

As his affinity for beads and sequins demonstrates, Norell's admitted greatest fashion influence was the Twenties. He drew upon this period for sheath dresses with their straight up-and-down lines, sometimes belted but never seamed at the waist. His low-waisted dresses, gathered into bouffant skirts (a version of the *robe de style*), and those sewn from the hips with flaring godet panels betrayed a late 1920s taste. He was fond of feathers and used ostrich for entire coats, and to edge sleeves and hems. The most popular coat in the Twenties had been fur-trimmed and Norell revived this look with wide fox cuffs, collars, and hem-bands, adding fur trim to dresses as well.

For nautical *ensembles*, Norell fittingly used red-white-and-blue combinations. His color sense was sharp and precise, and he contrasted black with pale beige, and paired turquoise or lime green with orange, lemon with navy, tomato with white. When he used prints, they were large-scale and dramatic. Strong color and clearly luxurious materials always highlighted the simple shapes of his clothes, which were not intricately cut, but which fell perfectly.

Norell appreciated and promoted a vision of American beauty that draws its elegance from a fresh, clean, healthy, and simple sportiness. He understood the limitations of the ready-to-wear industry and insisted that off-the-rack clothing be as fine as made-to-order.

Just before his retrospective at the Metropolitan Museum in 1972, he suffered a stroke that soon ended with his death. The House of Norell continued, with Gustave Tassell turning out bugle-beaded cardigans and columnar silk evening dresses in his predecessor's style, but this venture lasted only a few years.

This 1949 evening dress ran in Harper's Bazaar *with the caption: "fur, organdie, emeralds and warm blonde skin . . . "*

Pauline Trigère

PAULINE TRIGÈRE MAKES CLOTHES THAT ARE DRAMATIC THROUGH BOTH their simplicity and their honest practicality. There are hints in her work of other "designer's designers," those for whom complexity was the surest way of achieving the essence of simplicity: Vionnet, Grès, Charles James. In 1972 *Vogue* described a suit of Trigère's as being "taut *and* relaxed," no mean accomplishment, and one that has marked a career that has spanned the austerity-ridden war years, the playful Fifties, the rebellious Sixties and unglamorous Seventies, right into the unabashedly fashion-conscious Eighties.

Pauline Trigère was born a block away from the Place Pigalle in Paris to Russian-émigré parents sometime before World War I. Alexandre and Cécile Trigère, tailor and dressmaker respectively, had made military uniforms for the Russian aristocracy, and Pauline literally grew up in the world of fine tailoring. Pauline's first job was picking up pins and scraps of fabric from the floor. Before long, she was sewing on sleeves and cutting out toiles. Never dreaming of becoming a *couturière*, her first dress design was prompted by lack of money and a need for a dance frock. It was of plaid taffeta, its collar consisting of three layers of organdy edged with red, green, and blue piping. (For fun she made a version of this dress in 1971.)

Her parents dismissed her ambition to become a surgeon and at age fifteen she was apprenticed at Martial et Armand, which was a solid Parisian couture establishment from the turn of the century through the 1920s. It is said that her employer remarked after a few days that she already knew all he had to teach. She returned to working for her parents, where she met many American manufacturers and buyers, including Adele Simpson, who befriended her and told her of the New York fashion world.

With the approach of World War II, Pauline left Paris with her husband Razar Hadley, their two sons Jean-Pierre and Philippe, her mother, and her brother Robert in December 1937. Though headed for Chile, they wound up stopping permanently in New York where Trigère found work at Ben Gershel, the house where both an uncle and Adele Simpson worked. She later assisted Hollywood costume designer Travis Banton, who was designing for Hattie Carnegie, but this job ended when Pearl Harbor was attacked.

By 1942, when Pauline Trigère opened her own company with her brother at 18 East 53rd Street, her marriage had dissolved and there was very little money. Pauline designed and cut a collection of a dozen dresses and Robert toured the country showing them from a suitcase. Fortunately orders were not slow in coming, and by 1945 Trigère was a respected New York label. The business relocated twice

before finding its present location at 550 Seventh Avenue. By 1949, Trigère had won her first Coty Award.

In 1952 Trigère declared war on the New Look, telling *Mademoiselle* magazine that what she liked was a "walking column, slim and loose at the same time." Nor has Trigère herself counted on an "easy" silhouette of fitted bodice and gathered skirt. Slim and free-falling, her clothes are revelations of careful planning. Her narrow looks have included princess dresses and coats, slightly Empire-waisted ones, and haltered or strapless columnar evening dresses. She has sometimes employed fluid jerseys and chiffons, always in a tailored way, but it is her way with wool that has consistently been the most striking with even heavy tweeds being cut on the bias, looking weightless. Besides using sheer wool crepes and tweeds for afternoon and day dresses, Trigère has designed wool evening clothes that outshine anything in a traditional evening fabric.

Throughout her career, Trigère has never made clothes for the merely leisured; rather, her clothes satisfy the needs of women who are as busy as she herself is. Consequently, her clothes can be packed easily, combined, and counted on, for years. Being a woman designer, she says, has kept her perpetually aware of how clothes work in the wardrobe as well as on the body. This female intuition has resulted in lightweight, bias-cut, and unboned underwear and nightwear; faux-jewel necklines and giant Trigère "diamonds" for women who must leave their jewels in a safe; a blouse-like bodysuit that will not slide out of a waistband; monochromatic travelling wardrobes; and "intermission-length" theatre clothes, less fussy than evening gowns and more practical for hours of sitting. She has always advocated capes, not only because they flatter the greatest number of bodies, but also for the dash of movement they provide. Rarely has she made an evening dress that doesn't come with its own stole, bolero jacket, floor-length coat, or sleeveless mantle.

Trigère's own elegance and charm, somewhat Gallic in flavor, are renowned, as is her favorite method of keeping in tip-top physical and mental shape: standing on her head. She wears her own clothes superbly, enlivening her *ensembles* with printed scarves, tied her own way, and with her collection of handsome jewelry, including her signature turtles, which she perches on a shoulder, at each cuff of a suit jacket, or near a skirt's hem. Her favorite colors, when not black, or black and white, are warm—coral, flame red, tangerine. When she chooses a floral print, plaid, or striped fabric, it is likely to be both bold and, thanks to her skill with scissors, unusually placed on the body.

LEFT:

Scarf-printed evening dress, 1982.

BELOW:

Toga evening dress, late Sixties.

Hardy Amies

ALTHOUGH FAMOUS AS ONE OF THE THREE OFFICIAL DRESSMAKERS TO the Queen of England, Hardy Amies is known less for the pomp of his designs than for his mastery of a tailored understatement. He has proudly called himself a realist, and admits that he has always been drawn more to tailored clothes than to escapist, romantic evening looks. He got his start in the Thirties, when the tweed suit was tantamount to a day uniform for English women. During his fifty years as a designer he has never strayed far from concentrating on his coats and suits for country and town, with their built-in longevity.

In 1909, Hardy Amies was born to a mother well acquainted with the world of fashion, for she was a dressmaker who had worked for the London houses of Madame Durant and Miss Gray. Amies, who had been an undistinguished student, had tentatively chosen journalism for his career, when a newspaper editor advised him that he would have a better chance at a job with a few languages, rather than a university education, under his belt. He moved to France, where he worked as an English teacher in a small school, as a family tutor, and for a firm specializing in trans-Channel deliveries. For his second language he moved to Germany, where he worked himself up the ladder in a tile factory. Back in England he found what he had been looking for: an English-based company with German factories that would provide an opportunity for him to work part of the time in both countries. Amies became a trainee, then a travelling salesman with a specific territory in which to peddle the firm's weighing machines. This job, though plodding, provided a certain amount of free time and Amies amused himself by writing a three-act play described by one reader as dreadful, but somewhat promising.

So far there had been no hint of a designing career. But now, according to anecdote, Amies attended the annual Christmas ball given by a Mr. Singleton, owner of the fashion house that had once been Miss Gray's. Reporting on the party in a letter to a family friend, Amies waxed poetic about how beautiful Mrs. Singleton had looked in her black and silver dress. The letter was forwarded to Mrs. Singleton, who suggested to her husband that Amies might be just the person to replace Digby Morton, who had quit his job as a designer.

And so, in 1934, Hardy Amies became the manager and designer of LaChasse, the sportswear division of Mr. Singleton's Gray and Paulette, which was located in what had been the garages of the couture house. Begun in 1929, it was a rather novel operation, for it showed only couture sportswear, and Amies, with the aid of a very good staff, quickly learned how to supply his clientele with the sort of timeless, classic, and well-wearing clothes it sought.

Wenda Parkinson, photographed by her husband Norman, in a 1951 Hardy Amies suit.

World War II brought an end to Amies's LaChasse days. Hearing that the army needed linguists, he enlisted, giving his employer the opportunity to break their contract, something that might have happened anyway as Amies was developing a sense of his own worth and the idea that he might one day like to run his own establishment. When not involved in training—he would eventually serve in the Intelligence Corps—he spent leaves and other spare moments in London designing under an arrangement with Bourne & Hollingsworth, and also for a time having his own corner at Worth of London where a vendeuse showed Amies's own designs. He was a founding member of the Incorporated Council of British Fashion Designers, and as such, set an example by designing suits and other *ensembles* in accordance with the austerity regulations.

After the war, Amies was able to open his own house in a Georgian mansion, at 14 Savile Row, that had been damaged considerably when a bomb fell nearby. He found the building's history appealing, for it had not only been the prewar site of one of London's better dressmakers, but had also been home of the British dramatist Sheridan in the early nineteenth century. With a staff assembled from his previous posts, he moved in and prepared his first collection, which was shown in January 1946. The New Look was already in the air and for the most part, Amies worked with a gentler feeling of rounded shoulders and more feminine skirts complete with padded hips, otherwise sticking to his preference for discreet, beautifully tailored clothes.

Almost immediately his business acumen showed itself. He installed a boutique in Savile Row that sold accessories and ready-to-wear suits, coats, and sweaters rather than the Parisian kind of impulse-bought fripperies. To his delight, the ready-to-wear operation stole no thunder from his couture department. Both grew independently and steadily.

Commercially, Amies's greatest success was his men's clothing. Essentially through a succession of country-by-country licensing arrangements begun in 1959, he is responsible for—along with such women's designers as Pierre Cardin and Bill Blass—acquainting men with the desirability of the designer aesthetic and label. His viewpoint in this regard was quite British: rather than imbue his men's designs with the kind of quickly obsolete high style that seems to be par for the course when a designer switches his attentions to the other gender, he acted on his convictions that clothes should look comfortable in any circumstances, that they should strive to make the wearer look both richer and younger, and that they should never betray any lack of taste. Besides his men's clothing and his women's ready-to-

Hardy Amies suit.

wear ventures, he has also designed licensed products such as home furnishings, leather goods, and lingerie.

1950—the year he opened his boutique—was also the year he attracted the attention of the Queen, then the Princess Elizabeth. He had long been dressing one of her ladies-in-waiting and had been hopeful that the Queen too might approach him. His first designs for Her Royal Highness were worn during a Canadian royal tour and since then he has supplied many of her dress-and-coat *ensembles* as well as some of her grander evening dresses. One of the prettiest of these last was made somewhat in the Norman Hartnell style. Designed for a visit to California, it is made of flowing white silk, with its bead-embroidered bodice sporting meandering poppies, the state's flower. Such successful efforts, and the house's justifiably fine reputation for the best of wedding dresses, indicates Amies's awareness that the requirements of modern women sometimes revert to the most romantic of clothing traditions. For the most part however, he has concentrated on their other needs, admitting that his true love is tailoring rather than dressmaking, and leaving the more glamorous designs in the hands of Ken Fleetwood, his closest colleague, who now designs all the women's clothes.

"In the past," Amies told the London *Times*, "a sexy woman was one who lay on a sofa like an odalisque, smoking a cigarette. Now she is an athletic woman, and she certainly doesn't smoke." For these women, the Amies message has rarely wavered, although he now admits that the suit, once his mainstay, has become too dressy for contemporary life, so he and Fleetwood oblige the Amies customer with separates that can be worn together or apart. Nothing is more appropriate for this kind of look than tweeds, and Amies has always been very particular about them, decreeing that the best are the ones in the colors of the earth and that nothing in the design of the garment should detract from their subtlety.

Good taste and ease, both in physical comfort and the conviction that one is always suitably dressed, are what Amies has offered first Britain, and then the United States, Australia and New Zealand, Canada, South Africa, and Japan. In addition to the royal family, he has boasted at least one client of great sophistication: Vivien Leigh. This sophistication served him well when called upon to design the costumes for Stanley Kubrick's 1968 film *2001: A Space Odyssey*. The challenge here was to make clothes that were both interesting to look at and believable. It is confirmation of Amies's realist status that he succeeded by creating another permutation on the theme of "sportswear."

P*ink moiré ball gown.*

Geoffrey Beene

EVER SINCE HE WAS FIRED FROM A SEVENTH AVENUE DESIGN JOB FOR being too forward-thinking in his designing, Geoffrey Beene has been the one to watch for the news in fashion. He has not achieved this distinction by creating surrealistic space-age oddities, but by steadfastly promoting the notions of ease and practicality, made all the more appealing through his almost nostalgic standards of quality. His clothes, garment by garment, collection by collection, and decade by decade, promote strong feelings of both continuity and evolution.

Geoffrey Beene was born in Haynesville, Louisiana in 1927. After graduating from high school at the age of sixteen, he landed a scholarship to Tulane's pre-medical program. There, like so many designers, his dormant creativity was prompted by a dissatisfaction with his studies. He stuck it out at medical school for two years, and then transferred to the University of Southern California where, instead of enrolling, he took a job in the display department at I. Magnin, where he began sketching his own fashion designs. The store's president saw his work and decided that he had a talent worthy of pursuing, which led him to New York to study at the Traphagen School of Design, then to Paris where he attended both the school run by the Chambre Syndicale de la Couture Parisienne and the Académie Julian, and also worked for Molyneux. Back in New York he worked for Samuel Winston, but lost his job when he spilt mayonnaise on an antique chair. He then worked as assistant to the head designer at Harmay, a Seventh Avenue dress house, where he remained for seven years before being dismissed while on vacation. Next came an equally long stint with Teal Traina where his name was mentioned in the house's advertising and press releases. This job came to an end when Traina married one of his models, a close friend of Beene's, causing a friction that gave Beene the impetus he needed to strike out on his own. Geoffrey Beene Organization opened in 1962.

From the beginning, Beene's own designs were original, not merely decorated or watered-down versions of the going mode, as has often been the case on Seventh Avenue. His 1960s clothes were, above all else, youthful, with a *poupée*, or doll-like, style predominating: Empire-waisted short, or long, dresses made like jumpers with blouses underneath, trimmed with what we now think of as very Beene bands of braid and ribbons.

He showed his creativity with fabrics early on, choosing ones that had previously been thought of as formal and combining them with those that had previously been used only for day, resulting in a relaxed elegance. In 1967, for example, he showed dresses printed in a houndstooth plaid, inset with undulating bands of lace—a fresh ap-

PRECEDING PAGES:
Charmeuse tunic over printed silk skirt, 1985 (top); a portrait of Geoffrey Beene. PAGE 389: a 1985 ensemble.

RIGHT:
Beige linen and black gabardine tunic suit, 1985.

BELOW:
Seventies dress inspired by racing silks.

proach that still surfaces in his collections and has done much to invigorate the reputation of lace.

Beginning with his clothes for Harmay in the Sixties, and continuing today, Beene has advocated an easy fit, designing tank-top dresses, bloused jackets, toga-like evening dresses, sweater coats, drawstring-topped skirts, and strapless dresses, as well as many versions of pajamas. Today he is best known for clothes that follow the body, revealing it through his use of cutouts and transparent panels.

In his highest-priced collections—which he calls "couture" for their quality rather than because of custom fitting—as well as in his lower-priced Beene Boutique and Bazaar lines and his Beene Bag sportswear, he offers flexible wardrobes of interrelated pieces. These, like the clothes he wears himself, are not based on the traditional menswear elements of blazer, man-tailored shirt, and pleated trousers, but on smock jackets, tee-shirts, elasticized or drawstring running pants. He has done much to blur the distinction between "sportswear" and "other clothes" in his strapless Grecian tennis frocks, pailletted football jersey evening dresses, or jogging clothes with glittery piping.

Bernadine Morris has written in the *New York Times* of the "heirloom quality" of Beene's clothes. This is a result of old-world, but not old-fashioned, craftsmanship and detailing. He has chosen to contrast the ease of his clothes with their luxurious quality born of the fabrics themselves and his characteristic use of them in abstract patchworks, appliqués, and line stitching. For practical reasons he sometimes designs a reversible coat or jacket, giving the effect of having both a luxurious inside and outside, which recalls the finishing of the most beautiful couture garments of the early twentieth century. The fabrics are always the best of their kind, whether the expected silks of every description or the more homey mattress ticking, hopsacking, or blanket wool. His colors can be bright and bracing ("All the world seems to love red at sometime or another," he once told *Vogue*), or earthy and subtle.

Along with his variously priced collections, Beene has undertaken the usual variety of licensing agreements: hosiery, shoes, furs, eyeglasses, linens, perfumes, menswear, and a men's cologne. Unlike other Seventh Avenue designers, he has even set up a European office in Milan. He has won the Coty Award of American fashion more often than any other designer.

Given all this, it is striking that he is resistant to the blandishments of fame and publicity. He reserves his energies for his aesthetic vision, one that changes from year to year, yet remains true to its own fundamentals.

Perry Ellis

P ERRY ELLIS PROVES THAT SPORTSWEAR, RATHER THAN BEING THE
most limiting area in which to design, with the greatest number of
requirements and the greatest audience to please, is actually the most
pertinent arena for creativity in a decreasingly formal world. Though
most often seen wearing a pair of faded khakis and a partially unbut-
toned button-down shirt (an *ensemble* that can be viewed either as
unimaginatively Virginian or creative in its contrast to his nattier rivals),
Ellis has said that "sportswear allows me to do anything." With this
freedom he has made a category of clothing designed for the most
active of activities with a predetermined set of components, into an
unpretentious forum for examining the history and function of clothing.
His casual sweaters perpetuate Schiaparelli's trompe l'oeil whimsies
and his luxurious furs, cashmeres, and satins are inspired by Sonia
Delaunay whose designs were more art than fashion. He has been
acclaimed as the most innovative designer in America and these innovations are easy to recognize and applaud because they are so under-
standable in their way of taking off from existing traditional elements.

Perry Ellis was born in Portsmouth, Virginia in 1940. He did not
grow up with the ambition of becoming a fashion designer—his B.A.
from the College of William and Mary in business, and his Master's
in Retailing from New York University prepared him rather for life as
a department-store executive. Appropriately his first job was as sportswear buyer for the Richmond, Virginia department store Miller &
Rhoads. In 1968 he became a stylist for the highly traditional New
York-based firm John Meyer of Norwich. Gradually he began to design for this company, which specialized in ultracoordinated junior
sportswear for the status-conscious girl. In 1975 he became sportswear designer for Vera, owned by Manhattan Industries, and the following year had his own label for the company: Perry Ellis for Portfolio.
In 1978 he set up his own company, Perry Ellis Sportswear, again
with Manhattan Industries, and since then his clothes have escalated
in both quality and price. Ellis has lately branched out into men's
clothes, furs, legwear, shoes, scarves, sheets, and towels.

In the relatively short time he has been designing under his own
name, he has become known for a variety of looks. His hand-knitted
sweaters with dimple sleeves and single cable-knit braid have become a new category of sweaters as easily recognizable as the cable-
knit cardigan or Fair Isle pullover. Sometimes he uses tweedy wools
or cotton; sometimes sweaters have trompe l'oeil patterns (a necklace
and bracelet knit in at neck or wrist, a faux Peter Pan collar reminiscent of John Meyer blouses, or patterns that duplicate the skins of
zebra, tiger, and leopard). His sweaters might be very short (abbrevi-

RIGHT:
P *erry Ellis ensemble in
deep jewel tones, 1984.*

BELOW:
A *portrait of Perry
Ellis.*

RIGHT:
A 1981 ensemble *of challis.*

FOLLOWING PAGES:
E*llis ensembles, 1980: sweet, pale, and young.*

BELOW:
S*tripes for a suit* (top); *and a belt for a linen turnout.*

ated in some cases to being bandeaux) or very long, and these off proportions strike some observers as perfect.

For other separates he has used Irish tweeds, wide-waled corduroy, cotton sateen, linen, Oxford twill, Liberty prints, piqué, and challis. Although he names as his favorite colors such neutrals as putty, khaki, and sand, equally recognizable are his tones of deep, deck paint green, never before translated so perfectly into fabric, and equally deep port wines and marine blues. The clothes take all kinds of shapes and are worked out to be interchangeable among a wide variety of outfits. Long coats, almost to the ankle, blazers to the knee, and trousers cut off mid-shin but with waistband up below the bust are all cut full, sporting plenty of room. Cropped sweaters described as "shrunken," bolero jackets and skirts with extra-wide midriffs and belts buckled with the biggest buckles number among his more fitted efforts.

Ellis revels in the juxtaposition of the traditional and the offbeat. A woman's button-down Oxford cloth shirt has cuffless sleeves, and an *ensemble* put together for work may use a traditional blazer to curb the less traditional effect of culottes. Most recently he has added more luxurious evening fabrics to his repertoire: cashmere for sweaters that are dressed up by off-the-shoulder, mink-banded necklines; velvet for godet-flared Twenties chemises; jewel-toned charmeuse for his Delaunay patchworks; and sheer organdies for balloon-sleeved blouses that are teamed with velvet, satin, or linen, cotton, and wool. His main concern when designing is to give women utter freedom to get on with their lives. He gives them freedom of movement and, by interrelating all his different pieces, freedom to do things other than shop. As he has admitted, "clothes come pretty far down on my list of priorities," a feeling he shares with clients who choose sportswear for their every need.

Ralph Lauren

A DESIGNER'S WORK USUALLY LOOKS AS IF IT WERE INSPIRED BY A specific ideal of beauty, an idiosyncratic view of the needs of a particular kind of woman, or simply a need for a change. Ralph Lauren, one of the only designers to begin designing menswear and then branch out into women's and children's wear, admits that his approach to making clothes is different. Rather than dressing a single ideal, starting with one fabric, one silhouette, and one notion, he claims to imagine the scene of a certain activity and then proceed to dress each participant in the way most suitable to that moment in time and that part of the world. Thus he orchestrates scenarios, costuming such activities as cross-country skiing, crewing in a sailboat race, or playing croquet. Recently he has begun to provide his casts with sets and props, complementing his active-sports, spectator-sports, and candlelight-dinner clothes with household furnishings of faded chintz, tartans, sailcloth, flannel, or linen, along with fittings of mahogany, brass, and crystal.

That he designs for a group—the participants in any given tableau could be members of a family, old school friends, or a collection of summer community acquaintances spanning all ages—is significant. His clothes appeal to the fantasy of belonging: to clubs, boards, cliques, and ultimately to a former aristocracy. This American aristocracy is distinguished not so much by its custom-made Bugattis, liveried staffs, and tiaras (all of which seem removed from contemporary life), but by its choice of leisure activities, notably travel and sports. Today, most sports and most parts of the world are readily accessible and a nostalgia for a former quality of life is most easily expressed in terms of specific sports, and their locales, whose specific accoutrements form part, or perhaps all, of their appeal.

Almost every article of clothing Lauren designs for women is based on an article of gentleman's clothing, whether it is something specific for a sport: tennis whites, riding jackets, foul-weather gear; or something reminiscent of one of the aristocracy's haunts of old: Newport, Jamaica, the big-game wilds, or the English countryside. Typically, the androgyny of dressing women in men's clothing results in a kind of highlighted sexiness, but Lauren's clothes more aptly reflect a stiff-upper-lip reverence for the Platonic relationship. His advertisements rarely show a couple dressed in such a way as to speed up the courting process. They rather display the urge to belong to their group. Although he has been criticized for the derivative nature of his work (despite an allegiance to quality that has led him to improve upon the originals), many think of Lauren as the most American designer, for his work embodies typically American aspirations as well as a national habit for borrowing.

M ink and cashmere from 1983.

Ralph Lauren was born in 1939, not far from the Mosholu Parkway in the Bronx. (His father, a mural and house painter, changed the family name from Lifshitz to Lauren when Ralph was in his teens.) Ralph spent his childhood playing baseball and basketball, and his first design was actually a warm-up jacket for his neighborhood baseball team. He attended DeWitt Clinton High School in the Bronx and, at night, the City College of New York, where he took business courses. Meanwhile he worked at Alexander's, first as a stockboy and then as a salesman, ending up at Brooks Brothers after City College and a six-month stint in the Army. He also served as an assistant buyer at Allied Stores and as a salesman for a glove company before signing on as the New York representative for a Boston necktie manufacturer. He decided he wanted to design his own neckties and was sponsored in 1967 by Beau Brummel Ties, Inc. Lauren chose the name Polo for his line and set to work with characteristic perfectionism, choosing the finest fabrics, overseeing production to maintain top quality, and making his ties almost twice as wide as the then popular skinny ones. It took only six months for his wide tie to become de rigeur and in 1968 he began work on an entire menswear line, founded partially on a need for wider shirt collars and suit lapels to accommodate the widened ties, but also on an awareness of the market.

The Polo line, as well as all ensuing endeavors, was to reflect Lauren's personal taste in clothes. As early as high school he had set himself apart by wearing plaid madras shorts, white bucks, and hunting jackets, which he bought from "L.L. Bean, riding, hunting, and sporting goods stores." As he told *American Fabrics and Fashions* magazine: "When I saw the quality of their things deteriorate, I knew there was a wide

FAR RIGHT:
Ski sweaters hand-knit with appropriate motifs.

RIGHT:
Rugby-inspired Eighties rugby shirts.

open market." Lauren's design adaptations were an immediate success, and by 1970 he had won a Coty Menswear Award and was firmly ensconced in Bloomingdale's (the store that had initially refused to sell his ties unless he removed his label and narrowed them).

Lauren didn't begin his commercial foray into women's clothing until 1971, when he premiered his fitted, tailored cotton shirts available in the whole range of shirtings long familiar to men. His pima cottons and Oxford cloths were as welcome a sight to women frustrated by a dearth of natural fibers as his Neoclassicism was to those who had outgrown the psychedelic. At first he dressed women in literal versions of menswear: pleated trousers, wing-collared, pleated-front shirts with French cuffs, skirts of silk foulards and other necktie materials, and tweed hacking jackets. His early fly-front skirts were fashioned after trousers, and dresses were either elongated cashmere sweaters or knee-length shirts with curved hems and men's weekend grosgrain belts. Since then he has expanded his sources to include Edwardian lingerie, prairie clothing, Navajo blankets, cowboys and Indians, and early American samplers and patchwork quilts. More recently, he has begun to relax the shapes of his women's clothing, showing more unfitted jackets and blouses, as well as his dictates about what should be worn with what when, showing linen with velvet, tweed with charmeuse, and suede with lace. He has never designed women's evening clothes that are more elaborate than what men themselves wear at night.

In addition to his sources, Lauren has also expanded his markets. He now designs clothes for children, luggage and leather goods, eyeglasses, and home furnishings, as well as a line of denim, flannel, corduroy, and leather "roughwear." There are also Lauren fragrances and cosmetics, as well as more than three dozen Polo shops in North America, Europe, and the Far East. Moreover, in the movies, he has costumed Robert Redford for the title role in *The Great Gatsby* (1974). Diane Keaton and Woody Allen wore his clothes in the 1977 *Annie Hall*, thereby making Lauren responsible for two of the most important fashion archetypes of the Seventies.

Lauren, who is frequently photographed wearing a faded workshirt and jeans, makes clothes that hold the promise of lasting long enough to acquire the kind of patina cherished by the Ivy League and the English gentry. He also, like such establishments as Brooks Brothers, whose looks he sometimes adapts, continues to make many of the same clothes season after season, indicating that he must feel his client is one whose style is likely to be a lifelong commitment. This consistency, with his perfectionism, sets him apart from his competitors.

LEFT:

Trouser suit and blanket, both by Lauren, 1983.

BELOW:

Ralph Lauren for girls, 1981.

Kenzo

RIGHT:
Exuberant Kenzo
turnout.

BELOW:
A portrait of
Kenzo.

FOR THE DECADE-AND-A-HALF HE HAS BEEN DESIGNING PRÊT-À-PORTER, Kenzo has achieved whimsically striking results with his combinations of patterns, fabrics, and inspirations. From the first, he has dismissed the French couture, feeling that it is "too perfect" and therefore no longer applicable to contemporary dressing. His clothes, inspired by the young, are made with the irreverent exuberance of the youth he constantly watches in the streets of Paris.

Kenzo Takada was born in Himeji, in the Hyogo region of southern Japan, in 1939. Dissatisfied with the literature studies prescribed by his traditional innkeeper parents, he fled to Tokyo where he worked as a house painter and took night courses in studio art before being accepted into the predominantly female student body of the Bunka Gakuen School of Fashion. In 1960 he won a Japanese fashion award and began working for the Sanai department stores as a designer of girl's clothing.

In 1965 he moved to Paris. Overwhelmed at first, he took time to acclimate himself, then assembled a collection of fashion designs, five of which were purchased by the designer Louis Feraud. During the next several years he worked for various department stores, the Pisanti textile group, and Relations Textiles before he took over a former antique clothing store in April 1970, painting the store himself, cutting and sewing a collection of his own designs, and taking the designs around to various magazines. By November he had moved to 28, passage Choiseul, and almost immediately his clothes attracted notice. By 1971, Jungle JAP designs were being featured in American *Vogue* as the newest developments in the Paris boutique scene. (The name Jungle JAP—chosen for fun because JAP sounded good with Jungle and the first boutique had Rousseau landscapes for its decorative theme—caused an uproar in America, bringing Kenzo to begin using his own name.) These first collections revealed Kenzo's predilection for simplified schoolchild shapes like pullover vests, knee-length shorts, minicoats, and sweater dresses, made fresh by such vaguely foreign nuances as kimono sleeves (unusual in knitted clothing), oversized berets, and Japanese textiles.

Since then he has moved twice, first to the rue Cherche Midi and then to bigger, more formal quarters on the Place des Victoires. And he has launched any number of fashions: cap-sleeved sweaters worn over long-sleeved ones; trousers bloused into leg-warmers; knitted wool or gathered taffeta bubble dresses; hip-wrapped looks of all sorts; and a revival of the minidress featuring a lowered waist with lots of ruffles. He is much influenced by folk costumes, interpreting such varied pieces as Spanish boleros, Austrian loden jackets, Indian

trousers, Chinese tunics, Bedouin blankets, and Breton aprons, in appropriately ethnic fabrics, new or wild colors, or in East Asian batiks or Japanese woven textiles. Widely imitated, he has recently signed an agreement to be his own copyist. For the American concern The Limited he will design four collections a year in addition to the two French ones he also completes.

The diversity in Kenzo's range of design influences is seconded only by the cultural extremes he has experienced in his own life. From a traditional upbringing in Japan, to adopting France as home, to naming his perfume King Kong and transforming himself into a perfect replica of Minnie Mouse for his much-talked-about fortieth birthday bash, he has left no stone unturned. He has also remained the prototype of the young designer, the designer with a sense of humor about fashion, culture, and life, as well as a lively curiosity about clothing itself.

LEFT:
Suits with smock blouses from summer 1984.

ABOVE RIGHT:
Summer coats from 1984.

Giorgio Armani

S PORTSWEAR USED TO REFER TO THE CLOTHES WORN FOR ACTIVE sports, and in the case of women these were borrowed, in principle if not in fact, from their men. From riding habits came *tailleurs* for street and town wear and it wasn't until the Teens and Twenties that Chanel changed the direction of this increasingly tailored progression. When she appropriated both the details and the scale of men's clothing, turning a sports jacket into an overcoat or a tennis sweater into a jersey dress, women's clothing became "easy."

Giorgio Armani, often described as the "Chanel of the Eighties," has drawn upon the concepts of menswear dressing once again. Casting aside the Twenties fascination with the English nobleman's cast-offs and the Fifties fondness for Dad's shirt, he brings to his women's clothing an all-Italian tradition of natty precision. Like Chanel's, his translation is not a literal one. Armani's touch is also one of ease, stemming from an almost Spartan scorn for the trappings of the aristocracy, from antiques to formality of any kind. What Armani has done for women's clothing is exactly what he had done earlier for men's: rendered meaningless the chasm between the business uniform and the clothing worn for leisure, managing in all his designs to improve upon that insouciant perfection of the thing cadged from one's lover, recreating the beauty of the thing already worn in.

Born in 1934 in Piacenza, Italy, Giorgio Armani gave in to his family's wishes that he attend medical school, but after two years left for military service as a medical assistant. Almost incidentally, his first civilian job, in the mid-Fifties, was with the large Milanese department store La Rinascente, where his window displays were considered too avant-garde and he was transferred into the buying office. It was there that Armani learned not only about merchandising but also about fashion. A talented buyer has to be as aware and full of conviction as a designer, for he often has direct control over what garments will actually be produced from a line, modifying designs and demanding special colors and fabrics as he goes. After seven years in buying, Armani joined the Cerruti empire as a designer in 1961, breaking away to form his own business with his friend, former architectural draftsman Sergio Galeotti, in 1970. For five years he freelanced for various manufacturers, launching his own label in 1975 with the founding of Giorgio Armani Company. Today he designs five hundred items a year for twenty-nine different collections, ranging from his luxury line, Giorgio Armani, to the lower-priced Mani (known in this country as Giorgio Armani U.S.A.). His holdings include the chain of Emporio Armani shops, and he designs leathers for Mario Valentino and uniforms for the Italian Air Force.

RIGHT:
N *on-suit suit from Armani, 1985.*

BELOW:
A *rmani blazer, 1983.*

Perhaps nothing epitomizes the Armani style, which entails combatting rigidity, emphasizing fine tailoring, and taking a traditional item and making it new again, better than the blazer, which in his hands became loose-fitting, unlined, wrinkleable. The unconstructed blazer was successful for men, but Armani's women's version has singlehandedly dominated recent fashion, supplanting the dress-for-success look of matching jacket and skirt. "I love jackets," Armani told Bernadine Morris for the *New York Times*, "I always try and do something new with them." While the novelty may take the form of adding an extra pair of sleeves, tied like a scarf, more usually it is a play on proportion, texture, and color. Armani has made blazers as long as the skirts he shows with them, and he has cropped them, almost to a nipped-in waist, with very wide shoulders. He teams a blazer, in one of his specially designed patterned wools, with a skirt or pair of shorts, trousers, or culottes in a corresponding pattern. He experiments with role and function, transforming a topcoat into a dress, a vest into an overcoat, a second blouse knotted at the hips into a sash. His cut, while always impeccable, is not restricted by an allegiance to close fit, and he is capable of cutting a lapel to hang in a perfectly engineered but seemingly casual fold where the jacket buttons.

The most famous of a new breed of Italian designers—the Milanese group that includes Gianni Versace, Gianfranco Ferre, Mariucci Mandelli for Krizia, Laura Biagotti, and Luciano Soprani for Basile —Armani represents a break with the couture tradition. For him as well as for his colleagues, couture sportswear is its own entity. This group doesn't concentrate on a collection of elaborate evening dresses designed to attract the attention of the press and whose expense is underwritten by the profits of their other endeavors. Armani designs evening clothes, but not the kind that can be worn only by a rarefied and aristocratic few. Like all his clothes, they reflect a sensibility that derives from sportswear, and ultimately from decades spent dressing not women, but men.

RIGHT:

A*rmani's trompe l'oeil lapels, 1985.*

BELOW:

A *portrait of Giorgio Armani.*

Issey Miyake

H E IS NOT THE FIRST JAPANESE FASHION DESIGNER TO FIND AN INTER-
national audience, but he is the best known for an aesthetic that is
rooted in Japanese perceptions, customs, and values. If Hanae Mori
went to Paris to work within the couture tradition, and Kenzo to plug
into the energy of the prêt-à-porter, then Issey Miyake undertook something more ambitious and cerebral. After living in Paris and New
York, and being overwhelmed by the blue-jeans culture, he wanted to
do something intentionally pervasive, and as indigenous, but to his
own heritage. Once home, he searched for fabrics and shapes that
would provide a Japanese equivalent. What he came up with not only
assured him a place as a designer of international stature, it launched
Tokyo as a new fashion capital, one that found its inspiration not in
New York or Paris, but in itself.

Born in Hiroshima in 1939, Miyake attended the Tama Art University for five years, during which time he assembled his first fashion
collection, which he named "The Poem of Material and Stone." He
moved to Paris where he studied at the school of the Chambre Syndicale
de la Couture Parisienne and worked as an assistant to Guy Laroche
and Givenchy. Next was New York, where he served as a ready-to-
wear designer for Geoffrey Beene. When he returned to Tokyo in
1970, he founded the Issey Miyake Design Studio. By 1971 he had a
boutique of his own at Bloomingdale's.

Sashiko, a quilted cotton traditionally used for both workers' clothes
and for practitioners of the martial arts, was among the first native
materials Miyake chose for his contemporary fashions. He has since
gone on to investigate all forms of Japanese costume. Like Schiaparelli,
he has decorated thin jersey clothes with patterns from the great Japanese tattoo artists (and unlike her, dedicated his to the departed
souls of Janis Joplin, Jimi Hendrix, and Marilyn Monroe). His wire
constructions, lacquered and woven bamboo structures, and his molded
plastic pieces make reference to samurai armor. While the transparent woven bamboo and the realistic molding of the plastic tantalize,
their stiffness and defensiveness paradoxically repel and inhibit. He
has sought to utilize the principles of origami in folded clothing and
has even used a fabric called *tabi-ura*, formerly reserved for the bot-
toms of the fitted Japanese sock.

Miyake's use of wrapping and tying techniques for the fastenings of
his clothes is also based on Japanese tradition. The kimono, for instance, has no closure and is secured by the tying at the waist of the
obi. During his apprenticeship in the haute couture, Miyake became
impatient with the reverence accorded old-time methods of pattern-
making and began to feel that complicated and expensive workman-

RIGHT:
M iyake invests the wearer
with much of the
responsibility of the
designing process.

BELOW:
A 1984 dress-robe.

ship was lessening the importance of constructed clothes. As a result, he makes clothes more like the mantles worn by eighteenth-century Buddhist priests, where patchwork rectangles were meant to suggest the humility of tatters, while in actuality they were stitched from the finest of antique brocades out of respect to the stature of these wise men.

The most alien aspect of his design, and the most difficult to understand, is the space it maintains between body and garment. Designed to be applied to the body in multiple ways and with multiple meanings, the clothes are not constructed on the model as a second skin. Rather, Miyake invests the wearer with much of the responsibility of the designing process—the decision of how to wear the clothes. In addition to choosing the draping of a piece, the wearer can work with textural and color relationships in the combinations of the traditional Japanese fabrics. Besides the quilted cottons (also made in knitted form), basket-woven straw, black, gray, and indigo *ikats*, Japanese tie-dyed, puckered, and paper cloths, Miyake uses fabrics described by him as "whisker" linen, "downy hair" knit, and "dobby" double-weave linen.

Miyake is not alone in refining and purveying this inherently Japanese vision. In the late Seventies and early Eighties the West also became acquainted with other Japanese designers, including Kansai Yamamoto, Rei Kawakubo (who designs for the label *Comme des Garçons*), Yohji Yamamoto, and Mitsuhiro Matsudo. As a group, they make clothing that Karl Lagerfeld told the *New York Times Magazine* is forward looking. "They are so much better educated for the future," he continued. "They can be happy in a changing world. They don't compare clothes to the past as we do. They want the future."

Miyake, who has used avant-garde elements like laser-printed fabrics, is urging us into a new period. His loose, even formless, clothes, in seeming celebration of androgyny, mock the perfect-toned "me decade" body. In fashion, even the future is retrospective. With Miyake we have come back to the time when the couturier/designer provides the client with cloth to be used in any way the client sees fit.

LEFT:

Dobby weave poncho over sun-dried tunic and pants.

BELOW:

Antonio drawing of a Miyake turnout.

Bibliography

Adburgham, Alison. *Liberty's: A Biography of a Shop*. London: Allen & Unwin, 1975.

_____. *Shopping in Style: London from the Restoration to Edwardian Elegance*. London: Thames & Hudson, 1979.

Adolfus, F. *Some Memories of Paris*. New York: Henry Holt & Co., 1895.

Alsop, Susan Mary. *To Marietta: Letters from Paris, 1945–1960*. Garden City, N.Y.: Doubleday, 1975.

American Women of Style. New York: Costume Institute, Metropolitan Museum of Art, 1975.

Amies, Hardy. *Still Here*. London: Weidenfeld & Nicolson, 1984.

Baedeker, Karl. *Paris and Environs with Routes from London to Paris*. Leipzig: K. Baedeker, 1907, 1924, 1931.

Baillen, Claude. *Chanel Solitaire*. New York: Quadrangle, 1974.

Ballard, Bettina. *In My Fashion*. New York: David McKay, 1960.

Balmain, Pierre. *My Years and Seasons*. Garden City, N.Y.: Doubleday, 1965.

Barthes, Roland. *The Fashion System*. New York: Hill & Wang, 1983.

Batterberry, Michael, and Arlane Batterberry. *Mirror, Mirror*. New York: Holt, Rinehart & Winston, 1977.

Beaton, Cecil. *The Glass of Fashion*. London: Weidenfeld & Nicolson, 1954.

Bell, Quentin. *On Human Finery*. New York: Schocken Books, 1976.

La Belle Epoque. New York: Costume Institute, Metropolitan Museum of Art, 1982.

Bender, Marylin. *The Beautiful People*. New York: Coward-McCann, 1967.

Bentley, Nicolas. *The Victorian Scene: A Picture Book of the Period 1837–1901*. London: Weidenfeld & Nicolson, 1968.

Bernhard, Barbara. *Fashion in the 60s*. New York: St. Martin's, 1978.

Bertin, Celia. *Paris à la Mode*. London: Gollancz, 1956.

Black, J. Anderson, and Madge Garland. *A History of Fashion*. New York: Morrow, 1980.

Blum, Stella. *Victorian Fashions & Costume from Harper's Bazar, 1867–1898*. New York: Dover, 1974.

_____, and Louise Hamer. *Fabulous Fashion, 1907–1967*. New York: Costume Institute, Metropolitan Museum of Art, 1967.

Bond, David. *The Guinness Guide to Twentieth Century Fashion*. Middlesex, England: Guinness Superlatives Ltd., 1981.

Bonney, Therese, and Louise Bonney. *A Shopper's Guide to Paris*. New York: Robert M. McBride & Co., 1929.

Brady, James. *Superchic*. Boston: Little, Brown, 1974.

Brady, Maxine. *Bloomingdale's*. New York: Harcourt Brace Jovanovich, 1980.

Brainerd, Eleanor Hoyt. *In Vanity Fair: A Tale of Frocks and Femininity*. New York: Moffat, Yard & Co., 1906.

Bricktop [pseud.], and James Haskins. *Bricktop by Bricktop*. New York: Atheneum, 1983.

Brummell, Beau. *Male and Female Costume*. Garden City, N.Y.: Doubleday Doran & Co., 1932.

Burchell, S. C. *Imperial Masquerade: The Paris of Napoleon III*. New York: Atheneum, 1971.

Burris-Meyer, Elizabeth. *This Is Fashion*. New York: Harper, 1943.

Les Cahiers de la République des Sciences et des Arts. De la Mode, no. 39. Paris: Les Beaux Arts, rue de la Boetie.

Carter, Ernestine. *Twentieth Century Fashion, a Scrapbook: 1900 to Today*. London: Eyre Methuen, 1975.

_____. *The Changing World of Fashion*. New York: Putnam's, 1977.

_____. *Magic Names of Fashion*. Englewood Cliffs, N.J.: Prentice-Hall, 1980.

Cassin-Scott, Jack. *Costume and Fashion in Color, 1760–1920*. New York: Macmillan, 1971.

Chambers, Bernice. *Fashion Fundamentals*. New York: Prentice-Hall, 1947.

The Chanel Wardrobe and Casket of Costume Jewelry (catalogue). London: Christie Manson & Woods, December 1978.

Charles-Roux, Edmonde. *Chanel: Her Life, Her World and the Woman behind the Legend She Created*. New York: Knopf, 1975.

_____. *Chanel and Her World*. London: Weidenfeld & Nicolson, 1979.

Chase, Edna Woolman, and Ilka Chase. *Always in Vogue*. London: Gollancz, 1954.

Churchill, Allen. *The Upper Crust: An Informal History of New York's Highest Society*. Englewood Cliffs, N.J.: Prentice-Hall, 1970.

Coleman, Elizabeth Ann. *Changing Fashions, 1800–1970*. New York: Brooklyn Museum, 1972.

_____. *The Genius of Charles James*. New York: Brooklyn Museum, 1983.

Contini, Mila. *Fashion from Ancient Egypt to the Present Day*. New York: Crescent Books, 1965.

Crawford, M. D. C. *The Ways of Fashion*. New York: Fairchild, 1948.

Dache, Lilly. *Talking through My Hats*. New York: Coward-McCann, 1946.

Dahl-Wolfe, Louise. *A Photographer's Scrapbook*. New York: Marek, 1984.

Dariaux, Genevieve Antoine. *Elegance: A Complete Guide for Every Woman Who Wants To Be Well and Properly Dressed on All Occasions*. New York: Doubleday, 1964.

Dars, Christine. *A Fashion Parade: The Seeberger Collection*. London: Blond & Briggs, 1979.

d'Assailly, Gisele. *Ages of Elegance: Five Thousand Years of Fashion and Frivolity*. Paris: Hachette, 1968.

De Forest, Katharine. *Paris As It Is: An Intimate Account of Its People, Its Homelife and Its Places of Interest*. New York: Doubleday Page & Co., 1900.

De Gramont, Elisabeth. *La Femme et la Robe*. Paris: La Palatine, 1952.

DeGraw, Imelda G. *25 Years, 25 Couturiers*. Denver: Denver Museum, 1975.

DeMarly, Diana. *The History of the Haute Couture, 1850–1950*. London: Batsford, 1980.

_____. *Worth: Father of the Haute Couture*. New York: Holmes & Meir, 1980.

de Osma, Guillermo. *Mariano Fortuny: His Life and Work*. New York: Rizzoli, 1980.

de Pougy, Liane. *My Blue Notebooks*. New York: Harper & Row, 1980.

Descaves, Lucien, ed. *The Color of Paris: Historic, Personal and Local, by Messieurs les Académiciens Goncourt*. New York: Dodd, Mead & Co.

Deschodt, Anne-Marie. *Mariano Fortuny, un Magiciende Venise*. Tours, France: Editions du Regard, 1979.

Devlin, Polly. *Vogue Book of Fashion Photography, 1919–1979*. New York: Simon & Schuster, 1979.

di Grappa, Carol, ed. *Fashion: Theory*. New York: Lustrum Press, 1980.

Dior, Christian. *Dior by Dior*. London: Weidenfeld & Nicolson, 1957.

_____. *Talking about Fashion*. New York: Putnam's, 1954.

The Doges of Fashion: Disguise or Reality? Venice: Lanerossi, 1984.

Dorner, Jane. *Fashion: The Changing Shape of Fashion through the Years*. London: Octopus Books, 1974.

_____. *Fashion in the 40s and 50s*. London: Ian Allen, 1975.

Duff Gordon, Lady. *Discretions and Indiscretions*. London: Jarrolds, 1934.

B I B L I O G R A P H Y

417

Elégance et Création: Paris, 1945–1975. Paris: Musée de la Mode et du Costume, 1977.

Ellman, Richard. *The Artist as Critic: Critical Writings of Oscar Wilde*. Chicago: University of Chicago Press, 1968.

Erté. *Things I Remember*. New York: Quadrangle, 1975.

Etherington-Smith, Meredith. *Patou*. London: Hutchinson, 1983.

Evans, Mary. *Costume throughout the Ages*. Philadelphia: J. P. Lippincott Co., 1930.

Evolution of Fashion, 1835–1895. Kyoto: Kyoto Costume Institute, 1980.

Ewing, Elizabeth. *History of Twentieth Century Fashion*. London: Batsford, 1974.

Fairchild, John. *The Fashionable Savages*. Garden City, N.Y.: Doubleday, 1965.

Fairley, Roma. *A Bomb in the Collection: Fashion with the Lid Off*. Brighton, England: Clifton Books, 1969.

Fashion, 1900–1939. London: Scottish Arts Council; Victoria and Albert Museum, 1975.

Feldon, Leah. *Womanstyle*. New York: Potter, 1979.

Ferragamo, Salvatore. *Shoemaker of Dreams*. New York: Crown, 1972.

Fine Fashion. Philadelphia: Museum of Art, 1979.

Flanner, Janet. *Paris Was Yesterday, 1925–1939*. New York: Viking, 1972.

Fogarty, Anne. *Wife Dressing: The Fine Art of Being a Well-Dressed Wife*. New York: Julian Messner, 1959.

Fontenoy, Marquise de [Marguerite Cunliffe-Owens]. *Eve's Glossary: The Guidebook of a Mondaine*. Chicago: Herbert S. Stone, 1897.

Fortuny. New York: Fashion Institute of Technology, 1981.

Fortuny nella Belle Epoque. Milan: Electa, 1984.

Forty Years of Italian Fashion, 1940–1980 [organized by Bonizza Giordani Aragno]. Rome: The Made in Ltd., Fidevrart, 1983.

Fraser, Kennedy. *The Fashionable Mind: Reflections of Fashion, 1970–1981*. New York: Knopf, 1981.

Galante, Pierre. *Mademoiselle Chanel*. Chicago: Regnery, 1973.

Gallico, Paul. *Mrs. 'Arris Goes to Paris*. Garden City, N.Y.: Doubleday, 1960.

Garland, Madge. *The Changing Form of Fashion*. London: Dent, 1970.

Gersheim, Alison. *Victorian and Edwardian Fashion: A Photographic Survey*. New York: Dover, 1981.

Ginsburg, Madeline, comp. *Fashion, an Anthology*. London: Victoria and Albert Museum, 1971.

Glyn, Anthony [Sir Geofffrey Leo Simon Dart Davson]. *Elinor Glyn: A Biography*. Garden City, N.Y.: Doubleday, 1955.

Glynn, Prudence. *In Fashion*. New York: Allen & Unwin, 1978.

———. *Skin to Skin*. New York: Oxford University Press, 1982.

Gold, Arthur, and Robert Fitzdale. *Misia*. New York: Morrow Quill, 1981.

Greer, Howard. *Designing Male*. New York: Putnam's, 1951.

Haedrich, Marcel. *Coco Chanel: Her Life, Her Secrets*. Boston: Little, Brown, 1972.

Hall-Duncan, Nancy. *The History of Fashion Photography*. New York: Alpine Book Co., 1979.

Hamburger, Estelle. *Fashion Business: It's All Yours*. San Francisco: Canfield Press, 1976.

Hartley, L. P. *Eustace and Hilda: A Trilogy*. London: Faber & Faber, 1958.

Hartnell, Norman. *Silver and Gold*. London: Evans, 1955.

Haute Couture: Notes on Designers and Their Clothes in the Collection of the Royal Ontario Museum. Toronto: Royal Ontario Museum, 1969.

Hawes, Elizabeth. *Fashion Is Spinach*. New York: Random House, 1938.

———. *It's Still Spinach*. Boston: Little, Brown, 1954.

Head, Edith. *The Dress Doctor*. Boston: Little, Brown, 1959.

Hemline, Neckline, Streamline. University Park: Museum of Art, Pennsylvania State University, 1981.

Hibbert, Christopher. *The Royal Victorians: King Edward VII, His Family and His Friends*. Philadelphia: J. B. Lippincott, 1976.

A History of Fashion. London: House of Worth.

Hollander, Anne. *Seeing through Clothes*. New York: Avon, 1975.

Hommage à Schiaparelli. Paris: Musée de la Mode et du Costume, 1984.

Hommage aux Donateurs: Modes Françaises du XVIII Siècles à nos Jours. Paris: Musée de la Mode et du Costume, 1980.

Houck, Catherine. *The Fashion Encyclopedia*. New York: St. Martin's, 1982.

The House of Worth. New York: Brooklyn Museum, 1962.

The House of Worth: The Gilded Age, 1860–1918. New York: Museum of the City of New York, 1982.

Howell, Georgina. *In Vogue*. New York: Schocken, 1976.

Hulanicki, Barbara. *From A to Biba*. London: Hutchinson, 1983.

Immagini e Materiali del Laboratorio Fortuny. Venice: Comune di Venezia Marsilio Edition, 1978.

Jachimowicz, Elizabeth. *Eight Chicago Women and Their Fashion, 1860–1926*. Chicago: Chicago Historical Society, 1978.

Josephy, Helen, and Mary Margaret McBride. *Paris Is a Woman's Town*. New York: Coward-McCann, 1929.

Keenan, Brigid. *The Women We Wanted to Look Like*. New York: St. Martin's, 1977.

———. *Dior in Vogue*. New York: Crown, 1981.

Kennett, Frances. *The Collector's Book of Fashion*. New York: Crown, 1983.

Khornak, Lucille. *Fashion 2001*. New York: Viking, 1982.

Konig, Rene. *The Restless Image: A Sociology of Fashion*. London: Allen & Unwin, 1973.

Laker, Rosalind. *Banners of Silk*. New York: Doubleday, 1981.

Lambert, Eleanor. *The World of Fashion: People, Places, Resources*. New York: R. R. Bowker, 1976.

Langlade, Emile. *Rose Bertin: The Creator of Fashion at the Court of Marie Antoinette*. New York: Scribner's, 1913.

Langner, Lawrence. *The Importance of Wearing Clothes*. New York: Hastings House, 1959.

Latour, Anny. *Kings of Fashion*. New York: Coward-McCann, 1956.

Laver, James, ed. *Costume through the Ages*. New York: Simon & Schuster, 1963.

———. *Fashion, Art and Beauty*. New York: Costume Institute, Metropolitan Museum of Art, 1967.

———. *The Concise History of Costume and Fashion*. New York: Scribner's, 1969.

Lee, Sarah Tomerlin, ed. *American Fashion*. New York: Quadrangle, 1975.

Leigh, Dorian, and Laura Hobe. *The Girl Who Had Everything*. Garden City, N.Y.: Doubleday, 1980.

Lesse, Elizabeth. *Costume Design at the Movies*. New York: Frederick Ungar, 1977.

Levin, Phyllis Lee. *The Wheels of Fashion*. New York: Doubleday, 1965.

Loos, Anita. *A Girl Like I*. New York: Viking, 1966.

Lurie, Alison. *The Language of Clothes*. New York: Random House, 1981.

Lydig, Mrs. Philip. *Tragic Mansions*. New York: Boni & Liveright, 1927.

Lynam, Ruth. *Couture*. New York: Doubleday, 1972.

Madsen, Axel. *Living for Design: The Yves Saint Laurent Story*. New York: Delacorte Press, 1979.

Maxwell, Elsa. *R.S.V.P. Elsa Maxwell's Own Story.* Boston: Little, Brown, 1954.

McConathy, Dale, and Diana Vreeland. *Hollywood Costume.* New York: Abrams, 1976.

Mendes, Valerie D. *Twentieth Century Fashion: An Introduction to Women's Fashionable Dress, 1900 to 1980.* London: Victoria and Albert Museum, 1981.

Miyake, Issey. *East Meets West.* Tokyo: Heibonsha, 1978.

La Mode et ses Métiers du XVIII Siècle à nos Jours. Paris: Musée de la Mode et du Costume, 1981.

Mohrt, Françoise. *30 Ans d'Elégance et de Créations Rochas Mode, 1925–1955.* Paris: Jacques Damase, 1983.

Moore, Doris Langley. *Fashion through Fashion Plates, 1771–1970.* New York: Potter, 1971.

Morand, Paul. *Lewis and Irene.* New York: Boni & Liveright, 1925.

Morishita, Hiromo. *Inventive Clothes.* Kyoto: Kyoto Chamber of Commerce, 1975.

Mulassano, Adriana, and Alfa Castaldi. *I Mass-Moda: Fatti e Personaggi dell'Italian Look.* Florence: Spinelli, 1979.

Nicolson, Nigel. *Mary Curzon.* New York: Harper & Row, 1977.

Nuzzi, Christina. *Parisian Fashion.* New York: Rizzoli, 1980.

Packer, William. *Fashion Drawing in Vogue.* New York: Coward-McCann, 1983.

Palmer, Gretta. *A Shopping Guide to New York.* New York: McBride, 1930.

Paul Iribe, Précurseur de l'Art Deco. Paris: Bibliothèque Forney, 1983.

Penn, Irving, and Diana Vreeland. *Inventive Paris Clothes, 1909–1939.* New York: Viking, 1977.

Perkins, Alice K. *Paris Couturiers and Milliners.* New York: Fairchild, 1949.

Pickens, Mary Brooks. *The Fashion Dictionary.* New York: Funk & Wagnalls, 1957.

_____, and Dora Loves Miller. *Dressmakers of France.* New York: Harper, 1956.

Poiret, Paul. *King of Fashion: The Autobiography of Paul Poiret.* Philadelphia: J. B. Lippincott, 1931.

Polan, Brenda, ed. *The Fashion Year, 1938.* London: Zomba Books, 1983.

Richardson, Joanna. *La Vie Parisienne, 1852–1870.* New York: Viking, 1971.

Riley, Robert. *The Fashion Makers.* New York: Crown, 1968.

_____. *Givenchy: 30 Years.* New York: Fashion Institute of Technology, 1982.

Robinson, Julian. *Fashion in the Forties.* New York: Harcourt Brace Jovanovich, 1976.

_____. *The Golden Age of Style: Art Deco Fashion Illustration.* New York: Harcourt Brace Jovanovich, 1976.

_____. *Fashion in the Thirties.* London: Oresko Books, 1978.

Roshco, Bernard. *The Rag Race.* New York: Funk & Wagnalls, 1963.

Rudofsky, Bernard. *The Unfashionable Human Body.* New York: Anchor Press, 1974.

Rykiel, Sonia. *Et je la voudrais hue . . .* Paris: Bernard Grasset, 1979.

Saunders, Edith. *The Age of Worth, Couturier to the Empress Eugénie.* Bloomington: Indiana University Press, 1955.

Scavullo, Francesco. *Scavullo on Men.* New York: Random House, 1977.

_____. *Scavullo on Women.* New York: Harper & Row, 1982.

Schiaparelli, Elsa. *Shocking Life.* New York: Dutton, 1954.

Schreier, Barbara. *Mystique and Identity: Women's Fashions in the 1950s.* Norfolk, Va.: Chrysler Museum, 1984.

Seebohm, Caroline. *The Man Who Was Vogue.* New York: Viking, 1982.

Spanier, Ginette. *It Isn't All Mink.* London: Collins, 1959.

Stegemeyer, Ann. *Who's Who in Fashion.* New York: Fairchild, 1980.

Thurlow, Valerie. *Model in Paris.* London: Robert Hale, 1975.

Toklas, Alice B. *A New French Style.* Paris: J. F. Verly, 1946.

Trahey, Jane, ed. *Harper's Bazaar: 100 Years of the American Female.* New York: Random House, 1967.

Uzanne, Octave. *Fashions in Paris, 1787–1897.* New York: Scribner's, 1898.

Vanderbilt, Gloria. *Woman to Woman.* New York: Doubleday, 1979.

Vreeland, Diana. *Allure.* New York: Doubleday, 1980.

_____. *D.V.* New York: Knopf, 1984.

Watkins, Josephine Ellis, comp. *Who's Who in Fashion.* New York: Fairchild, 1975.

Waxman, Frances Shaefer. *A Shopping Guide to Paris and London.* New York: McBride, Nast and Comdan, 1912.

White, Emily, ed. *Fashion 85.* New York: St. Martin's, 1985.

White, Palmer. *Poiret.* New York: Potter, 1973.

Whiteman, Von. *Looking Back at Fashion, 1901–1939.* West Yorkshire, England: EP Publishing, 1978.

Wilcox, R. Turner. *The Mode in Costume.* New York: Scribner's, 1958.

Wiser, William. *The Crazy Years: Paris in the Twenties.* New York: Atheneum, 1983.

The World of Balenciaga. New York: Costume Institute, Metropolitan Museum of Art, 1972.

Worsley-Gough, Barbara. *Fashions in London.* London: Allan Wingate, 1952.

Worth, Jean-Philippe. *A Century of Fashion.* Boston: Little, Brown, 1928.

Yoxall, H. W. *A Fashion of Life.* New York: Taplinger, 1967.

Yves Saint Laurent. New York: Costume Institute, Metropolitan Museum of Art, 1983.

Zeldin, Theodore. *The French.* New York: Vintage, 1984.

PERIODICALS

American Fashions and Fabrics
L'Art et la Mode
Art, Gout, Beauté
Connoisseur
Les Elégances Parisiennes
Elle
Femina
La Femme Chic
Flair
Gazette du Bon Genre
Gazette du Bon Ton
Glamour
Godey's Magazine
Interview
Le Jardin des Modes
Life
Mademoiselle
Les Modes
New York Times
L'Officiel
The Tattler
Theatre Arts
Time
Town & Country
Vanity Fair
Vogue
W
Women's Wear Daily (WWD)

Index of Designers

ADRIAN

Pages 10, 195, 204–211, 222, 302, 352
After a successful career designing for the movies, Gilbert Adrian formed Adrian, Ltd. in 1941, with headquarters in Beverly Hills. He retired in 1952 and thereafter briefly designed a line of men's shirts and ties.

HARDY AMIES

Pages 194, 351, 382–387
Amies began designing under his own name in 1941. After the war he opened his house at 14 Savile Row, where his house is today. His design partner is Ken Fleetwood.

ARMANI

Pages 351, 408–411
Giorgio Armani began designing under his own name in 1974. Today, besides his top-level line, he designs both an Emporio Armani collection, and a line known in Italy as Mani and in the U.S.A. as Giorgio Armani.

Balmain

AUGUSTABERNARD

Pages 118, 156–157, 168
In 1919, Augustabernard opened her house in the rue Rivoli; in 1928 she moved to 3, rue du Faubourg St-Honoré, where she remained in business until 1935.

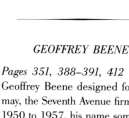

BALENCIAGA

Pages 11, 18, 134, 173, 196, 264, 289, 292, 298, 312, 318, 320–327, 342, 372
Balenciaga opened his house on the Avenue Georges V in 1937 where he remained until retiring in 1968.

Augustabernard

Eisa was the name of his Spanish couture houses in Madrid and Barcelona.

BALMAIN

Pages 216, 230, 238, 250, 252–257, 264, 286
Balmain opened his house at 44, rue François Premier in 1945. In addition to his first couture label, he has designed numerous boutique accessories and other lines. Since his death in 1982, his former righthand man, Erik Mortensen, has been the house's premier designer.

GEOFFREY BEENE

Pages 351, 388–391, 412
Geoffrey Beene designed for Harmay, the Seventh Avenue firm, from 1950 to 1957, his name sometimes featured in ads for the house. At Traina, Inc., where he next worked, his name appeared on the company label. He started designing for himself in 1962, opening Geoffrey Beene, Inc., on Seventh Avenue. Since then his label has appeared on an ever-growing number of lines.

BILL BLASS

Pages 231, 302–307, 384
After designing for the now defunct Seventh Avenue firm of Anna Miller, Ltd., Bill Blass worked with Maurice Rentner in 1959. By 1960 the company's advertisements read "Bill Blass for Maurice Rentner," and by 1961 he was made a vice president. Bill Blass, Ltd., was founded in 1970.

Balmain

Blass

BOUÉ SOEURS

Pages 23, 70–73
Mme. Sylvie Boué Montegut and the Baronne D'Etreillis (née Boué) founded their house in 1899 at 9, rue de la Paix. Their New York branch opened around 1916 and the house stayed in business through 1931.

CALLOT SOEURS

Pages 23, 40, 60–63, 158, 160
The House of Callot Soeurs, at 24, rue Taitbout, was founded in 1895 by Mesdames Marie Callot Gerber, Marthe Callot Bertrand, and Regina Callot Chantrelle. In 1914 the house moved to 9–11, Avenue Matignon and it was around this time that it began dating its labels. During the 1920s, Callot established branches in Nice, Biarritz, Buenos Aires, and London. By the time Mme. Gerber retired in 1937, the branches had closed and the house was absorbed into another house, Calvet. Designs continued to appear bearing the Callot label, however, until Calvet closed in 1948.

ROBERTO CAPUCCI

Pages 319, 336–337
Capucci opened his first *sartoria* in Rome in 1950. Ten years later he moved to Paris, to the rue Cambon, where he remained for six years. Back in Rome in 1966, he established his house in the Via Gregoriano, where it remains today.

PIERRE CARDIN

Pages 319, 338–341, 384
After working at the houses of Paquin, Schiaparelli, and Dior, Pierre Cardin founded his own house in 1950 in the rue Riche-

Callot Soeurs

Roberto Capucci

panse, presenting his first collection in 1953. His boutique, Eve, opened in 1954 at 118, rue du Faubourg St-Honoré, followed by Adam in 1957. In 1959 he established both a men's couture line and a prêt-à-porter line for women. Since then his boutiques, labels, and locations around the world have been countless.

BONNIE CASHIN

Pages 210, 350, 364–365
After costuming over forty Hollywood movies, Bonnie Cashin moved to New York in 1949 to try her hand at sportswear. Bonnie Cashin Limited was founded in 1953, and from her studio she has turned out designs for various manufacturers, most notably Phillip Sills and Ballantyne. In 1972 she established the Knittery for the manufacture of hand-knitted clothing from hand-spun yarns.

CHANEL

Pages 10, 14, 84, 118, 119, 120–137, 141, 148, 149, 163, 173, 194, 195, 196, 200, 202, 218, 224, 240, 274, 312, 314, 323, 354, 360, 408
Chanel began her hat business in 1908 in a basement apartment at 160, Boulevard Malesherbes. In 1912 she moved to 21, rue Cambon. Her houses in Deauville and Biarritz were opened in 1913 and 1916, respectively. In 1928 she moved into three floors of 31, rue Cambon, closing the house from 1939 to 1954. Following her death in 1971, her assistants Yvonne Dudel and Jean Cazaubon took over designing the couture, with Philippe Guibourgé in charge of the Chanel Boutique, launched in 1976. Accessories have been designed by Frances Stein since 1981, and in 1984, Karl Lagerfeld

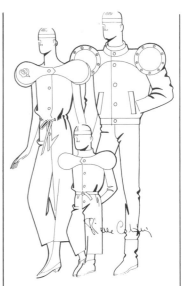

Pierre Cardin

Chanel

formally and officially took over as designer of both couture and ready-to-wear.

COURRÈGES

Pages 11, 319, 324, 342–347
After working for Balenciaga for ten years, André Courrèges opened his own house in 1961 at 48, Avenue Kleber. In 1965 he relocated to 40, rue François Premier and inaugurated his system of fashion levels. Prototypes is the label for the haute couture and Couture Future the deluxe ready-to-wear. In 1970 he added another tier, Hyperbole, for younger clients and budgets.

OSCAR DE LA RENTA

Pages 231, 298–301
Oscar de la Renta worked in Balenciaga's Eisa atelier in Madrid and in Paris for Antonio del Castillo before becoming a designer at Elizabeth Arden, New York, where his designs appeared as "by Oscar de la Renta for Elizabeth Arden." In 1965, after two years there, he began designing for Jane Derby, and it wasn't long before his name appeared alone on the label. Since Derby's death, the company has been known as Oscar de la Renta.

JEAN DESSÈS

Pages 230, 274–275, 280
Jean Dessès worked for the couture house Jane in the rue de la Paix beginning in 1925. In 1937 he opened his own house at 37, Avenue Georges V, moving in 1948 into the mansion formerly owned by the Eiffel family at 17, Avenue Matignon. From 1958 until his retirement in 1963, he was located at No. 12, Rond-Point-des-Champs-Elysées. In 1955 he inaugurated

Jean Dessès

Dior

both a prêt-à-porter line known as Diffusions and a boutique in Athens.

DIOR

Pages 10, 230, 231, 232–245, 250, 252, 254, 264, 286, 302, 310, 312, 314, 320, 323, 338
Christian Dior worked for both Robert Piguet and Lucien Lelong before opening his own house in 1947 at 30, Avenue Montaigne. In 1953 he hired the young Yves Saint Laurent, who, by 1955, was designing for the house and, upon Dior's death in 1957, was chosen to succeed him. Marc Bohan became the house couturier in 1960. Ready-to-wear was designed by Philippe Guibourgé during the 1970s and by Gérard Penneroux beginning in 1983. Christian Dior–New York began in 1949, and the London operation in 1955. Baby Dior was born in 1969; Miss Dior in 1966.

DOUCET

Pages 22, 38–40, 76, 160, 194
When Jacques Doucet established his *maison de couture* in 1871, it was a division of a house established over fifty years earlier by his grandmother as a lace shop on the Boulevard Saint-Martin. The house had moved in 1837 to 17, rue de la Paix and had been divided by Edouard Doucet in 1869 into two adjoining shops: a chemisier for men and a ladies' shop for lace and lace-trimmed lingerie. The couture house of Doucet was located next door at 21, rue de la Paix. Poiret worked there as a designer from 1897 to 1900 as did Vionnet (around 1903 to 1908). Jacques Doucet died in 1929 and his house merged to form Doueillet–Doucet, which lasted until 1932.

Dior

PERRY ELLIS

Pages 202, 351, 392–397
Perry Ellis worked as a department store sportswear buyer before joining John Meyer of Norwich as a design director in 1968. From there he went to Vera Companies in 1974, designing a line for them in 1975 with his own label: Portfolio. Perry Ellis Sportswear, Inc. was launched in 1978. In 1985 Perry Ellis revived the lesser-priced Portfolio line and, in addition, began to design an America line for Levi Strauss.

JACQUES FATH

Pages 230, 250, 264–269, 286
Jacques Fath opened his first couture house in 1937 at 32, rue de la Boëtie, moving in 1940 to rue François Premier and in 1944 to Avenue Pierre Premier de Serbie. He opened a New York boutique in 1951 and, beginning about 1950, designed ready-to-wear collections for Joseph Halpert that were sold all over the United States. In 1954 he initiated a line for young women called Fath Université. After his death that same year, his wife, Geneviève, operated the house until its closing in 1957.

FORTUNY

Pages 10, 78, 90, 92–99, 274, 352
Mariano Fortuny made his first garments in 1906, stencilled silk Knossos scarves for a Paris ballet performance. The following year he created his first pleated Delphos dress, patenting the process in 1909. By 1912 he was producing a large variety of stencilled velvet robes, cloaks, dresses, wall hangings, and cushions at his Palazzo Orfei in Venice, and displaying them in a Paris shop at 2, rue de

Perry Ellis

Marignon and one in London at 29 Maddox Street. By 1924 he had moved his Paris location to 67, rue Pierre Charron. After his death in 1949, the Contessa Gozzi, an associate and owner of the Fortuny shop at 509 Madison Avenue in New York, took over management of the Fortuny factory in Venice. Production of the pleated dresses halted in 1953 and Fortuny today produces only the stencilled cotton furnishing materials.

GALANOS

Pages 231, 294–297
James Galanos worked for Hattie Carnegie in New York, Robert Piguet in Paris, and Davidow back in New York before moving to Los Angeles and founding his own business in 1951. Since 1953 he has been showing his California-designed-and-made collections in New York.

GALLENGA

Pages 90, 100–101
Maria Monaci Gallenga was an artist who began making clothes in 1914, showing them in Rome and in Florence, where her studio was located in the Via de'Tornabuoni. She frequently incorporated her signature into the pattern of her materials. By the Twenties she sometimes also used a printed label.

GIVENCHY

Pages 194, 224, 231, 280, 286–293, 324, 412
Hubert de Givenchy worked for Jacques Fath, Robert Piguet, Lucien Lelong, and Schiaparelli before opening his own house in the Avenue Alfred de Vigny in

1952. In 1957 he relocated to his present address of 3, Avenue Georges V.

GRÈS

Pages 10, 118, 119, 150–155, 318, 354, 378
Born Germaine Barton, Grès briefly worked for the House of Premet before designing under a version of her own name, Alix Barton, at 8, rue Miromesnil. In 1934 she moved to 83, rue du Faubourg St-Honoré, where she was the head designer at Alix until 1940. She opened her own house in 1942 – adopting her husband's painting name of Grès – at 1, rue de la Paix, her present location. Her first prêt-à-porter collection was shown in spring 1985.

JACQUES GRIFFE

Pages 148, 230, 270–273
After working for a tailor in Toulouse, then in Paris for the House of Vionnet, Jacques Griffe opened his own house in the rue Gaillon in 1942. In 1946 he moved to 29, rue du Faubourg St-Honoré, moving again to take over Molyneux's establishment at 5, rue Royale in 1950. His boutique line was called Jacques Griffe Evolution and he also designed Griffe Prêt-à-porter. He retired in 1974.

HALSTON

Pages 119, 178–183, 362
Halston trained briefly with Charles James and with the milliner Lilly Daché before becoming the custom hat designer at New York's Bergdorf Goodman in 1958. He branched out from millinery when Bergdorf's gave him his own boutique in 1966. Halston, Ltd. was founded

Givenchy

Grès

in 1968 at 813 Madison Avenue, where his designs took up several floors, the couture at the top, then moved to the Olympic Towers in 1978.

NORMAN HARTNELL

Pages 230, 276–279, 387
Norman Hartnell, Ltd. opened at 26 Bruton Street in London in 1924. Briefly, in the late Twenties, the house showed in a Paris branch on the rue de Ponthieu. Sir Norman Hartnell designed ready-to-wear for various manufacturers before beginning with his own in 1963. He died in 1979.

HEIM

Pages 230, 258–263, 350
The House of Heim was established by furriers Isidore and Jeanne Heim in 1898 at 48, rue Lafitte. Jacques Heim began designing couture for his parents' house in 1923 and the house moved in 1934 to 50, Avenue Matignon, and again in the 1950s to 15, Avenue Matignon. Heim Jeunes Filles, specializing in wedding dresses, was begun in 1937, and prêt-à-porter activities, under the label Heim Actualité, started in the early 1950s. Jacques Heim retired in 1967, succeeded by his son Philippe, who is the present director.

CHARLES JAMES

Pages 177, 178, 183, 318, 319, 328–335, 378
Charles James started his career in 1924 in Chicago as a milliner using the name of Boucheron. He began designing clothes and headed to London via New York, where he spent most of the 1930s

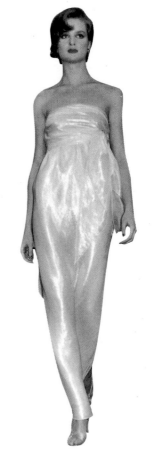

Halston

designing clothing under versions of his own name at various addresses, occasionally showing in Paris. Just before World War II he returned to New York, where he initiated multiple businesses over the years until retiring as an active designer in 1958. He died in 1978.

Norma Kamali

NORMA KAMALI

Pages 351, 366–371

Together with her husband, Eddie, Norma Kamali opened a boutique on East 53rd Street in New York in 1968, where she sold her own designs as well as those of other designers. The boutique moved to Madison Avenue in 1974. When she divorced her husband, she started OMO, at 6 West 56th Street, moving across the street in 1984 to number 11.

KENZO

Pages 351, 404–407

Kenzo leased his first Paris shop in 1969, opening in 1970 at the Passage Choiseul and moving in 1972 to the rue Grenelle. Since 1976 his headquarters have been located at 3, Place des Victoires and, although the company name is still Jungle JAP, the label has been known in America as Kenzo since 1976.

KARL LAGERFELD

Pages 134, 143, 195, 216–221, 280, 415

Karl Lagerfeld worked for the houses of Patou and Balmain before becoming a designer at Chloé, a deluxe prêt-à-porter house, in 1964. During his twenty years there he freelanced for several other houses, including Fendi, where he has designed furs and clothes since 1972. In 1983 he

Karl Lagerfeld

began designing couture for the House of Chanel, and has since begun designing prêt-à-porter there too. In 1984 he ended his connection with Chloé and presented the first collection under his own label: Lagerfeld.

LANVIN

Pages 23, 48–57, 240, 250, 276, 298, 350

Jeanne Lanvin founded her house in 1890 as a millinery business at 22, rue du Faubourg St-Honoré, the same building in which the house thrives today. She had expanded into designing ladies' and children's clothing by 1900, and by 1926 had opened, across the street, Lanvin Tailleur for men, where she also conducted a shop for sportsclothes. In 1929 she initiated a fur branch on the Rond-Point-des-Champs-Elysées. After her death in 1946, her daughter, the Comtesse de Polignac, took over the design direction, hiring Antonio del Castillo in 1950 as the house's couturier. When the comtesse died in 1958, the house was bequeathed to Yves Lanvin, nephew of Jeanne and father of Bernard Lanvin, the present director. Castillo left in 1963 and was replaced by Jules-François Crahay as couturier. In 1982, Bernard's wife Maryll Lanvin began designing prêt-à-porter for the house, and since the 1984 retirement of Crahay, has taken on more and more of the design responsibilities.

RALPH LAUREN

Pages 351, 398–403

Polo began as a line of men's neckties Lauren designed for Beau Brummel in 1967. It rapidly expanded into a complete collection of men's clothing in 1968, with the addition of women's shirts in

Lanvin

Lanvin

1971, and women's separates in 1972. Since then Ralph Lauren has brought out lines of Rough-wear, boys' wear, and girls' wear.

Ralph Lauren

LIBERTY & CO.

Pages 84, 90, 102–105
In 1875, Arthur Lasenby Liberty founded his emporium in London, selling Oriental imports of great variety. Shortly thereafter, Liberty's began dyeing imported fabrics, then moving into the production and printing of its own fabrics. The costume department opened in 1884 under the direction of E. W. Godwin, an architect and costume historian. Its output of clothing based on classical and artistic dress was also sold in the Paris Liberty's, founded in 1890 at 38, Avenue de L'Opéra. The Paris branch moved in the 1920s to the Boulevard des Capucines, but closed 1932, the same year of Paul Poiret's brief affiliation with the firm. For the past fifty years, Liberty's has operated much as it first did, as a kind of eclectic department store.

LOUISEBOULANGER

Pages 10, 118, 156, 158–159, 168
Louiseboulanger worked as a de-signer for the House of Chéruit before opening her own in 1923 at 3, rue de Berri. In 1933 the house closed briefly, with Louiseboulan-ger designing for Callot Soeurs be-fore relocating her house to 6, rue Royale. The house closed in 1939.

LUCILE

Pages 23, 64–69, 144, 276, 320
The then Mrs. Wallace started a dressmaking establishment in Lon-don's Davies Street in 1890. In 1894 she changed her business's name to Maison Lucile and moved

Liberty & Co.

to Old Burlington Street. She next moved to 17 Hanover Square, 14 Georges Street (1898–1900), and finally to 23 Hanover Square in 1900, the year she married Sir Cosmo Duff Gordon. Lucile, Ltd. was formed in 1903. In 1910 she opened a New York branch at 17 West 36th Street, in 1911 a Paris branch at 11, rue de Penthièvres, and in 1913 moved the New York house to 37–39 West 57th Street, and opened a Chicago one at 1400 Lake Shore Drive. In 1918 she sold the London house, closed the Chi-cago one, and reopened the Paris branch. In 1924 she moved the New York house to East 54th Street and in 1930 she went into semi-retirement, announcing she would only design for a limited clientele. She died in 1935.

CLAIRE McCARDELL

Pages 11, 350, 352–359, 372
McCardell worked as a knitwear designer before becoming assistant to designer Robert Turk, accom-panying him to the firm of Town-ley, where she remained for eight years until the firm's 1938 closing. A stint at Hattie Carnegie followed. Townley reopened in January 1941, and McCardell emerged as the main designer, with her name on the label, and she remained there —becoming a vice president and partner in 1952—until her death in 1958.

MARY McFADDEN

Pages 90, 106–109
McFadden was working as a spe-cial projects editor at *Vogue* in New York when the clothes she had designed for herself attracted notice. She began having them made up for small orders, some of which Bendel's bought, and in 1973 she went into business. Mary

Lucile

McFadden, Inc. was formed in 1976.

MAINBOCHER

Pages 118, 119, 166–173, 177, 194, 199, 230, 312, 323, 352
Mainbocher opened his couture house in Paris in 1930 at 12, Avenue Georges V. When he closed it in 1940, he relocated to New York, opening a house at 6 East 57th Street. In 1960 he moved his house to 609 Fifth Avenue where it existed until his 1971 retirement.

VERA MAXWELL

Pages 350, 360–363
Vera Maxwell began designing around 1930, working during the Thirties for several sportswear firms: Adler & Adler, Max Millstein, and Glenhunt. She opened Vera Maxwell Originals in 1947, maintaining the firm, except for a 1964–1970 "fallow" period, until her retirement in 1985.

Vera Maxwell

ISSEY MIYAKE

Pages 351, 412–415
Miyake studied art and design in Japan before working in Paris for Guy LaRoche and Givenchy, and in New York for Geoffrey Beene. He established Miyake Design Studio in Japan in 1970.

MOLYNEUX

Pages 84, 118, 144–149, 166, 194, 195, 240, 254, 270, 323
Edward Molyneux worked for Lucile in England before opening a *maison de couture* in Paris in 1919 at 14, rue Royale. By 1921 he had moved to 5, rue Royale where his house would remain un-

til December 31, 1950. His Monte Carlo branch opened in 1925, one in Cannes in 1927, and a London one in 1932. During World War II his business was inoperative. In 1965 he came out of retirement to begin Studio Molyneux, a prêt-à-porter concern. He died in 1974.

NORELL

Pages 11, 173, 194, 351, 372–377
Norman Norell studied fashion illustration and worked as a movie costumer before beginning to design fashion for Charles Armour in 1924, and Hattie Carnegie in 1928. He remained at Carnegie's until 1940 when he moved to the firm of Traina, where he was offered a salary cut in exchange for having his name on the label. In 1960 Traina retired and Norell presented his first collection under his own name, continuing to do so until his death in 1972. Gustave Tassell designed for Norell until 1976.

PAQUIN

Pages 23, 42–46, 338
Paquin opened in Paris in 1890 at 3, rue de la Paix, and in 1896, Paquin London, at 39 Dover Street, became the first foreign branch of a French couture house. During the Twenties, Paquin had branches in Buenos Aires, Madrid, and New York, the last known as Paquin-Joire. By the Thirties, Paquin was under the direction of Madame del Pombo, and by the end of World War II the Paris Paquin had been merged with the London Paquin and Worth, sharing the Paris Worth address of 120, rue du Faubourg St-Honoré and its London location at 50 Grosvenor Street. Although Paquin closed in 1956, Worth was bought and sold again.

Jean Patou

Paquin

JEAN PATOU

Pages 10, 84, 118, 138–143, 148, 216, 250, 320, 350, 352

Patou launched several businesses before opening a couture house under his own name. He began in 1910 with a fur and dressmaking establishment, switching in 1911 to a tailoring one. In 1912 he initiated Maison Parry, his first success. He had acquired the *hôtel particulier* at 7, rue St. Florentin (where Patou remains today), just before World War I, but was not able to open officially until 1919. In 1924 he opened branches in Deauville and Biarritz, followed by one in Monte Carlo. After his death in 1936, the house continued to be run by Raymond Barbas, husband of Patou's sister Madeleine and grandfather of the present president, Jean de Mouy. Marc Bohan and Gérard Pipart were hired as designers in 1953; Karl Lagerfeld in 1960, Michel Gona in 1963, and Angelo Tarlazzi in 1973. Christian La Croix, the couturier there today, has been with the house since 1980.

Jean Patou

POIRET

Pages 10, 22, 23, 33, 40, 42, 46, 74–87, 98, 103, 118, 143, 194, 199, 338

Paul Poiret worked as a designer for the houses of Doucet (1897–1900) and Worth (1901–1904) before opening his own at 5, rue Auber in 1904. He relocated to 26, Avenue d'Antin in 1909. His school, Martine, was founded in 1911, and its output of furnishing fabrics and furniture was sold in its own shop. In 1925 he moved to 1, Rond-Point-des-Champs-Elysées, where he remained until being closed down by his backers in 1929. He began a new house, called Passy 10–17 in 1931 which lasted barely six months. He worked last as a designer for Lib-

erty's, but only briefly during 1932. He died in 1944.

ZANDRA RHODES

Pages 90, 112–115

Zandra Rhodes started out in London designing fabrics for a print-works set up by her and a partner. She then began designing clothes made of materials she designed. These were sold through another organization—the Fulham Road Clothes Shop—created by her and several partners. By 1969 she was on her own and since 1975 has operated Zandra Rhodes Limited, with headquarters in London.

NINA RICCI

Pages 230, 246–251

Nina Ricci, with her son Robert, founded her house in Paris in 1932 at 22, rue des Capucines. During the Fifties, Madame Ricci became more involved with overseeing general management and less with actual designing, hiring Jules-François Crahay in 1954 as couturier. Since 1963 the house designer has been Gérard Pipart. Madame Ricci died in 1970, and was succeeded by her son, who moved the house to its present location at 39, Avenue Montaigne.

MARCEL ROCHAS

Pages 10, 195, 222–225

Marcel Rochas opened his couture house in Paris in 1925 at 100, rue du Faubourg St-Honoré, on the Place Beauvau. He moved in 1931 to 14, Avenue Matignon and in 1937 opened a New York house at 32 East 67th Street. Since his death in 1954 the house has continued to produce perfumes and accessories. Today it is located at 33, rue François Premier.

Poiret

Nina Ricci

MAGGY ROUFF

Pages 195, 199, 212–215, 350
Maggy Rouff opened in 1929 at 136, Avenue des Champs Elysées, where the house remained until the *couturière*'s retirement in 1948. Then, with her daughter as designer, it moved to Avenue Matignon where it remained until 1960. Between 1960 and 1966, with designers Jean Marie Armand and Serge Matta, the address was on the Avenue Marceau. In 1966 the house moved a last time to 14, Avenue Montaigne with Guy Douvier as the designer. Maggy Rouff died in 1971.

SONIA RYKIEL

Pages 119, 184–191
Sonia Rykiel began designing sweaters in 1963, which she sold in conjunction with her husband's Paris boutique, Laura. She opened her own boutique in 1968 at 6, rue de Grenelle, and since then has opened others all over the world.

YVES SAINT LAURENT

Pages 11, 202, 216, 218, 231, 242, 245, 280, 298, 308–315, 374
In 1957, Yves Saint Laurent was chosen as head designer for the House of Christian Dior, where he had worked as an assistant designer since 1953. After leaving for his military duty in 1959, and returning to find his post filled by Marc Bohan, he set about opening his own house, which he did in 1962 in the rue Spontini. His first ready-to-wear boutique was opened in 1966 and his *maison de couture* moved in 1974 to 5, Avenue Marceau.

Marcel Rochas

SCHIAPARELLI

Pages 10, 168, 194, 195, 196–203, 218, 222, 312, 320, 338, 350, 392, 412
Elsa Schiaparelli began designing, out of an upper-floor apartment at 4, rue de la Paix in 1927, with a line of sweaters. By 1930 she was able to move to a ground floor space in the same building where she offered designs "Pour la Ville" and "Pour la Nuit," as well as "Pour le Sport." She moved to 21, Place Vendôme in 1934—the same year she opened a London branch at 36 Upper Grosvenor Street. Closed during part of the war, she reopened in 1945 and continued her couture and boutique collections until 1954, when she quit the couture for good. Until her death in 1971, she designed for various licensing arrangements: *lunettes*, wigs, stockings, jewelry, swimwear, and some clothing. Schiaparelli, on the Place Vendôme, still dispenses perfumes as well as prêt-à-porter and boutique items.

Yves Saint Laurent

PAULINE TRIGÈRE

Pages 351, 378–381
Pauline Trigère had worked at various fashion companies before introducing a collection of about a dozen pieces of her own in 1942. The new company, at 18 East 53rd Street, was managed by her brother, Robert. Trigère moved twice—to East 47th and West 57th Streets—before settling at 550 Seventh Avenue, its present headquarters.

VALENTINA

Pages 118, 174–177
In 1928 Valentina Schlee opened Valentina Gowns Incorporated at 145 West 30th Street, then moved into a townhouse at 27 East 67th

Pauline Trigère

Street in the 1940s. She retired in 1957.

VALENTINO

Pages 231, 280–285

Valentino Garavani worked in Paris for the couturiers Jean Dessès and Guy LaRoche before returning to Italy and opening his own couture house in Rome's Via Condotti in 1959. In 1967 he moved into the Via Gregoriana, his present head-quarters, and in 1969 he inaugurated his prêt-à-porter, which was to be the first of many other lines.

VIONNET

Pages 10, 14, 40, 63, 84, 118, 148, 149, 160–165, 240, 270, 273, 318, 352, 354, 357, 378

Madeleine Vionnet worked for the Paris houses of Vincent, Bechoff–David, Callot Soeurs, and Doucet, and for the London house of Kate Reilly before opening her own Paris establishment in 1912 at 222, rue de Rivoli. She closed during World War I and reopened in 1919, moving in 1922 to 50, Avenue Montaigne, where she remained until closing permanently in 1940. During 1924 she advertised a New York office at 657–659 Fifth Avenue and in 1925 a Biarritz branch in the Rotonde de Casino.

Valentino

WORTH

Pages 10, 11, 12–13, 17, 22, 24–36, 42, 74, 76, 143, 144, 194, 196, 232, 245, 302, 312, 338, 350

The House of Worth et Bobergh was founded in 1858 at 7, rue de la Paix by Otto Bobergh and Charles Frederick Worth. When Bobergh left the firm in 1870, Worth continued alone. After his death in 1895, the business was continued by his sons: Gaston Worth as business manager, Jean-Philippe Worth as couturier. From 1901 to 1904 Paul Poiret was a designer. In 1911 the London branch opened at 4 New Burlington Street, moving to 3 Hanover Square in 1922. By 1922 Gaston Worth had died, and the business was continued by his two sons with Jacques Worth as financial director and Jean-Charles Worth as couturier. During the 1920s Worth maintained branches in Cannes and Biarritz and by 1930 there was another London location at 221 Regent Street. In 1936 the Paris house moved to 120, rue du Faubourg St-Honoré, and Jacques Worth's son Gaston became the couturier. At the end of World War II the Paris Worth had been merged into the Paris house of Paquin and joined with the London Worth and Paquin, now at 50 Grosvenor Street. In 1956 this combined house closed, but in 1968 Worth was sold again.

Worth

Photo Credits

Photographs © Katherine Abbé, courtesy the Washburn Gallery, New York: pages 50–51, 94.

Photograph © ANSA/Photo Trends: page 283.

Illustrations © Antonio: pages 16, 109, 220–221, 300, 304 (bottom), 305, 316–317, 415.

Photographs courtesy House of Armani: pages 409, 410, 411.

Photographs © Eve Arnold/Magnum Photos: pages 151, 340, 392.

Photographs courtesy House of Balmain: spine (bottom), page 419 (left, middle).

Photograph by Yutaka Banno, courtesy Issey Miyake: page 414.

Photograph © Bassano/Camera Press/Photo Trends: page 276.

Photographs © Cecil Beaton, courtesy Sotheby's, London: pages 19, 159, 169, 198, 201, 203, 241, 321, 331, 373, 419 (right, top).

Photograph © Cecil Beaton/Photo Trends: page 320.

Photograph © Robyn Beeche, courtesy Zandra Rhodes: page 113.

Photographs courtesy Geoffrey Beene: pages 388 (both), 389, 391.

Photographs © The Bettmann Archive: pages 120, 390.

Photographs courtesy The Bill Blass Limited Archives: pages 17, 303, 304 (top), 306, 307, 419 (right, middle).

Photograph © Michel Boutefeu, courtesy Pierre Cardin: page 338.

Photograph courtesy House of Capucci: page 420 (left, bottom).

Photographs courtesy Pierre Cardin: pages 341 (both), 420 (right, top).

Photograph © Henri Cartier-Bresson/Magnum: page 319.

Photographs courtesy House of Chanel: pages 130, 131.

Photograph courtesy Chloe House: page 424 (left, bottom).

Photograph by Jean Coquin, © Pierre Balmain: page 254.

Photographs courtesy House of Courrèges: pages 9 (b), 343, 344, 345, 346, 347.

Photographs by Ted Croner: pages 60, 92, 101, 105, 116–117, 124, 128, 164–165.

Photographs © Louise Dahl-Wolfe (courtesy the Edward C. Blum Design Laboratory, The Fashion Institute of Technology): pages 233, 261, 356, 377, 385; courtesy Staley-Wise Gallery, N.Y.: page 355; courtesy Vera Maxwell: page 361.

Photographs by Loomis Dean, *Life* magazine, © Time, Inc.: pages 9 (a), 237.

Photographs courtesy House of Dior: pages 235, 245, 421 (left, bottom; right, bottom).

Photograph © Robert Doisneau/Photo Researchers, Inc., courtesy Time Life: pages 2–3.

Photograph by Page Doughty, courtesy Mr. and Mrs. Adrian McCardell: pages 358–359.

Photograph by Alfred Eisenstaedt, *Life* magazine, © Time, Inc.: page 147.

Photograph courtesy Perry Ellis: page 422 (left, top).

Photographs © John Engstead, from the collection of Joseph Simms (courtesy the Edward C. Blum Design Laboratory, The Fashion Institute of Technology): pages 208, 211.

Photograph courtesy Fairchild Publications, Women's Wear Daily: page 295.

Photographs by N. R. Farbman, *Life* magazine, © Time, Inc.: pages 58, 269, © 1951; 255.

Photographs courtesy Lillian Farley: pages 65, 66, 67, 68.

Photograph © Hans Feurer, courtesy Kenzo: 348–349.

Photograph © Sandi Fellman: page 380.

Photograph © E. Fornaciari/Gamma Liaison: page 281.

Photograph © John French, courtesy Life Picture Service, Inc.: page 279.

Photograph by Joe Gafney, courtesy House of Givenchy: pages 290–291.

Photographs © Lynton Gardiner, courtesy The Museum of the City of New York: pages 25, 26, 28, 29.

Photographs courtesy House of Givenchy: pages 286, 287, 289 (top), 423 (left, top).

Photograph © Alex Gotfryd: front cover.

Photographs courtesy House of Grès: pages 150, 154, 423 (left, bottom).

Photographs © Brian Hagiwara, courtesy *Connoisseur* magazine: pages 296 (right), 297.

Photograph courtesy Halston: page 423 (right, top).

Photographs courtesy J. Heim House: pages 14, 258 (both), 263 (far left).

Photographs by Horst: pages 8 (c), 107, 110–111, 122, 123, 175, 176, 199, 219, 311, 315.

Photograph © Hoyningen-Huene: page 155.

Photograph courtesy Kamali: page 424 (left, top).

Photograph © Art Kane: pages 332–333.

Photographs © Lucille Khornak, from her book *Fashion: 2001*: pages 121, 152–153, 216 (bottom), 217.

Photographs © The Kobal Collection: pages 8 (d), 197, 202, 204, 206, 207, 234, 292, 293.

Photograph © F. Kompalitch courtesy House of Kenzo: page 406.

Photographs courtesy Lanvin: spine (top), pages 48, 49, 52, 56, 57, 424 (right, top).

Photographs © Dan Lecca: pages 184, 337.

Photograph by Nina Leen, *Life* magazine, © 1946 Time, Inc.: page 267.

Photographs © Erica Lennard: pages 185, 394 (both), 395.

Photograph © Cindy Lewis: page 301.

Photographs courtesy The Library of Congress: pages 43, 420 (left, middle).

Photograph © Ralf Lindquist/Camera Press/Photo Trends: page 325.

Photographs © Lipnitzki-Viollet, courtesy Roger-Viollet: pages 55, 59, 62, 74, 79, 82, 83, 86–87, 126, 135, 139, 162, 170, 170–171, 215, 223, 247, 274, 428 (left, top).

Photographs © Roxanne Lowit: pages 106, 108, 129, 133, 136–137, 179. 182, 188 (both), 191, 192–193, 244, 289 (bottom).

Photograph courtesy Peter Hope Lumley: page 144.

Photograph © Butch Martin, courtesy Kamali, N.Y.: pages 370–371.

Photographs courtesy Vera Maxwell: pages 360, 362 (both), 363, 426 (left, top).

Photographs © Willy Maywald: pages 146, 239, 242, 259, 262, 263 (right, top and bottom), 264, 266, 270, 273, 275, 322.

Photographs © Frances McLaughlin-Gill: pages 253, 271, 326.

Photograph © Jeannette Montgomery, courtesy Staley-Wise Gallery, N.Y.: page 302.

Photograph by Christopher Moore, courtesy Peter Hope Lumley: page 386.

Photographs © The Museum of the City of New York: pages 34–35.

Photographs © The Museum of Modern Art Film Stills Archives, New York: pages 127, 379.

Photograph courtesy The New York Public Library at Lincoln Center: page 91.

Photograph by Fiorenzo Niccoli, courtesy Capucci, Milan: page 336.

Illustration courtesy Lisa Nirenberg: page 73.

Photograph © Claus Ohm, courtesy Yves Saint Laurent: page 312 (bottom).

Photograph by Philippe Ortiz, courtesy The Library of Congress: page 47.

Photographs © Norman Parkinson: pages 145, 383.

Photographs © Gordon Parks: pages 228–229.

Photograph by Gordon Parks, *Life* magazine, © 1951 Time, Inc.: page 238.

Photographs courtesy House of Patou: pages 140, 141, 427 (left, middle).

Photographs courtesy Pictorial Parade: pages 143, 278 (left), 339.

Photographs © Dustin Pittman, courtesy Fairchild Publications, Women's Wear Daily: pages 299, 365.

Photographs © Ken Probst: pages 296 (left), 408, 413.

Photographs by John Rawlings (courtesy the Edward C. Blum Design Laboratory, The Fashion Institute of Technology): pages 205, 268, 329, 335, 354, 374, 375.

Photographs © Man Ray: pages 30, 167.

Photograph courtesy R. J. Reynolds Tobacco Co., Winston-Salem, N.C.: page 96.

Photograph © Stan Ribton, courtesy Zandra Rhodes: page 115.

Photographs courtesy Nina Ricci: pages 246, 248, 249 (both), 251, 427 (right, bottom).

Photograph © Jacques Rouchon, courtesy House of Dior: page 236 (bottom).

Photographs courtesy House of Rykiel: pages 186–187, 191.

Photograph courtesy Yves Saint Laurent: page 428 (right, top).

Photograph © Scoop/Gamma Liaison: page 404.

Photographs © Seeberger Frères, courtesy Bibliothèque Nationale: pages 11, 164, 165, 196, 212, 214, 226–227 (all), 427 (right, top), 429 (right, top).

Photographs © Daniel Simon/Gamma Liaison: pages 1, 4, 18, 189, 240 (both), 243, 257, 288, 309, 310, 312 (top), 313, 314, 405, 407, 412, back cover.

Photograph © Amanda Sposito, courtesy House of Valentino: page 429 (left, middle).

Photograph © John Swannell, courtesy Zandra Rhodes: page 114.

Photograph © Syndication International/Photo Trends: page 278 (right).

Photographs courtesy House of Trigère: pages 380, 381, 428 (right, bottom).

Photographs © Deborah Turbeville: pages 180–181, 284–285, 393, 396–397.

Photograph © P. Vauthey/Sygma: page 216 (top).

Photographs © Sacha Van Dorssen: pages 8 (b), 88–89, 93, 97.

Photographs courtesy the Victoria and Albert Museum (crown copyright): pages 103, 425 (left, bottom).

Photographs courtesy *Vogue*. Copyright © 1935 (renewed 1963), 1939 (renewed 1967), 1943 (renewed 1971), 1944 (renewed 1972), 1945 (renewed 1973), 1946 (renewed 1974), 1948 (renewed 1976), 1949 (renewed 1977), 1950 (renewed 1978), 1951 (renewed 1979), 1952 (renewed 1980), 1975, 1977, 1979, by The Conde Nast Publications Inc.

Photographs © Barbra Walz: pages 328, 378.

Photograph courtesy Katherine McCardell Webb: page 353.

Photographs by Bruce Weber, courtesy Ralph Lauren: pages 9 (c), 399, 400, 401, 402, 403, 425 (left, top).

Photographs © Theo Westenberger/Gamma Liaison: pages 366, 367, 369.

Photograph by Mike Yavel, courtesy House of Patou: page 142.

Original material was photographed by: David Arky, Dennis Cowley, Joel Feder, Caroline Rennolds Milbank, and Irving Salero.

Original material provided for photography courtesy The

Cooper-Hewitt Museum: pages 8 (a), 41, 44, 61.
Original material provided for photography courtesy The
Costume Institute, The Metropolitan Museum of Art:
pages 44, 53, 77, 80, 85, 99, 138, 148, 149, 157,
161, 173, 213, 224 (both), 225, 236, 265, 272,
277, 324, 419 (left, bottom), 421 (left, top).
Original material provided for photography courtesy the
collection of Keith De Lellis: pages 30, 75, 167.
Original material provided for photography courtesy The
Edward C. Blum Design Laboratory, Fashion Institute
of Technology: pages 20–21, 39, 42, 46, 54, 70,
71, 72, 420 (right, bottom), 424 (right, bottom),

426 (right, top and bottom).
Original material provided for photography courtesy the
collection of Leonard Fox: page 45.
Original material provided for photography courtesy La
Vieille Russie: page 128.
Original material provided for photography courtesy the
collection of Wendy Lebing: page 60.
Original material for photography provided courtesy the
collection of Caroline Rennolds Milbank: page 37.
Original material provided for photography courtesy the
collection of Susan Nirenberg: pages 12, 32.
Original material provided for photography courtesy the

collection of Sandy Schreier: pages 101, 105.
Original material provided for photography courtesy Sotheby
Parke-Bernet: pages 116–117, 124, 164–165.
Original material provided for photography courtesy the
collection of Mark Walsh: page 92.

We have endeavored to obtain the necessary permission
to reprint the photographs and drawings in this volume
and to provide proper copyright acknowledgments. We
welcome information on any error or oversight, which we
will correct in subsequent printings.

Acknowledgments

LIKE FASHION, THIS BOOK HAS CHANGED MUCH AND
often since its inception. Throughout, and in every
aspect of putting it together, I have been amazed
and touched by the generosity of those who offered
their help, either concretely by giving freely of information and photographs, or less tangibly, with
support and interest. I am grateful to each and every
person who listened to my description of the project,
especially those who heard about it in its earliest,
crudest stages and were still encouraging. I would
like to thank my husband, who barely knew me when
he said "get going," and also Andy Stewart, for having pretty much the same reaction.

Almost all of the research was accomplished by
my looking at couturier and designer clothes all over
the country or by losing myself in old magazines
and newspapers. Therefore it was refreshing, and
inspiring, to meet with some of the actual designers,
and I thank the following for their patience and their
gifts of gab: Bill Blass, Bonnie Cashin, Perry Ellis,
James Galanos, Christian LaCroix at Jean Patou,
Ralph Lauren, Zandra Rhodes, and Valentina. I
would also like to thank Miss Martha, at whose store
(unbeknownst to her) some of these meetings took
place.

Fashion photographs are judged by their visual
appeal, by who took them and occasionally for what
they show. For this book, we could only use photographs that depicted clothes attributed to our list of
designers. Consequently, our search for illustrations
was long and arduous. I would like to thank Marya
Dalrymple for getting us off on the right foot, Leora
Kahn for photo research on the East Coast, Paul
Rankin for his indefatigable scouring of Paris, and
Cindy Deubel for filling in holes once the book's
design was underway. I am also grateful for the
advice, assistance, or actual photographs of: Keith
Douglas de Lellis, Nancy Hall-Duncan, Horst P.
Horst, Francis McLaughlin-Gill, Jeannette Mont-
gomery, Willy Maywald and his assistant Jutta

Niemann, Irving Salero, Vincent Vallarino, and Les-
lie Van Breen.

Ted Croner's photographs of couturier clothing
and accessories provide a special close-up look at
fashion and he deserves kudos for following me to
the ends of New York to shoot Chanel suits, Callot
headdresses, and countless labels and details. Other
photographs of labels and of fashion illustrations
were taken smilingly and beautifully by David Arky,
as well as by Page Doughty, Jean Neder, Alexandra
Palmer, Margaret Rennolds, Irving Salero, and Cynthia Young. Equally important were those who lent
examples of couturier clothing, labels, and accessories to be photographed; here I would like to thank
Christie's East, Linda Donahue, William Doyle
Galleries, Cora Ginsburg, Martin Kamer, Kent State
University Museum, Amelie Rennolds, Sandy
Schreier, Suman Shenoi, Sotheby's New York, Mark
Walsh, Nina Winthrop, and a la Vieille Russie. For
special help shooting labels, I thank Titi Halle,
Karen Meyerhoff, and Gina Silvester. I am also grateful to the following for permitting their fashion
photographs, illustrations, and drawings to be
reproduced: The Costume Institute at the Metropoli-
tan Museum of Art, Lillian T. Farley, the Special
Collections at the Fashion Institute of Technology,
the Leonard Fox Gallery, Mrs. Susan Nirenberg, and
Mrs. Eugene Webb.

Not surprisingly, some of the best photographs,
documents, and concrete information came from the
houses of the designers themselves. I am thus in-
debted to: Peter Hope Lumley for Hardy Amies,
Giorgio Armani, Claudine de Diebach and Marie-
Christine Brarda at Pierre Balmain, Richard
Lambertson and Kevin Ryan at Geoffrey Beene, Tom
Fallon and Linda Edgerley at Bill Blass, Dorrie Davis
and France at Chloé, Alexandra Tchernoff and Eliza-
beth Flory for Christian Dior, Betty Knoff at Givenchy,
Giles Soudant at Grès, Mrs. Price at Norman
Hartnell, Philippe Heim, Claire Mugnier-Pollet at

Kenzo, Laurence Nachet at Lanvin, Anne Marie
Rozelle at Ralph Lauren, Beth Wohlgenerter at Mary
McFadden, Vera Maxwell, Jun Kanai for Issey
Miyake, Jean de Mouy at Jean Patou, Gill Curry at
Zandra Rhodes, Beatrice Keller at Nina Ricci,
Françoise Mohrt at Marcel Rochas, Jane at Sonia
Rykiel, Gabrielle Buchaert at Yves Saint Laurent,
Juliana Russo at Schiaparelli, Pauline Trigère, An-
gela Istok at Valentino.

I would like to thank the following people for their
help with specific fashion information, suggestions
about the book's format, or knowledge about books
and publishing in general: Vera Bacal, Tina Chow,
the Contessa Gozzi, Lindy Hess, Sally Kirkland,
Mrs. Adrian L. McCardell, Jean de Mouy, and Joyce
Volk.

For much help, but especially for reading the
manuscript, I am grateful to: Holly Brubach, Har-
old Koda, Michael Pollan, and Sally Wood.

It surprises me how long I have been intrigued by
fashion, and I am much obliged to those who recognized and encouraged my early interest. The people who follow deserve special thanks either for
guiding me into this field of study or keeping me
interested in it as I go along: Katel le Bhouris, Ann
Coleman, Mildred Davis, Linda Donahue, Jean
Druesedow, Cora Ginsburg, Phyllis Magidson, Jo
Ann Olian, Alexandra Palmer, the late Mary Brooks
Picken, Shannon Rodgers, Anne Schirmeister, Laura
Sinderbrand, Mark Walsh, and Grace Wells.

Last but not least, there are those whose various
talents came into play on an almost daily basis in
preparing the manuscript. Without them it truly
couldn't have been done, and I like to think of them
as the book's godmothers: Margot Dockrell, Lillian
Farley, Mary Kennedy, Lisa Nirenberg, Lisa Pearson,
and Sandy Schreier. At the end of this list, but more
appropriately heading it, is my mother, Seymour
Rennolds. Thank you all.

CM New York May 1985

Design

J. C. Suarès

Laurence Vetu

Caroline Ginesi
JoDee Stringham

Production

Katherine van Kessel

Carol Chien

Photo Research

Cynthia Deubel
Leora Kahn
Paul Rankin

Composed in Bodoni Book, Design Fine Line, and Design Medium
by U.S. Lithograph, Arkotype Inc., and Marvin Kommel Productions,
New York, New York
Printed and bound by Toppan Printing Company, Ltd.,
Tokyo, Japan